UNDISCOVERED ENDS

*Available from HarperCollins*Publishers
by the same author

BUILDING THE GLOBAL VILLAGE
(Fount Paperbacks)

BRUCE KENT

UNDISCOVERED ENDS

HarperCollins*Religious*

HarperCollins*Religious*
Part of HarperCollins*Publishers*
77–85 Fulham Palace Road
Hammersmith, London w6 8jb

First published in Great Britain
in 1992 by HarperCollins*Religious*

1 3 5 7 9 8 6 4 2

A catalogue record for this book is
available from the British Library

ISBN 0 00 215996 1

Set in Linotron Ehrhardt by
Rowland Phototypesetting Ltd
Bury St Edmunds, Suffolk

Printed and bound in Great Britain by
HarperCollinsManufacturing, Glasgow

This book is dedicated to the three wise women
without whose gifts it would not have been possible:

Joan Cavender, who can read my writing
Jackie O'Driscoll OP, who can outwit computers
and
Valerie Flessati, who can spell

BRUCE KENT
Feast of the Epiphany, 1992

From quiet homes and first beginnings
Out to the undiscovered ends
There's nothing worth the wear of winning
But laughter and the love of friends.

HILAIRE BELLOC

Contents

List of Illustrations

Cartoon warfare from *The Sun* (*News International*)

... and *The Star*. (*Star Newspapers Ltd*)

CND's 25th birthday party in 1983, Westminster Central Hall. I hold the cake with (from left) Michael Foot, Pat Arrowsmith, Annajoy David, Olive Gibbs, Joan Ruddock, Sir Richard Acland. (*CND*)

Greater London Council, Nuclear Free Nagasaki Day 1984, with Donald Soper and Illtyd Harrington. (*Greater London Council*)

CND rally 1985 with Meg Beresford (next CND General Secretary), Alf Dubs and Glenys Kinnock. (*Melanie Friend*)

Arrest at Sculthorpe, January 1986.

With Jesse Jackson, Geneva press conference 1985. (*Samual F. Yette*)

Sean MacBride and Bishop Tutu, Roebuck Castle, Dublin 1984.

Ron Todd explains the way forward *en route* to Burghfield, 1986. (*David Rumsey*)

Arriving at Burghfield, Hiroshima Day 1986, George Galloway (later MP) on right. (*Press Association*)

Keeping the Battleship Iowa out of Portsmouth 1989. (*Peter Blunt*)

With Lord Soper after a Gulf War Protest at Downing Street 1991. (*Nigel Tanburn*)

Valerie learns to paddle, Ottawa River 1991.

CHAPTER ONE

My War Part I – Going West

That I was born at 5.30 p.m. on 22nd June 1929 was, my mother told me, due to a tram. For reasons never explained she decided to have me not in Hampstead Garden Suburb, or Hendon, where she had been living, but in Blackheath. In Dr Pink's nursing home, to be precise. I was slow to arrive, so Dr Pink, or his partner Dr White, is supposed to have advised my mother to take a tram up and down Blackheath Hill.

It is said that I was not only slow to arrive, but also took my time with most things. My brother George, eighteen months older, had to dress me long after I should have been able to look after myself, and I don't think I've ever been properly grateful. I'm not sure if I ever helped to dress my sister, Rosemary, after she arrived two years later, but I certainly could not have given her the care and attention she deserved. There is still a picture in the family album of a dear little girl, perhaps three years old, dashing straight across the main sea front at Brighton, through all the traffic, with an ear-to-ear smile.

By all reasonable standards it was a happy pre-war family and a most contented comfortable childhood. Hampstead Garden Suburb life in the 1930s was easy indeed. There were nannies, in series, there were cooks at times, and usually maids in black and white looking like Lyons Cornerhouse Nippies. We always had a house, a garden, a dog and a car, or even two. My father, Kenneth, and my mother, Molly, were both Canadians. He had survived the First World War – just. Enlisting under age in the Canadian Horse Artillery, he went to France in 1916. At one stage he was gassed and at Vimy he nearly lost a leg and, but for one of his horses and the gun carriage which took the blast of a shell, his life. He used to point out to us children Charing Cross station, where he arrived on a stretcher, and Charing Cross Hospital, as it then was, where he spent his first few days back from the front. I was very proud of a picture in some album which showed him in uniform entirely confident, standing up in his stirrups as the horse reared to full height, in his training camp at Petawawa, Ontario. His leg was an endless reminder of that war. Until almost the day he died, from time to time little scraps of metal would work their way to the surface and break the skin.

He rarely spoke about the war. Only after he died, many years later, did we discover his wartime diaries, from which he, or the censor, excluded almost any reference to the fighting itself. What was revealing was the careful listing, night after night, of whichever psalm he had said before he went to sleep.

The most moving family relic of the First World War is a letter written by my uncle Tom, recovering from his wounds, to his mother back in Des Joachims, Quebec, in 1917. He was serving in the Canadian Rangers and his short letter was written on YMCA paper ("For God, King and Country" at the top) from a hospital in Shoreham. He wasted no words:

> Many of the Rangers are wounded and many are taking their last long rest beneath the mud of Flanders and many a mother's heart is breaking for her boy who will never return. However death is nothing over there, lives are cheap and a live dog is better than a dead lion. I hope this bloody muddy war soon ends, goodbye love to all Tom.

Poor Tom. We never met him, though he survived the war. It was said that he had gone out to Western Canada and was not well. I'm sure that he must have had breakdowns as a result of what he saw and suffered in France.

It was never possible for us children to forget the Great War. Our comic books were full of ridiculous-looking Germans, and there were always grown-ups with tales to tell. Armistice Day was an awesome event for a five- or six-year-old. At eleven o'clock, whatever the day, everything and everybody stopped in their tracks. In the two minutes of total silence the guns could be heard booming

from Hyde Park. Memories were actively fed by cigarette card collections. Ships of the Royal Navy came with Player's large boxes,
and Uniforms of the Empire from some brand I've forgotten. I liked
the Empire. So many uniforms and so many fearsome looking men
of almost every colour. All "ours".

How did my Canadian parents come to be living in London? Eight
years after the War, in 1926, my father was sent from Canada to
London to start a branch of the American Armstrong Cork Company, which was based in Lancaster, Pennsylvania. My mother followed a year afterwards and married him at once in St Edward's
Catholic Church in Golders Green, under the shadow of the Crema-
torium and down the hill from the Jewish cemetery. They knew no
one in London, so the two church cleaners acted as witnesses.

Catholicism was not Father's choice. A Presbyterian brought up in
Montreal, he was full of Belfast-type sectarianism, and his animosity
to "Rome" was pretty clear. That he tolerated, for love of my
mother, so many things Catholic despite his background was, I later
realized, a great tribute to him. My mother came from an entirely
different world, with Irish and some French roots grounded in
strong Catholicism. She was one of eleven children, eight of whom
survived, and her home was miles out in the wonderful backwoods
of Northern Quebec. There her father, Thomas Marion, bought
furs, sold timber, ran the village store and drove a sledge pulled
through the snow by two horses, Toss and Fly.

History landed these two young Canadians in Golders Green,
and they married despite the distinct lack of enthusiasm shown by
parents on both sides. The business prospered and we all took
happily to being part of the English middle class. Actually I hardly
knew that there was any other class, or if there was one, how it
managed. We lived in a world apart. On Sundays the muffin man
walked down Meadway with his wicker basket, green baize cloth
and bell. The Walls ice-cream three-wheel bicycle went past, with
lovely triangular water-ices for a penny. We went to nursery schools
and mucked about with sand and Plasticine. It was regularly Cow-
boys and Indians in the garden, though I was once discovered playing Doctors and Nurses with a girl from the end of the road – but
Nanny put a stop to that! I also got into grave trouble for killing two

goldfish, by pulling them out of their bowl and dropping them on the carpet, which crime I could only justify by saying, "They bit me."

I burst into tears at the sad sight when three very tired cart-horses arrived at our house one day, having pulled loads of coal up from Golders Green as a result of an order placed by my brother as a prank. They had to pull it all back again. Then there was the United Dairy van with the horse which seemed so huge to me, the reins running the full length of its enormous brown back. My brother and I from time to time fell out, and I had to hit him on the head on one occasion with one of my father's golf clubs. To be made to apologize went right against the grain. But we also had an agreeable partnership, making tiny pin-holes in the family cigarettes before parties (try it!) and engaging in healthy competitions, one of which was to find out who could pee furthest out of the bedroom window. In an early photo he can be seen holding me on to a minute pony on Littlehampton beach. We also used to visit Frinton, Bexhill and Lyme Regis fishing for mackerel. Just before the Second World War, at Hunstanton we both got up before the lark to go down to the local stables together and clear out horse manure in hope of a ride down the beach, through the sea.

On Sundays, Mother and we three children went with absolute regularity to Mass at St Edward's. I have almost no recollection of what went on at Mass except for lighting candles afterwards and moving chairs forward when people stood up. If you moved them forward slowly and carefully enough you could make the people in front very uncomfortable when they tried to kneel down! The high point of the year was of course Christmas midnight Mass and the parish crib. The Golders Green crib was at all times unique. In amongst the oxen and the sheep a couple of ducks used to "float" on a piece of mirror. "Why shouldn't Jesus have ducks?" I thought.

All this bliss nearly came to an end with a mastoid operation in a private clinic (naturally) somewhere in the Harley Street area. I think I should get total remission from purgatory for the pain of that operation, as every day yards of gauze were stuffed into the hole behind my ear. My partner in mastoid was an Indian prince of my age. We played together but, sadly, we failed to keep in touch

4

afterwards. The white bandage around his brown face was most impressive. The one compensation for the operation was that for a long time I could fold my ear behind the mastoid scar, which was something no other boy at school could manage.

Wellbury was a preparatory boarding school near Hitchin run by a convert Anglican clergyman and his ever-growing family. On a very wet night after a long day spent by my father examining various Catholic prep schools, our Headmaster had had the sense to offer him a very large whisky. That sealed matters and the hunt for a school was over. As a school it seemed very typical of that time. Beatings were part of the regular routine, as anyone could see from the boys' black and blue bottoms at any swimming session. Today the Head might be called a sadist. We played cricket, learned a lot about the Roman Catholic martyrs, went for walks in the woods, and thought General Franco a very good thing. One by one the Head would take us off to explain "the facts of life". I suppose I got "the facts" from him at the age of seven or eight, and I thought they were quite ridiculous. What stupid things for grown-ups to do to each other. Quite disgusting!

Religion was a fundamental part of the school life. At an early age we learnt the difference between venial sins and mortal sins. Getting martyred clearly had its advantages. If you got martyred, then all sins were wiped out whether you had been to confession or not and even if you had not yet managed that very difficult "perfect" act of contrition. So we used to envy the martyrs who had avoided all risk of hell. Having heard about Lourdes, several of us constructed personal shrines in the woods and organized our own processions. None were ever as good as the official Corpus Christi procession which wandered around the grounds while a priest held the monstrance under a canopy and I walked backwards throwing flowers out of a basket.

Confession and Communion were central to our lives, though I think one of my confessions must have astounded the school chaplain, young Father Andrew Beck, a very nice man who ended up in later years as an educational expert and Archbishop of Liverpool. At the age of about eight I told him through the confessional grille that I had committed adultery. He was kind enough not to say

5

"Nonsense." The confusion arose because no-one would tell us exactly what adultery was, and yet it was there in bold print in the Catechism. I had spent an afternoon examining the private parts of a dead mole, which I had found on the tennis court, to find out whether it was a lady mole or a gentleman. I realized that this was not what good boys did, and concluded that the forbidden sin of adultery must include the secret examination of the private parts of moles. So the trip to the confessional was perfectly logical. I am sure Father Andrew gave me absolution. The spiritual crisis was over.

We had a master who, because he could ski, went off to fight for the Finns against the dreadful Communist Russians. This was a wonderful example and he became a hero to the boys on the scale of St Thomas More. We already, of course, knew that odd things were going on in Europe. There was a great rush back from a holiday in France in 1938 in case a war started. Despite a very rough trip from St Malo to Southampton I managed to hold on, but was finally and substantially sick inside our Southampton hotel all over a wonderful red carpet. Years later, in a dockside radio station in Southampton, I realized that I was in what once had been that same hotel. Meanwhile the Headmaster got ready for war. In a special circular letter the parents were reassured. "Had war broken out Wellbury would have been as well provided for as any place in England . . ." We apparently behaved with British phlegm. "Throughout the preparations the boys showed their usual abundance of common sense." When it actually started it didn't seem to amount to much more than gas masks. I did my bit by growing several large lettuces and sending them by parcel post to Hampstead Garden Suburb for the support of my parents. Disappointingly, they arrived in a very miserable condition.

Then the real war started and there were maps in the classroom showing the bulges across France. According to the previous history which we understood, the bulges were meant to go backwards and forwards for some years. This time they didn't. They kept moving rapidly westwards as if the Germans didn't know the rules. I was more interested in winning the three-legged race, which I succeeded in doing with a boy called Bamford, who I think went off eventually

6

to make tractors in Birmingham. We won triumphantly, but they forgot to give me a prize, so I cried most of the night. I don't think Bamford was such a drip. I was, however, the regular winner of the kipper competition, which meant eating an entire kipper – bones, head and all – faster than anyone else.

The westward bulges on the map of France in our prep school classroom had also been noticed by my father. In the summer of 1940 he decided that the best place for his wife and children to be for the rest of the war would be back in Canada with close relations. All I remember is a train trip to Liverpool, exploring a very large ship, called the *Duchess of Richmond*, in the company of a friendly Cunard steward called Mr Rimmer, admiring the seagulls and waving goodbye. It was all too interesting to feel the slightest sense of regret, especially as the ship was full of other middle- and upper-class English children on their way to America and Canada for the duration. The idea that England might be taken over by the Germans in our absence never occurred to me. In fact a teenage Bonham-Carter (Norman, as I discovered over fifty years later) at one point got up on a saloon table to assure everyone in sight that England would win. We were not escaping and we would soon be back. He was very uplifting. Of even greater interest was the sight of Ireland on the left, Scotland on the right and a patrol plane above us as we headed out on a lovely sunny day into the Atlantic. We zigzagged across it with no other ship in sight for the next week. We children were mostly concerned with the ship's gym, which was provided with an electric horse which was worked to death during the journey. My mother had, I'm sure, submarines in mind, and she was right. The next liner to follow us was sunk in mid-Atlantic.

With much hooting and many strange lights the port of Halifax finally turned up. The most interesting part of arriving at Halifax was the train, which had sleeping compartments and two-tier bunks. My uncle Jack, my father's brother – a total stranger to us all – slept in the bunk below. I spent a long time hanging from the top bunk like a small monkey, looking at this new face with the moustache which snored quietly as the train set off on the long journey to Montreal and quite a new life.

Gone were cooks, nannies, maids and the like. We had first to get used to what seemed like hundreds of new relations on both sides. Then we had to find somewhere to live and ended up in various apartments on Sherbrooke Street in the very English and upper-class suburb of Westmount. I didn't mind living in an apartment. There were always a lot of interesting cooking smells, and during the winter you could get on the roof and throw snowballs at people a long way below.

School life, too, was very, very different. We were sent to a Protestant day-school, on an English model – Lower Canada College. My father could cope with Catholic schools on his own ground in England, but not on the family patch of Montreal, where the English did not mix with the French, did not speak French and lived in English enclaves in the best bits of the town. When there was some danger of my sister being sent to one of the few mixed schools a telegram from London put an end to that. Rosemary was a very patient girl. For most of the time I was in Canada I had a large Brownie Box camera and she was my most frequent model. There are pictures of her posing in front of flag-poles and town halls and sitting on walls and in front of park greenhouses. One more successful than most is of her looking very proud and all dressed up for winter in one of those horse-drawn sledges which used to take tourists around the town. All three of us had to sink or swim in a very different world in which one escaped from school at around four o'clock and didn't have to go at all at weekends. George and I – Kents II and IV, to be distinguished from our cousins, Kents I and III – got on well enough. Softball replaced cricket and ice-skating replaced anything when there was a chance.

Now that it was under threat, my religion took on much greater significance, and I fought for it to the point of winning the Scripture Prize and beating the Protestants. There were sticky moments, as, for instance, when Mr Mustard, our very amiable history teacher, came to the Reformation and assured the class that by putting money into the hands of statues Catholics thought they were freed from their sins. "Have you ever seen such a statue?" I piped from the back of the class. Mr Mustard, an honest man, admitted that he had not, and I sat down to the applause of the class. Religious differences did not matter too much when it came to success in putting down

8

a teacher! The most remarkable teacher by a very long way was a young radical, full of astonishing ideas, called Hugh McClennan. He became my hero and must have been very bored by the experience, though he never showed it. It was only well after I had left school that I learnt that my hero had turned into a famous Canadian novelist. I read his *Barometer Rising*, about a First World War catastrophe in Halifax, from cover to cover. Various school reports still crumble in family archives. In October 1942 my mother was told that "he could work harder". Fair enough. By April 1943 I apparently *was* working harder, but my spelling was "weak" and writing was "poor". Not much has changed since then. School drama was always enjoyable and I starred in *A Midsummer Night's Dream*. But I doubt if many masters would today write on a school report, as one of mine did in April 1942, "I am anticipating a good performance from his Bottom."

School, on a day basis, was now only part of life. There was so much more. Dreadful dancing classes, for one thing. Little did we know it, but we were now part of Montreal's junior high society and went to parties with famous families like the Molsons and the Redpaths. As English evacuees we were quite important. Parties were formal and you had to know how to dance. So we had to go to various classes under the eagle eye of a famous Miss Edwards who clasped us, still barely in our teens, to her generous bosom as we learnt the waltz and the foxtrot. The hokey cokey was always much more fun and usually ended up with a hot and sweaty football scrum of which Miss Edwards did not much approve. These activities prepared us for dances which we had to attend in dinner-jacket and black tie, partnered by girls in long dresses and equipped with dance cards. You had to book yourself up for a dance in advance, and it was a sad evening for girls who did not get their cards signed up. The best dance was of course the one in the middle – the supper dance. After clumping around the floor for a bit you filled a plate as high as possible and sat munching next to the girl of your choice. Gluttony, not lust, was the main feature of those evenings.

I only mention such dances because they now sound so bizarre. But they were the done thing then. What we really enjoyed was rather different. Visiting a cousin in Montreal West, for instance, and going there by tram. In those days about a mile of unbuilt-up land separated Montreal from Montreal West, and the trams travelled, bells clanging, at what was probably about thirty-five miles per hour but felt like sixty, rocking from side to side all the way. Another batch of cousins lived out in Hudson Heights, or did so during holidays. There was always something to do there and money to earn, as a caddy, at the local golf club. I have to say that those early experiences put me off golf for life, however eagerly I banked the dollars that came my way.

The social centre for young people was the Yacht Club, and the high point of amorous adventure was the Club hayride, which meant a couple of dozen or so early teenagers being pulled by large horses through the evening in a farm-cart deep in hay. Whatever happened to Sue Leslie, I wonder, at whose feet I worshipped but who always went on hayrides with other people, knowing nothing of my devotion? At least dear blonde Sue, with the bobby socks and the blue eyes, was a Catholic, and I always felt that this should have given me a special priority. It didn't. She seemed to be equally happy with Protestants, even though meeting her at Mass in our church in Montreal should have given me an advantage. It did not. I was lost for words.

Protestants had, of course, their good points. As a result of some tragic cinema accident years before in the Province of Quebec, children under the age of sixteen were not allowed into cinemas. This meant a great deal of deviousness, like sitting on fire-escapes and peering in from outside, or clapping a large hat on one's head and attempting to look sixteen. That rarely worked. So the Protestant Church Hall in Westmount was a place of pilgrimage every Friday or Saturday night. There were cartoons, cowboy films and even sometimes Hedy Lamarr. How the church escaped the rules of Quebec I have no idea, but we were all delighted that it did.

Montreal, for all its joys, of which the best was tobogganing in Murray Park, was not where I felt happiest. My favourite spot was not even the summer camp where we always spent a couple of weeks in July – Camp Nominingue, set on a lake in the Laurentian Hills. It was an ideal location and a paradise for small boys. Most of the helpers were students from University on holiday, and they did a great deal to improve on the knowledge of "the facts of life" imparted with such care at Wellbury. In fact some of the student "counsellors" were extremely crude, but most of it went over my head.

Each boy was given his own small wooden Indian shield. As you became proficient in swimming or riding or first aid or canoeing, another feather was added to the head-dress on your shield. The aim was to earn as many feathers as possible. We lived in tents, went on canoe trips and had marvellous camp-fires. Children brought up in England don't know what most of them miss in Canadian summer camps. The wonders of a three-day canoe trip, sleeping under the stars and smoking pine needles wrapped in toilet paper.

Camp Nominingue was, however, only my second favourite place. Real paradise was a week or two in winter or summer spent in my grandmother's village of Rapides des Joachims, miles up the Ottawa River. It was pronounced locally as "De Swisha". Grandmother herself was rather a scary old lady. She was rarely well, lived in a darkened room in the large house, said her prayers and was looked after by my senior aunt. We used to visit her with some trepidation, though she was always very kindly. Anyone coming from Montreal had to bring with them a bottle of St Joseph's oil from the vast shrine still being built on the side of Mount Royal. I never appeared without one, which may have caused her on one memorable occasion to rise from her bed, point a boney finger at me and say, "That boy is going to be a priest." I think I laughed at the time.

Grandmother's house stood at the entrance to the village; it was wooden and had a long porch. The head of a large and rather miserable-looking moose hung on the porch wall, gazing gloomily across the river. The village consisted of twenty or thirty other small houses, the store and the church – Catholic, of course. The road through the village went only up to various hunting and logging camps. There was no resident priest, but a special room was always kept by Grandmother for the visiting priest who came nearly every week to say Mass.

It was the area we loved so much. Great rapids (today producing electricity) thundered down into the bay. Wolves could be heard howling in the winter. The ice on the river was then feet deep, and men would cut out great blocks and heave them into the barn where, packed with sawdust, they would last the season, until they were broken up with ice-picks and taken to the kitchen. We had our family brown cow, with its own bell in Swiss style, and we would be sent off into the woods to find it and bring it back for milking. There were endless warnings of what we should do (i.e. run) if we met a black bear, but the nearest we ever got to that was finding a cub well up a tree, with no sign of its mother.

The river was vast, a third of a mile across, and logs, escaping from timber booms, crashed down the rapids and ended up on the rocks of the bay. Six logs, two short planks, a few nails and a pole made a raft as solid as a house on which one could drift all day – even towards the cabin of the old Indian, Ponas, on the other side. Ponas terrified us, because adults threatened us with him. He used to cross the river in his skiff from time to time to get sugar and tobacco at our store. Increasingly deaf, he died one day under the wheels of a train while walking the tracks through the forest towards Pembroke.

It was, of course, "our store". It was all that was left of the Marion Trading Company after my grandfather, so the story went, had been defrauded of his money by agents who took an entire season of furs down to New York and never came back. The store smelt wonderful. Flour, sugar, tobacco, leather, heavy boots, axes, rope, paraffin: it was all there on shelves and in great bins. The Americans called there to get fishing tackle, cartridges and beer on their way north. I did quite well out of the Americans through collecting frogs and selling them live at two for a nickel (five cents) as fishing bait. It was a pretty disgusting trade, granted the fate of the frogs, but business, even then, was business. The store doubled as the Post Office and telephone exchange. A private phone call was impossible in those days. By the number of clicks one could almost tell how many others up the line were getting all the gossip. In my life phone tapping has a long history.

Fire was the ever-present danger during the summer. Family tradition had it that as a great fire swept down towards the house and the river in the 1920s, Grandmother just put St Joseph's statue on the wooden pier where the paddle steamer used to call, and waited. The fire retreated, beaten by her prayers, we never doubted.

So it also retreated in my own and only personal forest fire. On some trip north with my uncle Henry we stopped for petrol at a friend's garage, only to hear cars rushing down the highway on the way to our village. We followed, and as our car crossed the iron bridge over the rapids orange and black flames were raging over the treetops. It had started when the fire warden's assistant had tried to thin some paint by putting it on a portable gas fire. Not a good idea! But it gave me the opportunity to run around, full of esteem and self-importance, with pails of water. It destroyed many trees but eventually the wind changed and the threat to the village disappeared. By the beginning of 1943 there were suggestions from my father that it was time we came home. The war seemed to be going in "our" direction and he, who loved his family, was fed up with the separation. So by Easter it was decided, over the heads of us children, that we would try to get a passage across the Atlantic. This turned out to be rather complicated – and no wonder, granted the chaos the world was in. A route was discovered which involved trains to New York and Philadelphia, and then a neutral Portuguese ship across to Lisbon. After a stay in Lisbon we were promised a flight in a Sunderland seaplane to neutral Ireland, and finally another to Portsmouth.

When it was all signed and sealed the *Montreal Star* reported that a plane carrying Leslie Howard had been shot down in the Bay of Biscay on just the same journey. We children tore out the piece of news from the paper. But this effort at deception was as unsuccessful as most of the others I have ever attempted. Mother knew the worst, but the scheme was going ahead anyway.

It turned out to be a rather wonderful journey. Not only did it include a trip up the Empire State Building and one to the Zoo in Central Park, but also we discovered in New York a shop with small tortoises on which you could paint the name of your beloved. I wanted to send one back to Sue Leslie but was forbidden to do so. The SS *Nyassa* was waiting for us in Philadelphia. It carried grain and passengers across the Atlantic with its sister ship, the SS *Serpa Pinto*, which we all thought to be a much more exciting ship, since a U-boat had stopped it in mid-Atlantic on its last crossing and removed a German spy. We were all anxious to discover a German spy but entirely failed to do so. Our route took us one day right through the biggest convoy anyone could imagine. The sea in the middle of the Atlantic was full of grey ships heading towards Africa. They showed no lights. We chugged on, lit up like a Christmas tree, with vast Portuguese flags painted on each side.

For a day or two we dropped anchor under the lee of the island of Terceira in the Azores, drenched in the scent which rolled down from the eucalyptus trees. The purpose of this diversion was to take on board what seemed, at the time, like most of the Portuguese army. Second- and third-class passengers were suddenly promoted and the whole of the steerage was handed over to hundreds of young soldiers who cooked, slept and sang wonderful songs under the stars right beneath our noses. We left them and the ship in the River Tagus as we disembarked for Lisbon. Only once did I ever hear of the SS *Nyassa* again: I think it was doing something illegal between Greece and the Lebanon in the 1950s.

In Lisbon we stayed with friends in the cork business and actually sat in cafés where there were Germans at the next table. As spies (and what else could they be?) they looked pretty run-of-the-mill.

Another idyllic few weeks passed with beaches, bicycles, picnics in pine forests and even a donkey. But Mother was not wasting time. The queue to get on the planes for home was very long and large groups were hard to place. So she persuaded someone at the Embassy that my brother and I were priority passengers, since we were due at boarding school. Why the same excuse did not work for my sister I have no idea. So some time in September 1943 we boys were taken together to a large Sunderland flying boat in the estuary. I have no memories of the flight except that the passengers faced each other and that a lady with a fur coat was unwise enough to wrap it around several blocks of chocolate and put it in the locker above her head, unaware of the hot pipes. We thought that the furry lump of chocolate that emerged in the morning was very funny, but all she could do was moan about her ruined coat.

Foynes was our destination, on the Shannon, and from Foynes quite a large group of parentless children were taken to Limerick. The Head Porter of the hotel into which we were placed deserved a post-war award. He turned out to be friend, adviser and very gentle disciplinarian to a group of kids who were quite ready to get up to anything. On other trips to Limerick I've tried to place the hotel, but it all now belongs to a different world. Another week and another plane, with white screens over its passenger windows, presumably so that passengers would not spot any military secrets, and we splashed down in Portsmouth Harbour. We were soon on the London train, which was blacked out with blue windows and very dim bulbs. There must have been a reunion at Waterloo with my father, but I can't remember it. I do remember acutely wondering in the next few days how this new personality, so confident and with so many jolly and noisy male friends, was going to fit into my life. I did not have long to wonder. The autumn term at Stonyhurst College, flagship of English Jesuit education, had already started and we had been found places there. Off we went again, taken by an elderly company salesman from Yorkshire called Mr Mutch, who was doing a favour for my father. Understanding Mr Mutch's accent was a considerable problem and wondering where on earth we were being sent was another. In the dark, the taxi from Whalley Station finally turned down the long drive to the College and Mr Mutch, far from being a Catholic, was as nervous as we were. They put us, while waiting, into a parlour with paintings and silver and old woodwork. Mr Mutch was given a strange antique three-legged chair, which promptly broke when he sat on it. He could not get back into the taxi fast enough, and that was the last we ever saw of him. Another new life was about to start.

CHAPTER TWO

My War Part II – Going East

The move to an English Catholic boarding-school in wartime from a Canadian Protestant day-school in what was effectively peacetime was a profound shock. We did not even arrive at the beginning of term, so we could not get any protection by being new boys amongst others. One dark autumn night Mr Mutch deposited us at the school. By the morning we were objects of considerable curiosity. It was a case of sink or swim. New nicknames were soon invented. In Canada I had been "Pepin" after the son of Charlemagne ("short, brutish and strong" according to our Canadian school history book). Now I became "Butch" because of the marked Canadian accent which I had acquired in the previous three years and because the rest of the boys assumed that with that kind of accent there had to be a New York gangster connection. "Butch" seemed to suit. My brother, already very tall for his age, was more logically christened "Tiny".

For the first six months I hated Stonyhurst. School never stopped. You couldn't escape at the end of the day and go home. Every minute of time was organized and regulated. You could only mix with certain groups of boys at certain times. The food was atrocious after the rich pickings of unrationed Canada. Awful pies used to appear with crusts made of some kind of potato mixture and slices of potato floating in greasy water within. We were given lumps of margarine which often enough, out of perversity, we would put on the end of knives and flick up to the ceiling. With any luck in the summer they would drip on to someone else. Memory has no doubt made all this much worse than it was, but I will certainly never forget receiving food parcels from home consisting mostly of peanut butter and Ryvita sandwiches. These I would smuggle up to the dormitory

16

at once and eat on my own, as fast as possible, in case I should have to share them with anyone else. The dormitory itself was a new experience. We all had cubicles with wooden partitions up to about six feet high, open at the top, with a white curtain over the entrance. The curtain was closed at night after prayers, and deep silence fell. A Jesuit patrolled the dormitories in case of hanky-panky but did so in ghostly silence. There were special Jesuit slippers with thick felt soles which glided over the polished wooden floors. The only way, inside the cubicle, of knowing that a Jesuit had passed was the sudden movement of the curtains. Under each bed there was a chamber pot to be emptied in the morning if used during the night. They were rather fine pots, with the school arms in green on the front. Below was the school motto, "Quant je puis". We thought that was brilliantly funny at the time.

Those first six months were not amusing. I suppose if I hadn't been already so conditioned to doing whatever grown-ups said, I might have refused to return after Christmas 1943. But it never occurred to me that such was an option, and I was not ready to cross swords with my father. In the new year I started to adapt so successfully that by 1946 I was sorry to leave, and did so with affection and happy memories. It took me another twenty years at least to realize how effectively I had been processed for English establishment life and values.

It was a gradual development. Discipline was, for instance, very strict, but I doubt if it was worse than that of other similar schools of the same period. Corporal punishment was routine. It was delivered on to the hands with a rubbery, leathery instrument called the ferula or "the tolly". Doses were ordered in numbers. You were told to get nine, or twice nine, or six, or twice six. Twice nine was about the top of the list for really outrageous crimes. My brother once got twice nine three days in a row but I can't remember how he earned them. He gained awe and admiration from the rest of the boys.

Distribution of punishment was all very clinical. If a master, lay or clerical, ordered a dose, then you had to wait till after lunch or after supper. Then you presented yourself, with other delinquents, outside the Prefect of Discipline's office. When your turn came you went inside and told whoever was on duty what you had been ordered to "get". He wrote all that down in a book and then held each wrist in turn while smashing the tolly down on your open hand. It was agonizing, but you couldn't afford to cry when you stepped back into the corridor. You walked over to the hot pipes and sat on them with your hands on the pipes and your head down. After a while the pain went, but your fingers looked like red sausages for many hours later.

That was the most regulated form of corporal punishment in an educational climate which accepted it as normal. The most barbaric form was that which boys were allowed to inflict on other boys. The School Committee was made up of a dozen or more senior boys, and they were given powers of supervision. If a crime against the authority of the Committee was committed, the Head Boy went to the Headmaster and asked for the right to cane the offender. I do not remember this right ever being denied. Once or twice a term the Committee would gather after supper in the Committee room, with no master present, send for some guilty wretch and proceed to flog him on his (trousered) backside. When I reached the dizzy heights of school seniority I once took part in such a performance, and I am ashamed of that evening even today. Such was the level of self-righteous sadism that each Committee member wanted his whack, so the cane was passed from hand to hand. The unfortunate victim was a boy called Travers. I met him a long time later, grown much bigger than me by then. He reminded me that I had once flogged him. I couldn't think of much to say in response to that, and he was decent enough not to pursue the conversation.

But I can't say that fear of getting flogged was an ever-present feeling. There was much too much that was positive also going on. The Lancashire countryside was fantastic and there were long walks and runs over the fells. My first fell run was a disaster. Never a good runner, I had read somewhere that sugar could be guaranteed to provide a rapid supply of extra energy. Saving up my sugar rations for several days, I swallowed the lot just before setting off, under the impression that thus I would zoom to the front. In fact I was sick. We never got as far as Pendle, which stood, humped up, to the south-east. Only long years afterwards did I climb it or hear anything about witches or George Fox or the history of the area. True, we were once taken down a coal-mine near Wigan, and I wrote an essay about it afterwards. Never did I want to go down those dark holes again.

Games featured prominently on the programme. Cricket in summer and rugger in winter. Cricket I have always found to be impressively boring, but I discovered a fielding position (long stop?) which became something else at the end of each over, so that one could remain in more or less the same spot, ruminating, for most of the game when not in the pavilion. Rugger was the alternative school religion, and being largish and lumpish, I was put in the scrum. This meant a lot of grunting and shoving and getting your fingers around other peoples' ears and trying not to get within tackling range of some dashing opposition wing streaking towards you with the ball.

Public schools all have their own networks, and so we chased up and down rugby pitches at Rossall and Sedburgh and once even at King William's on the Isle of Man. That was an interesting adventure, since it meant a flight from Liverpool in a very small plane across the water. Our most obvious opponent in games would have been the equally prestigious Benedictine school, Ampleforth, on the other side of the Pennines. But there had been a falling out between the two schools at the time over some sporting event, and it was generally agreed that since Ampleforth cheated we could do without Ampleforth on our fixture lists. No doubt Ampleforth's views were rather similar in return.

My cultural formation moved forward in all sorts of unperceived ways. The Stonyhurst dining hall was a magnificent place with coats of arms, moulded plaster ceiling, the table that Cromwell is supposed to have slept on at the far end, and portraits up and down the walls. Seven of them were pictures of rather grim Stonyhurst Old Boys who had won the Victoria Cross. This much we did know about Stonyhurst. We won more VCs than anyone else and would go on doing so. In this we were *the* best.

The Cadet Corps was an integral part of the school. A kindly Irish Guards NCO, Sergeant Major Barry, ran the show and various masters, including Jesuits, turned out to be Major this or Captain that on Wednesday afternoons. We marched up and down with great vigour and from time to time went off on exercises with blank cartridges which we shoved into antique carbines that looked as if they belonged to the Boer War. Anyway, the banging about was real enough and much enjoyed. So also was a hair-raising slide down a long wire over a brook while hanging on to toggle ropes. I'm no longer quite sure what toggle ropes were, but I do know that the ground looked a long way down. From time to time Old Boys in uniform would return to the school and these we worshipped. Our turn next. In fact, when one Old Boy, a pilot in the Fleet Air Arm, flew his plane one morning with a roar and a wail down the length of the playground, we were disgusted afterwards to find out that the Prefect of Discipline had actually reported him to the Navy. A really dirty trick unworthy of the school!

The Cadet Corps and school life criss-crossed in various ways. If you were promoted to the School Committee you almost always became a Sergeant in the Cadet Corps as well, and vice versa. On the Feast of Corpus Christi boys in uniform, with their rifles, guarded the Blessed Sacrament under the eye of Sergeant Major Barry, as the procession wound its way around the school grounds. Never did I hear tell of a conscientious objector, though I think we once did see a film called *The Four Feathers* which involved a decent chap refusing to do something for his regiment and spending the rest of the film, and a lot of Sudanese torture, redeeming himself. No wonder most of us could not wait to finish school and get our Commissions before the war ended. Serving as an Other Rank had happened to certain Old Boys, but it was the kind of failure we very much hoped would not come our way. Other Ranks came, after all, from other, lesser schools, not from our sort of school. We knew, of course, that other schools existed, but we had nothing to do with them – not even with the highly reputable Jesuit boys' grammar school in Preston only a few miles away. There were two worlds in the country, and we knew which one we belonged to.

Stonyhurst did sponsor a boys' club in Ladbroke Grove, Notting Hill, and we London boys were encouraged to visit the club during the holidays, which we were glad to do as a kind of favour. Once we invited some of the Ladbroke Grove boys up to Stonyhurst to play cricket, and they stayed for a weekend. There was much discussion about them and their curious ways and odd hygiene. Smelly feet, we decided. That we were going out of our way to encourage the lower orders was perfectly clear.

All this was rather odd, since there was no aristocratic tradition at Stonyhurst. Most of the boys came from professional or successful business backgrounds, and apart from its VCs the school had no great claim to national fame. We had our professors, judges and parliamentarians, but even now Paul Johnson's is the only contemporary name which would be nationally known. I was, for a time, in the same class as Paul. He was a wiry, active, slim redhead with radical tendencies who used to upset our history teacher, little Father "Pussy" Rea, by supporting the revolutionaries rather than the monarchy when we started to study the events of France in 1789. (Pussy Rea was easily upset. When bananas reappeared in 1946 someone accused the Jesuits in class of eating those intended for the boys only. He almost had a seizure, especially since it was not fair. There was a grown-up banana ration as well.) Paul went into life's orbit with a strong swing to the left, which he has subsequently wildly over-corrected.

If, at the time, I name-dropped it was always about Charles Laughton the actor, and only because I happened to have his desk. One of the sensible bits of school tradition was that a small brass plate with your name on it went on the front of your desk when you left the school. My desk had once been his, as his brass plate proved, and I always hoped that in the future people would be pointing out the connection between us. Not that I had any other connection. As an actor I was frustrated by a strong Canadian accent and was never allowed to repeat the Montreal triumph of *A Midsummer Night's Dream*. It was even worse. To get me a part where I would not actually have to say anything, and thus reveal the accent, a kindly Jesuit arranged for me to be Hamlet's father's ghost's double. I was known as "tis here", since my job was to appear, all done up in rope armour and silver paint, at the other side of the stage so that when Bernardo on the left pointed to the ghost and said "tis here", and was followed by Horatio on the right crying "tis here", there would be no loss of time. Thus our *Hamlet* had two identical ghosts, of which I was the second, non-vocal one. My two seconds on stage must have been the shortest Shakespearian appearance ever. If I had a dramatic success it was in getting through about three quarters of Chesterton's *Lepanto* at some recitation before getting lost in a fit of coughing. "Dim drums throbbing in the hills half heard" still rolls around my head from time to time.

The older one became at school, the more independence one had. I think it was forbidden, but nevertheless most of us managed to escape occasionally for large four-shilling teas, with bacon and eggs, in friendly farmhouses. A School Committee member, Tony Lawn, subsequently a prison chaplain, tried to stop such indulgence and nearly provoked a riot. The refectory table drummed with banging spoons and three hundred boys chanted "Lawn needs mowing." I thought the ceiling would come down, but he smiled and Nelson's eye continued to be applied. Farm teas survived. One of the difficulties for the Committee was its own corruption. Smoking was meant to be forbidden, but Committee members broke that rule, when they felt like it, sitting around the fireplace in the Committee room itself and blowing the smoke up the chimney.

Smaller boys were of course carefully guarded from bigger ones. The school not only had the House system of vertical division, but the horizontal division of "playrooms" for all recreation. Improper relationships were to be averted. They were not, of course. Most senior boys had their "tarts", which meant just a nice little boy much flattered by attention from higher up. All this was the result of the all-male (matron apart) society, but it never came to anything I ever heard of in terms of sexual activity, though notes were passed and winks and nods exchanged. All in all, though dirty jokes abounded, I think sexual experience in any area was minimal.

Many were the dark warnings of what might happen if one broke the sixth commandment. The Spiritual Director was a very nice old Jesuit, Christopher (invariably "Jerry") Wilmot, reputed to be an aristocrat and to have silk underwear, who would call us in for an update on "the facts of life". But when the interview was over and mortal sins had been separated from venials he always had a bar of chocolate to mark the event.

The Jesuits lived in a separate wing of the College in little rooms with coal fires, green baize doors and often a smell of pipe-smoke. They were a decent lot and if I lost touch with most of them that was only because the Society did not leave its men in one place for very long. For several of them my father had a great respect and I don't think he ever regretted finding us a place there. However, that happened rather by accident. In his London club under Bush House in the Aldwych he used to play bridge with a lawyer friend whose son, Paul Crane, was a Jesuit. Over the bridge table some time early in 1943 our school fate was settled and young Paul was asked to negotiate our admission to Stonyhurst. This was a school which could trace its origins back to its foundation in St Omer in 1592 during the days of Catholic persecution in England. It had returned to Stonyhurst, then the country house of a Catholic squire, in 1794, as persecution eased. Many priests and some colleges then fleeing the French Revolution found sanctuary in England. Its academic standards were high, though the names of its classes, by 1943, sounded quaint – Grammar, Syntax, Rhetoric and so on. Each class was divided into two sections. Those in Grammar I knew they were the hopeful high-flyers. The Grammar II boys were less ambitious, but everyone went in for the Lower School Certificate and most for the Higher as well. Oxbridge was the ultimate aim.

The Catholic faith was as important as any academic achievement and personal piety was a high priority. Daily Mass, Benediction, Confession, the Rosary and Our Lady's Sodality were all part of the normal routine. For a small boy the most striking bit of liturgy came with one of the great feasts: Corpus Christi, I think. The Brother Sacristan used to tie all the candles in the great College church together with some kind of taper or fuse. Then he lit one end, and all around the church the fire ran, from candle to candle, and there seemed to be hundreds of them, until the whole place glowed with light.

As ever, the example of the martyrs, like Edmund Campion, was held out in front of us. Ours was clearly the one true church. Our role was to defend it and protect it. Attacks on it could be swept aside as either ignorant or malevolent. We had a marvellous book called *The Question Box* with about three hundred objections to the

23

Catholic faith summarized and confounded. Communism and atheism were easily routed. It never turned out to be quite so easy, I discovered in later years. Narrow, I suppose, would be a fair description of our religious training, but it carried with it a great sense of awe and a conviction that this world was not enough. A great Ampleforth headmaster is supposed to have said, when asked at a Headmasters' conference about the real purpose of education, that *he* was preparing *his* boys for death. A Stonyhurst Head could have said much the same. The reply would not have been out of place. Within a few years of leaving school, nice amiable "Tubby" Maycock, with whom I shared a bench, was shot in Korea, a country of which I had probably never heard, in a war about which I understood almost nothing. But while we were being prepared for death and the next world, we were certainly not being prepared for many changes in this one.

This new wartime boarding-school life made growing together again as a family even more difficult. My father was a stranger, with his own life and friends, many connected with the Home Guard in which he was still actively involved. His official duty used to consist of guarding the West Hampstead railway tunnel, should the Germans have ever decided to invade it. There was a great deal of larking about as well with exercises. Once they even commandeered United Dairy's milk floats for a surprise assault on "enemy" units hidden on Hampstead Heath. For a long time after 1945 Sten gun bullets rolled around in the drawers of his desk amongst his Freemason's regalia. Not that he used the regalia anymore. He must have joined a Lodge in the 1930s but became bored with the theatrics quite early on.

We wanted to get on well with this new father, and indeed he tried hard. A great giving of presents by way of ending rifts or bridging gaps, one of his first holiday gestures was to take us down to Gamages to buy a puppy, so Micky the corgi joined the family. Probably because of his wartime diet, Micky's front legs bowed outwards rather alarmingly, but this deformity did nothing to slow him down if any enemy dog appeared on his patch. I remember my fury as I listened to two women in a Golders Green queue just in front of me pointing to Micky and saying in tones of outrage, "It's really cruel to keep a little doggy like that – he ought to be put down." We didn't think so and I said so loudly.

Father's generous gestures were offset by his drinking. Probably many other men separated by war from their families took that road. Off-licences around the area would ring up to say, "I've got a bottle of this or that for Mr Kent." I knew nothing about drinking, though I could tell when the conversation was out of gear and the jokes were getting more laughs than they deserved. It was only when he could not get the key into the front door one night that I realized what was going on, and then how easy it was for his good humour to turn to cruelty and verbal abuse. For children to be ever uncertain how a parent is going to respond is terrifying. Too many times we waited for him to come home from Bush House or the factory in Kingsbury for the regulation 7 p.m. dinner and went on waiting till we heard the key looking for the keyhole. Never was there a better Jekyll and Hyde. Sober, and he was the nicest man in the world to be with and the most generous. Drunk, and he could be very cruel. He was well aware that he had what is today called "a drink problem", and he did his best to control it. There were long periods when he got on the wagon and stayed there. But he never succeeded in escaping the alcohol trap on a permanent basis. Holidays at home from school were therefore uncertain times.

They were also lonely times. One of the disadvantages of a boarding-school is that you are not likely to have friends around the corner. I had three in London. One in Kensington, which meant the no. 28 bus from Golders Green, another in Streatham, which meant the no. 68 bus from Chalk Farm, and another next to South Kensington tube station. Brian's mother in Kensington had a flat in Duke's Lane overlooking the ruins of the Carmelite church. Washing up in her kitchen was quite easy. Every now and then one of her worst plates or saucers would go spinning across the road to see if we could hit the wreckage of the high altar. Geoff in Streatham had another wonderful mother, a loving and powerful Irish lady. We celebrated VE Night with her in Trafalgar Square, which was teeming with thousands of others. When she discovered, in a pub subsequently, that she had lost her glove in the crowd, she ordered poor Geoff back into the crowd to find it. And he did. My friend

Joe in South Kensington was Polish with very distinguished parents who had followed General Anders halfway round the world.

Holidays meant looking at the anti-aircraft guns on the Heath, the barrage balloons on the golf course and the rolls of barbed wire. It meant watching searchlights poking their way around the sky. It meant having a series of young Canadian airmen coming to stay, which was always good news, since I usually ended up with some decent socks or an Air Force blue shirt. Not until the flying bombs of 1944 did I know what it was to be under attack. On a clear day there was not much of a problem. They could be seen as well as heard. I remember watching one glide from over Hampstead, after its engine had cut out, towards Muswell Hill until it disappeared with a "crump" and a cloud of smoke. God knows how many it killed on the Archway Road. But in cloud or mist doodle-bugs were not a spectator sport. More than once, crossing the Heath, I heard the motor cut and leapt into the ditch, waiting in fear till a "crump" was heard somewhere else. My father brought us a series of pictures of the damage done by one that had plunged down at a busy time into the Aldwych just by Houghton Street, the LSE and his Bush House office. Twisted buses, legless horses and bundles wrapped in raincoats were the first I knew of war at the receiving end. Micky the corgi knew more than we did. He did not have to wait for sirens to know when to get into the family shelter. By that time the real air war was going on over Germany. We would stand on our balcony in the early summer mornings watching the start of those thousand-bomber raids. More little silver dots up in the sky than one could ever count all droning steadily south-east. I don't think it ever occurred to me that the scenes of the Aldwych were going to be repeated many, many times over in Germany.

Holidays also meant doing our bit. Once my brother and I were sent, more for our safety than for the war effort, I suspect, to a farm in Yorkshire next to the Castle Howard estate for the harvest. That meant a lot of hard work, balanced by enormous meals. But it also meant the chance to explore Castle Howard and its Grecian follies, as we crept through the long grass with airguns in search of rabbits. At the time Castle Howard stood empty after a fire. But I was utterly amazed when I first stood up and saw the length of its long grey east face. If there were keepers, they never got near us, though we got plenty of their rabbits.

My real war effort consisted of two school harvest camps in Hampshire. We lived under canvas on a farm at Over Wallop, with showers in an RAF camp opposite. A Jesuit was in charge, with some other masters. Every day we went off on bikes to various farms. I had to cycle through Middle Wallop to Nether Wallop, where Mr Pond would be waiting for me. It was all cutting and stooking and lifting. Hard work and a fairly good laugh at the same time. Barley, I discovered, travels up the inside of your trousers under its own steam and can cause embarrassing itches. There were always lively moments when the cutter got towards the centre of the field and trapped animals made a final dash for freedom. Some managed it, but the tractor driver with his gun was a good shot. One day he even brought down a little red fox which had nearly made it to the far fence.

There was an American camp up on the hill which had been abandoned after D Day, and we went looking around it for useful debris. We didn't get much. A few knives and forks, some magazines, a New Testament and, on the floor, what I later identified as a condom, in a used condition. So much for the spoils of war. Evenings were spent in the Nether Wallop pub before winding our way back to camp. The harvest camp would hardly be worth mentioning were it not for the fact that it gave me my first experience of mass hysteria – an awful warning ever since. Some of "our" boys had had angry words with some boys, unidentified, from Middle Wallop. The rumour went round our camp and escalated every night that "they" intended to do our camp and us over. We glared at Middle Wallop boys as we rode through their village. They no doubt glared back at us. From tent to tent the message went that we had to protect ourselves, so we got sticks for the purpose. We also raided those convenient little wartime roadside ammunition dumps where large black tins of thunder-flashes were stored. Thus armed, we decided one evening to sort out Middle Wallop before Middle Wallop sorted us out. Down we went to the village one night, letting off our thunder-flashes and looking for the enemy. They were not to be found. The supposed leader of the enemy was known, so we went to his parents' cottage, opened the front door, and barged in. Thank God no one was there. We all came out the back door and started to feel a little foolish. Back at camp a very angry priest was waiting, to be joined shortly by the RAF duty officer and the local bobby. The Wallops were not used to riots and criminal trespass. That evening should have put us all in court and on probation at least, but it didn't. The camp broke up a few days later and all was forgotten. But I have never forgotten, because I have seen international relations work on exactly the same principles so many times since. Paranoia is not confined to schoolboys.

Our war was winding to an end. We saw the horrors of the concentration camps in photographs as they appeared after VE Day in May 1945. On, I suppose, 7th August that year, I was standing on the corner of Baker Street and Marylebone Road when I saw the newspaper headline about a Wonder Bomb destroying a Japanese city. Great news, thought I, and greater news when the war in the Far East ended a few days later.

But I still had eighteen months to go at school in pursuit of Higher Certificates. When Oxford suddenly sent for me to be interviewed for a scholarship my academic reputation rose rapidly, only to fall as rapidly when I did not succeed. But the glory of staying, as a possible scholarship boy, in Oxford's Eastgate Hotel! I fortified myself for the interview by going to morning Mass and suspected nothing untoward in the Iffley Road church until the priest started *in English*, "I will go unto the altar of God." In English! I fled. I would not betray the martyrs for the false idols of Canterbury and Lambeth.

Not that I had any ideas of priesthood. The Jesuits had dropped enough hints. Our kindly but very nervous Rector, Father Swindells, interviewed most of the top form, and we all knew pretty well what he meant when it came to "Have you decided what God wants from you for the future?" We all thought we did, and it was not the Jesuits. Nor was it particularly marriage. Girls were people you met when you visited your sister at her school. Not till I was in the Army did I "go out" with one. I did earn a certain reputation with friends, however, by betting them that, in the Trafalgar Square Joe Lyons, I would successfully chat up a group of ATS girls several years older and centuries more sophisticated than me. The bet was on for ten shillings. I just went over to the girls, explained the situation and promised them tea for two shillings if they would chat for a couple of minutes. I returned triumphant.

At Christmas 1946 I finally left, with regret, the school which I had hated in 1943 – confident, aggressively Catholic and with almost no idea what to do for the six months before my eighteenth birthday and my call-up. My father had qualified as an engineer at McGill in Montreal, so I thought that engineering might be quite a good idea for me too. It was not. I spent a couple of unhappy months in a Lexham Gardens crammer trying to work out complicated bits of mathematics and to understand log tables. Having a Higher Certificate in English, History and French was of no help whatever, and "intensive personal tuition" meant that once or twice a day someone would ask how you were getting on. It was not possible to admit that one was utterly lost. So till the summer of that year I transferred to a nice old gentleman in Paddington who sat by a gas fire, ate jammy doughnuts, had pictures of Brasenose on the wall and really did believe in personal tuition. But not in logarithms. He got me through whatever Latin hurdles were necessary for Oxford, and I prepared for June and my call-up papers – that is, until I was struck by the Bright Idea.

CHAPTER THREE

Spit, Polish and Heroic Witness

It was while I was chewing over Latin constructions and very irregular Latin verbs with Mr Gardiner, my kindly and venerable tutor, in the spring of 1947, that the Bright Idea came. The Bright Idea was to get out of the country for a trip around Europe by bicycle before my call-up papers could arrive on my eighteenth birthday in June. This was not the scheme of a would-be draft dodger. On the contrary, getting into the Forces was essential for anyone's self-respect. In my head I was already dropping by parachute wearing a lovely red beret or zooming off a carrier for the Fleet Air Arm. But why not a little tour first? So it was planned. The cycle – a nice three-speed-gear Raleigh costing all of £12 – was bought on the Edgware Road and I signed up for the YHA. It was quite a remarkable trip. For one thing, despite fifty miles or so a day cranking my way from Dieppe down to Mont St Michel and around to Chartres, I was very homesick. Seventeen and three quarter year-olds are not meant to winge, still less weep about being away from home, but for some days I managed both. For another thing, I soon discovered that Higher Certificate French was not really enough. The French were not up to it and my Churchillian accent was not readily understood.

But the scenery was wonderful and the roads were long, straight and dotted with distance markers. Kind old ladies were ready with jugs of water and even sometimes cider for a thirsty traveller. Once in a while the wreckage of war was all too visible. I remember a picnic in a wood which was crossed with trenches and gun pits and littered with empty cartridges and rusting metal. Youth Hostels were much more free and easy than anything on the primmer British Isles. Near Cannes I went to bed in a nearly empty room, which in the morning I found to be a packed one full of both sexes: another new experience. Hygiene was still primitive there. For the first time I had to balance on a plank over a very unattractive pit. The Lord held me up. In the same hostel I learned a new fact of life. Girls were not as refined as I had thought. A couple of them from Lancashire were in the hostel, and in the course of their breakfast one pushed a jar of jam off the table on to the stone floor. "Bugger!" said the other. I could hardly believe my ears. The words which my schoolmates and I had used daringly, rarely, and well away from our parents, were known to and used by girls – innocent girls! I had much still to learn.

Growing thinner and browner, I eventually headed for the Spanish border, passing Carcassonne, with its ancient walls. The youth hostel there turned out to be an old chapel with a blue ceiling. Catholics in England, I felt sure, would not allow holy places to have such a secular purpose. With such priggish thoughts, the frontier came in sight in a rather curious way. The French and the Spanish had between them closed the border to rail traffic after the Spanish Civil War, and it was necessary to heave the cycle up to the top of some mountain pass before getting clearance to whizz down into Port Bou. The target I had in mind was Palamos on the Costa Brava, where the company for which my father worked had a cork factory. It was, long before package holidays, a dream-like place: the blue water, the little bay, the long siestas, the lazy hours on the beach, the lovely girls. I forgot Canada's Sue Leslie and replaced her with Catalonia's Janine, equally adorable but on the spot. It was a complete waste of time. To take her to the cinema required on her part a family conference. To take her to a dance meant that her mother and her aunt, in black, would take up defensive positions on the balcony and, hawk-eyed, watch every move below. So I drank beer, forgot the cycle, learned enough bridge (from an American who, I learned later, worked for the CIA) to remember not to trump my partner's ace and every night swayed around in a great circle as we danced the Sardana in rope sandals to reedy piping music. It was a wonderful couple of weeks, and the welcome from the town's upper-middle-class beach set could not have been warmer. Apart from Janine's mother and the aunt there were no flies in my ointment.

The plan had been to cycle back through Andorra, which seemed an interesting and odd sort of place, so finally I set off in that direction with many a sad backwards look. Progress was now much faster because I had learnt the art of hanging, with one hand, onto the backs of lorries as they went up the hills. No-one seemed to mind too much, and my mother was not around to point out the dangers of such rapid progress.

My political education began in some remote Catalan village when I was shown the voting slips for the Referendum which General Franco had ordered. What it was all about I wasn't quite sure, but everyone knew that a *"Sí"* answer was the one expected. That probably wasn't too difficult to achieve. All the voting slips I saw had *"Sí"* printed on them before they were given to the voters. Democracy made easy.

In all I was away for about two months and got back to Victoria Station eventually with a load of new experiences, some skills as a Catalonian dancer and the leanest and healthiest body I was ever going to have. Sun-tan covered the normal baby face which usually made me feel embarrassingly young.

The tan wore off by the time the call-up papers arrived in October, and my father deposited me at the guardhouse of the Hounslow No. 7 Primary Training Centre – a collection of army huts surrounded by a high wire fence with enough gaps in it to make unauthorized exits quite easy. For me the classless society of Hut 53 lasted only six weeks. Pip Permaine the trainee butcher and Ray Spain with the Brylcreemed hair, my first mates – where are you now? It was all a considerable challenge and major culture-shock. Drilling seemed to occupy a great deal of the day. Right turns, left turns, boots crashing down, about turns. Most of our hair was removed and we were sent into showers like sheep into a dip. Amiable abuse from sergeants and corporals, who might as well have served in the SS as far as I was concerned, was the order of the day. "Kent – what do you think you are? A pregnant nun?" I thought that was a deeply wounding question. But such questions, I soon discovered, needed no answers – just a series of ingratiating grunts. A pregnant nun? Such an outrageous idea had never occurred to me.

The main Rubicon I had to cross was Night Prayers. Often enough at school we had been told of courageous young Catholics who had not been ashamed to say their Night Prayers. There was I in this strange hut with twenty or thirty other eighteen-year-olds – a few were from public school but most were from God knows where, and I had to decide whether to go in for my Heroic Witness. Heroism won and I got down on my knees on the first night. With a proper sense of virtue I got up again after a few minutes. No-one seemed to have paid much attention. But I did. Further up the hut was another youth also on his knees. It was John White, and he was C of E. An Anglican saying Night Prayers! I felt really devalued. It was RCs who made heroic gestures, not members of Henry VIII's decadent, unfaithful C of E. I was quite cross.

There were yet more opportunities for Heroic Witness. Church parade, for instance. It was Remembrance Sunday and we were all to be marched off to church – a C of E church. I knew my duty and told the corporal, who told the sergeant, who told the officer. As a result RCs "fell out" and we thus gathered, almost a platoon of us – recusants and dissidents who would not bow to Caesar or offer incense to false gods. Sergeant Murphy took charge and we marched down Hounslow High Street to the Catholic parish church. That was enough for Sergeant Murphy. He told us in brisk terms when we got there that we could either go in or bugger off, just as we liked. But if we weren't back in an hour's time he would have our guts for garters. That was *not* the sort of piety we had learnt at school.

School still dominated the scene. When we had done enough right turns and left turns we had the Interviews. An officer actually talked to us individually. Mine took one look at my papers and saw that I had been to Stonyhurst. So had he. Handshakes and smiles! Did I play rugger? Would I like to go for a permanent commission? And so forth. I really didn't know what to suggest, but clearly the old school magic had worked and I was soon off to Belfast's Palace Barracks, of sinister reputation many years later, where the 28th Training Battalion, nursery of would-be officers and senior NCOs, was based.

Belfast meant long train journeys sitting on duffle bags, often in the guard's van, from Euston up to Stranraer and over to Larne. The crossing was short enough, but there was always time for someone to be sick over everyone else. Belfast was an entirely new world. I had learnt at school a great deal about the history of the French Revolution and could tell anyone far more than they would ever want to know about the Chartists. The Tudors I knew backwards. But Ireland was virgin territory. Not a clue about Irish politics had ever entered my head. Belfast was just a funny place with rather gloomy buildings and a lot of notices in the "Prepare to meet thy God" style. We didn't have much to do with Belfast, though I remember that the Rainbow Milk (sic) Bar was a surprisingly regular meeting-place for squaddies off duty. It was dimly known that there had been trouble with the IRA in the past and we were advised not to wear our heavy belts if going up the Falls Road. The belt with its brass clasps could be easily reversed and turned into a kind of club, which might be provocative. But I never even found the Falls Road, let alone went up it, so the situation did not arise. What I did find was the Malone Road and the welcoming and elderly Mr and Mrs Paisley, again business friends of my father, who provided excellent teas and large hot baths. I was not the only one to enjoy their hospitality. Another soldier, with more class than I would ever have and much interesting chat, would also turn up there sometimes. Thus Jeremy Thorpe's path through life and mine crossed accidentally over Mrs Paisley's scones and jam. An even higher-class recruit, but not a sharer of Malone Road teas, was a youthful Nicholas Ridley: he was very handsome, well turned out, and clearly going somewhere in life.

It was an interesting few months. Heroic Witness did not stop me going into the Protestant Sandy's Soldier's Home, which was inside the barracks and better than the NAAFI. There were large teas on Sundays, but one had to be careful not to be caught by the hymn-singing which followed. You could buy two (or was it three?) Woodbines in a little green packet. On four shillings a day, economy was essential, and we smokers would often fix beady eyes on other people's fags, hoping for a few puffs at the end of the butt. Security at the camp was minimal. We were never issued with ammunition on sentry duty and often enough we were provided with sticks, not rifles. "On" sentry duty could be a misnomer. One idle squad, which I helped to organize, arranged to do its spell on duty in the officers' garage, asleep in the back of their cars. The next shift would wake us and then take over. The IRA missed their opportunity.

From time to time we were hauled off for State occasions like the opening of Parliament at Stormont. That is a building I will never forget since it was the scene of a ceremonial disaster. One of the tricks of looking smart – a main objective – was to thread on string a series of small weights, probably old bullet heads, into a kind of "necklace". This necklace would go inside the trousers at the bottom of the leg, so that the trousers hung neatly over the gaiters.

At our Stormont parades there was a great deal of stamping about and many cries of "Halt!" and "Present arms!" During one inspection, as the General got near me, I had to stamp once too often. Out of my left leg popped my "necklace" and down it went over my foot. The gaiter vanished from sight. It was not a pretty picture, and the General said so. Stormont remains an unhappy memory.

Religious life now had two aspects. At the barracks it was religion as I had known it, though it was some surprise to discover at Christmas midnight Mass that many of the crudest and most impious of the ATS and the Catering Corps turned out, for that event at least, to be co-religionists. Churches in Belfast City were confusing. At the altar end things seemed roughly the same as what I was used to. At the door end it was all very different: Gaelic newspapers, hurley matches, pilgrimages to Knock and invitations to take the Pledge never to touch strong drink.

It was at Easter 1948 that I first really ran up against the invisible religious barriers which cut across the Province. I was asked to spend the weekend with the friends of some friends near Maghera-felt. They were a linen family, considerable local squires and very hospitable people. On the Easter Saturday night quite a crowd gathered around the family table, and I was there in my uniform, proud of my (acting unpaid) lance corporal's stripes. After all, one has to start somewhere on the way up. I was asked if I would be joining the family at church the next morning. Without any idea of the significance of what I was saying, I said I would sooner go to Mass.

35

Nice families cover up appalling gaffes by guests quite soon, and the silence was only momentary. But after the meal I heard the son of the house insist to his father that I was a guest and that while I was there I would be treated as one. The next day I was dropped from the family car on its way to their church, and I made my way on foot to the local Catholic church. To be fair, the arrival in a remote church on Easter Sunday morning of a lance corporal in uniform caused its own little flutter of amazement amongst the ranks of Rome.

My time in Belfast was fast running out. One by one my mates went off to Officer selection boards in England and rumours of their successes or awful failures came back to us. Our platoon began to evaporate. We had trained as far as we could train. Hand-grenades, PIAT bombs, Bren guns and rifles were all old friends, with the procedures for their use learnt by numbers. We had frozen under the shadow of the Mountains of Mourne, which actually seemed to sweep down to Ballykinlar camp. I had spent a week or so in a military hospital with an infected hand, which did not stop me from gathering up enough coal to make sure that, when the lights went out, our one central stove glowed deep red, a pillar of fire by night. It dawned on me that I was the last of my entry and still I had not been called to a selection board. In the interim, while waiting, I had risen to positions of power never subsequently repeated. At Palace Barracks I was made responsible for dishing out coke (of the heating sort) to the married quarters and, when not so powerfully engaged, I used to sit in the Quartermaster's store slicing up vast, solid currant-cake blocks which looked as if they had been stamped out by some huge kitchen hammer. I grew idle and plump, but still there was no call. Perhaps the country no longer wanted fresh-faced second lieutenants? Finally I went in desperation to the Company office to ask what had happened to Kent 022. Amazement and much shuffling of papers. A confused orderly sergeant explained that I had already gone. No, I replied, I was here. This was no vision – it was me, corporeal, present, still getting four shillings a day. More shuffling until it was revealed that indeed Kent 044 had been sent and that Kent 022's papers had, by a paper clip, got attached to Kent 044's. For some weeks I had apparently been a non-person.

A very nice Rifle Brigade (I was only in the Royal Fusiliers) company sergeant major apologized profoundly, and I was rapidly on my way to Catterick in Yorkshire and the War Office Selection Board, where my leadership qualities were to be tested.

When faced with a massive wall I made all "my men" crawl up it and then required them to pull me up afterwards by a rope, which seemed to go down well with the examiners. The most dramatic part of the examination was being faced with a table on which lay an old-fashioned lavatory chain comprised of a series of hooks ending up with a porcelain handle. It lay in pieces in front of me. So also did the kind of bicycle pump which involved a spring, a leathery washer and a metal tube. Both of these had to be assembled as fast as possible. It was no great problem, but I apparently managed some sort of record. Such skills, quite unsuspected, had a profound effect on my future military career.

On the way by car to Richmond, where another examination was waiting, I prized open the envelope which held the Catterick results. Under my name was the recommendation, "This man has considerable mechanical aptitude. He should be sent to Officer Cadet Training School and transferred to the Royal Armoured Corps." The providence of God and his wonderful ways were evident, as a paper clip, a lavatory chain and a bicycle pump determined my future direction.

The first stop on the new road was Aldershot's Mons Officer Cadet School in the spring of 1948, where a lot more stamping and banging went on together with a great deal of crawling through the undergrowth, map reading and study of the Manual of Military Law. The training was in two stages. After some weeks of basic officer training, the Artillery cadets and the Armoured Corps cadets were separated to go their different ways. A great party in a Farnham hotel marked the end of the first stage, and I disgraced myself by getting rapidly and disgustingly drunk. One of our instructors and I, I dimly remember, stood on a table and tried to sing "Alouette". How wonderfully witty we thought we were. On the bus back to Aldershot it seemed that the bus was crossing the Atlantic in a storm. Faced with our "spider" of six interconnected huts back in the barracks, I lay down dismally on what ought to have been my bed. It would have been, were I in the right hut. When I was finally put to bed in the right place, the roof rose and fell and the lights seemed to have an orbit all of their own. Horrible sickness struck. Finding in the morning that you have been sick into your own boots is not a nice discovery. Finally, by noon the next day, miserable and queasy, I managed to get a taxi to take me the mile or so up to the Armoured Corps area. Never have I been in such an entirely disgusting state again, nor would I wish the experience on anyone else.

It took two or three days to get back on form and to realize that the British class system had struck again. This time I was on the wrong side of the rails. The Armoured Corps cadets were divided into Royal Tank Regiment would-be officers and their Cavalry counterparts. The Cavalry lot were quite clear about their social status. One would have thought that most of their parents, male and female, had taken part in the Charge of the Light Brigade. We of the Tanks were the yobbos of the operation. There was not a title amongst us and most of us were not on speaking terms with horses.

Actually, the Cavalry may well have saved our lives, as things turned out. One of the nasty ideas of the management was that cadets, during their training, should undergo long-distance runs, carrying most of their equipment. It started at two miles and worked up over the weeks to six, eight and even ten miles, at a kind of exhausted half run, half dog-trot. The ever-present fear of being RTUed (Returned to Unit) drove everyone madly on to complete every task that was ever set. So it was with the long-distance runs. One blazingly hot day in the summer of 1948 we of the Armoured Corps, perhaps twenty of us, with a hundred of our former colleagues, the Artillery cadets, were scheduled for one of the longest runs. Then we, the yobbos of the Royal Tank Regiment, discovered that the dashing Cavalry cadets had all got permission to escape the run on the pretext of getting their London tailors to check their uniforms and, I suppose, to sharpen their swords. That left eight or ten of us, amongst whom a mutiny broke out.

We decided to go swimming in Aldershot, in the hope that the duty Sergeant would assume that all the Armoured Corps cadets had a legitimate excuse. In the event we were praised for our initiative. So hot was the day and so long the run that exhaustion set in.

A number of the Artillery cadets were very ill and at least one died on the roadside of heat-stroke that afternoon. There was a great Press outrage. An inquiry followed and the Commandant and others were reprimanded. Our Major was praised for his initiative in letting us off, and we basked in his glory. Rules, it seems, were sometimes there to be broken.

So the summer passed with various battles between Red Army and Blue Army, plenty of thunder-flashes and all kinds of assaults on the Waterloo to Basingstoke railway line. There was, of course, also a great deal of interest in hygiene. I do not easily forget the very large-scale yellowish fly that was on display at the Army School of Hygiene (I think that was what it was called), or the lurid accounts of where such flies went during the day and what they did. Boots were beaten into black ivory with toothbrush handles and kit layouts would have been the pride of any religious order. There were cadets who even slept on the floor before kit inspections the following day rather than disturb the layouts on their beds. Do they, I wonder, still make flat circles of their leather bootlaces, tie the circles together with thread and then polish the final result?

There were few eventualities for which we were not trained; we were even trained for the quelling of civil disorder and riotous behaviour. Were we ever called upon to take on that role, the procedure would be quite clear. We would bring a file of riflemen in V-formation towards the centre of the disturbance; each man would be numbered in advance so that no names would be used. Other soldiers would make sure that the exit roads from the square or town centre were clear. The mob would be told to disperse. If they failed to do so we were to identify someone clearly – e.g. "man in red jumper climbing lamp post" – and to follow up with "No. 1, fire!" or "No. 2, fire!" etc. The shooting was to be to kill. No messing about with firing over their heads. I suppose I scribbled all this down in those big buff notebooks without once thinking that "the square" might be in Birmingham or Glasgow or Belfast. It was always somewhere else, never defined. In such cases of dire emergency the job would be to restore order and the rule of law. I'm sure I would then have bumped off Trafalgar Square Poll Tax rioters if told to do so.

Hopes of seeing the world at the expense of the Ministry of Defence evaporated at once when, bursting like Aesop's frog in my new uniform with its officer's single pip on each shoulder, I got my orders to report to the 6th Royal Tank Regiment stationed on a disused airfield somewhere between Worksop and Retford. Down the drain went hopes of Hong Kong, Singapore, or even Germany. Worksop? I had to look it up on a map.

On my last day in Aldershot I happened to notice a rather miserable-looking soldier in fatigues with a bucket being chased along by a military policeman. It was Paddy, one of my early mates from Hounslow – one of the RC awkward squad. Clearly we had followed very different paths since then. I felt like Black Beauty watching poor old Ginger on his way to the knacker's yard. Our eyes met in recognition and that was that.

At Scofton near Worksop they were waiting for us. A friendly large lad called Mike Pillar (who went off to Rhodesia on demob) and I finally reported late one evening at the 6th RTR Officers' Mess, which was a kind of extended Nissen hut miles from any-where. A number of young officers greeted us warmly and took us to the bar, where the Padre appeared. He was a sympathetic and interested Padre. He wanted to know if we had any problems of a personal nature, and though the bar seemed to be an odd place for this sort of questioning, we both fell over ourselves assuring him that such personal problems had never crossed our minds. Dis-covering that I was rather rigidly RC, he then inquired in a friendly way about Mike's level of devotion and practice. Finally he explained that it was customary for new officers to attend morning service on their first day of duty, and would Mike kindly bring the cruets of water and wine to the Chapel hut. Which is exactly what Mike tried to do the next morning, only to find the entire Mess howling with laughter at breakfast, when he returned in confusion with his full cruets. The Padre turned out to be a captain and the 6 RTR joker, with a football shirt down his front and a piece of white plastic around his neck.

So we settled in. As defenders of the realm we were not exactly in the front line. Our job was to clean, paint, and generally keep operational the dozens of Comet tanks which were parked in vast hangars around the old airfield and which were kept for summer use by the Territorial Army. The Cold War had not yet really got under way, and no-one had in mind a sudden rush from Worksop to stop the Red Hordes at Calais. Palestine and Malaya were the only operational areas, and it seemed unlikely that the 6 RTR would be called on to sort out either situation. So we manicured our tanks, took long walks around the airfield, went to dances in the Retford Town Hall and generally idled our hours away, drinking rum and orange in the Mess. The other second lieutenants were a friendly lot with a variety of eccentric habits. One kept a small hawk which he trained to swoop down the length of our hut in pursuit of lumps of meat. This activity made quiet letter writing difficult. We all had batmen provided, so at the age of nineteen I became part proprietor of an amiable but rather dopey lad. So dopey, in fact, that once, when asked to light the stove, he did so, neglecting to remove my best boots, which were sitting on top of it. By the time I got back the soles had sprung open and what looked like tar was oozing out of the seams. Perhaps he was not as dopey as I thought, because after that I looked after my own gear and bothered him no longer.

The 6 RTR was not exactly a plum posting. Most of the senior officers were hanging on after war service, looking for something to do in civilian life. The Colonel was a boozer and painfully interested in Mess games. It was embarrassing to watch middle-aged Majors throwing bread rolls at each other or pretending to be interested in Mess post-dinner football, just to keep the Colonel happy and to ensure that on their way out they did not get a final negative report. One officer was sent to us from another regiment to await a Court Martial on pay fraud charges. By the time the Court Martial finally came round, months later, he had turned into an alcoholic.

With this Regimental Mess nonsense went a lot of good laughs as well. Keeping the tank with the bent gun away from the inspectors was one of them. One troop, on exercise near Scarborough, had actually managed to lose a tank over a cliff. It had been meant to bog itself down in a deep pit prior to a lesson on getting tanks out of deep pits. But, in fixed first gear, after the driver had jumped out, it had managed to circle the pit and chug along to the cliff-top, over which it slowly rolled. It bounced down the cliff, did a kind of pole-vault on its gun and landed on its tracks on the beach. Amazingly, it only took a new starter motor to get it going, and then it was driven along to a promenade and onto the awaiting tank transporter. What those on the beach thought as a tank appeared around the breakwaters I do not know. But the end result was a tank with a gently curved gun barrel. Whenever the REME (Royal Electrical and Mechanical Engineers) inspectors arrived a kind of shell game went on. We always managed to produce the right number of tanks, but one was always inspected twice and one not at all. I did not see the tank go over the cliff, though I might just as well have done, considering how often the tale was told.

What I did see was some quite remarkable tank gunnery. One of our firing ranges was at Cowden on the east coast. There shells were fired at targets out on the sea. One day a couple of trawlers, ignoring the various flags, sailed into the range area a long way out to sea. Since they ignored our signals, the officer in charge cleared the sea very efficiently. One tank was backed into a ditch to give the gun greater range, and a couple of live shells were dropped a few hundred yards ahead of the trawlers, which rapidly did 180° turns. I suppose we would all have been up for manslaughter or murder if he hadn't got the bearing right, but it seemed like a good wheeze at the time.

There were few discipline problems. Most of the troopers were conscripts, as we were, and not anxious to cause trouble. One of mine did steal someone else's trousers with the wallet still in it and was shipped off to Wakefield prison to await trial. In the best young officer tradition I dashed off after him with various gifts from "the lads", convinced that he must be innocent. Now I'm not quite so sure. My pink baby face got someone else into serious trouble at about the same time. On the bus back from Worksop one night I was at the front and one of the more seasoned troopers was at the back. With a few pints rolling about inside him he started to tell the rest of the bus what he thought of an army which sent boys straight out of school to give orders to men like him. From the general he then moved to me, the specific, and the passengers had their attention drawn to my effing cheeks, effing chin and effing immaturity.

I could not get off the bus fast enough when we got to camp, pretending that I had not heard a word. But a Sergeant Major in civvies had. A charge of insubordination was laid, and the wretch went off for three months to an effing glasshouse to teach him not to be rude to young officers.

I wondered what would happen when next we met and hoped that it would be in a public and protected place. It was not. We ran into each other three months later, more or less, on the far side of the dining hall, out of sight of anyone else and with only green fields for miles around. He got closer and closer and my blood pumped faster and faster. A couple of feet away, and he suddenly and smartly saluted. Cowardice dripping off me, I could not have been more relieved.

Before long I got a bit bored with tanks and the maintenance thereof and managed to get myself posted to a wireless course at Bovingdon in Dorset, which was the Mecca of all armoured enthusiasts. This meant a great deal of swanning around the West Country in fifteen-hundredweight trucks full of wireless gear, rigging up aerials and chasing yet more Blue and Red armies. I learned much about communication which has served me well since – the most important lesson being that 100% attention to verbal instruction drops rapidly to about zero within twenty minutes. How did nineteenth-century preachers ever manage? That wasn't the only useful skill I learned. "Man management" is probably an unfashionable term today, but there was a lot of good sense in it. Teamwork was essential to get anything done, and the key to teamwork was "putting everyone in the picture". Not a few voluntary organizations could learn useful tips of this nature from the military. Certainly, the importance of encouraging people and giving initiative its head I have never forgotten.

Bovingdon was a good break and probably put me on course for another change of direction. Attached to the camp was a really good Catholic chaplain who had not the slightest ambition to be one of the boys but who was simple, straight and interesting. He lent me Graham Greene's *The Power and the Glory* and thus put a small seed about priests into my head which came to full flower a few months later – with fairly dire family consequences.

Back from Bovingdon I came as a qualified wireless instructor. Theory did not much matter. Practical steps did. If a wireless failed to work, we looked up a large chart and sorted out the valves, symptom by symptom, until it did. I now had mystique as an "expert" on something at last, and to mark this new status I was put in charge of the fleet of Daimler Dingo scout cars in order to run wireless exercises. It was like having a dozen private taxis permanently at my disposal, and most afternoons I spent on "test runs" and thus learned much about the beauty spots of middle England. The hot summer of 1949 we spent in Norfolk at the Stamford training area, so I was able to add Norwich, Lincoln, King's Lynn and most of the sandy Norfolk coast to my list of "test run" targets. No Dingoes were better tested than mine. Interesting little vehicles, they were. By switching one small lever there were as many reverse gears as forward ones, which, I suppose, could get you out of trouble rapidly, but resulted in very peculiar steering when in reverse at speed.

Heroic Witness was by no means dead. There were a lot of Poles in our regiment, understandably not very interested in going home. Since they were Poles I assumed they had to be Catholics. It seemed clear to me that they would hardly want to miss Mass on the Feast of the Assumption, even if they were stranded on the Stamford training area. So off I went to the Adjutant who kindly organized a three-tonner to take all these Poles and any other of my allegedly devoted RCs up to Mass in the Convent at Swaffham. Full details of this religious expedition were provided in Regimental orders. Bright and early on the right day I waited by my truck, whose driver looked very sceptical indeed. How right he was! Not a single soldier turned up to save me from ridicule as I appeared alone in the Convent chapel. I didn't mind a bit of Heroic Witness, but being laughed at by the Adjutant was not part of the plan.

What *was* the plan was not quite clear. Brasenose College, unwilling to dish out a scholarship, was at least ready to offer me a place and ridiculously, because I had got into the Army by October 1947, I was entitled to a full wartime grant. The seed sown at Bovingdon really burst out at Easter 1949, when I went back to Stonyhurst for the annual retreat for Old Boys and fell under the spell of a dramatic and powerful preacher, Father Joseph Christie, SJ. As far as I was

44

concerned he could run rings around Billy Graham. Suddenly all was clear. The best way that I could live my life and bring Truth to the world and Good News to the poor was to become a priest. Of course, as a Jesuit. They seemed to me to be to the rest of the clergy what the Paratroopers were to the rest of the Army.

The conviction of vocation and destiny was powerful and lasting. I broke this certainty to my father with the crudeness of the young and with hardly a thought about his feelings. I knew he would object. I knew that such objections had to be rolled out of the way. God's will came first. It was not a happy few months. Father had swallowed the idea of children who were Catholics and had kept his promises about education. But he had never dreamt that one of his sons might want to be a priest. That was too much. For a week he left home. There were rows of every description, with my Catholic mother trying to pour oil on waters, but clearly on my side. Eventually a truce was agreed. I would go to Oxford for three years, and if I then persisted with clerical ideas there would be no further objections. So it turned out and the treaty was kept. Very decently he bought me a 350 cc Royal Enfield motorbike to seal the deal, though it nearly in the end eliminated one party to it. Hurtling round the North Circular road late that winter near Henley's corner, the front wheel hit some ice and I and the bike did a series of circular slides in and out of various cars and lorries. I should have been dead, for those were pre-helmet days, but suffered only torn trousers and a bent brake lever. The Royal Enfield therefore took me, not to a seminary, but to Oxford in the autumn of 1949 after nearly two years of National Service, which I regretted not at all.

CHAPTER FOUR

Oxford's Lotus-eating Years

Everyone says that University years go past at an unexpected speed, and so they certainly did for me. Mine were three interesting, active years, but looking back now, I can see that they were spent in a world which had little enough to do with any other. Long after leaving Oxford I discovered the estates out on the Botley Road beyond the station and others up the Cowley Road. I have, indeed, no memory whatsoever of seeing the car factories, let alone of visiting them. Only when I read Olive Gibbs' fascinating autobiography, *Our Olive* did I realize what I had missed. Olive grew up in the 1920s in near poverty in workmen's flats near the Castle and worked her way with skill and persistence until she, a lifelong courageous supporter and eventually Vice president of CND, became the Mayor of Oxford in 1974. But her world was not my world. Even the changes brought in by the first Labour government after 1945 were passing over my head. Ours was a *Daily Telegraph* and *Sunday Express* family at home, so left-wing politics were not our cup of tea. My father more than once complained that the little socialist creep, Harold Wilson, had actually moved during the war into the Hampstead Garden Suburb, where he clearly did not belong. Mention of Aneurin Bevan would produce volcanic signs of paternal disapproval.

But I was comfortable at Oxford with a generous Government grant and no shortage of things to do. It was not difficult to find friends. Some of my old friends from school and from the Army came at the same time. The College system made making new ones quite easy. The atmosphere was one of austere luxury, if that is possible. There were coal fires cleaned out by "Scouts" who woke you, tidied you up and even ran errands for you. After rugger or

46

football you could collect a tray of tea plus buns and cakes, take it to the baths, put it on the wooden soap rack in front of you and enjoy multiple pleasures. It was rather a Charlie's Aunt world. Everyone, for their first year, had a sitting-room and a bedroom. To go to the lavatory meant a chilly expedition to be postponed as long as possible. If you closed your outer door you were "sporting your oak" and did not want to be disturbed. Why you might not want to be disturbed I only discovered when I barged in, knocking as I opened, on a now well-known journalist. How was I to know what was going on, and were they actually committing mortal sin, I wondered?

Early attitudes were not easily, or in fact ever, shaken off. No-one could have been more conformist than I. Within a few days someone pointed across the square at a skinny but ordinary-looking youth and said, "That's Alan – he's a Marxist." I stared. A Marxist! The embodiment of all evil! Stealers of private property and deniers of the One True God. I continued to stare with amazement. He just looked so ordinary.

Gross over-estimates of my own intelligence and of the brilliance of the arguments with which I had been fitted out were soon exposed. My first essay was marked with a Greek squiggle. This, I assumed, had to be an Alpha. I was crushingly told it was a Gamma and soon started to have some humility forced on me. I went one night to some philosophical circle where the non-existence of God was being discussed. So I crashed in on the conversation with Aquinas and the five knock-down proofs of the existence of God, which I had been assured worked everywhere. They did not seem to work very well in Brasenose, at least as presented by me.

Life soon got into an agreeable routine, most of which revolved around the weekly essay. It had to be presented for a tutorial on Friday mornings. From Monday to Thursday a crescendo built up as one carefully postponed getting down to writing the wretched thing until the last possible moment. I was reading law, for no better reason that someone had given me the biography of Marshall Hall, a great defence advocate, and I saw myself as dominating juries in the style of American films. It was a choice of subject I never regretted. Law gave one a grounding in history and philosophy and above all taught its students to read documents carefully and not to make opinions into facts unless the evidence was there. So, in my way, I enjoyed ploughing through Crime, Tort, Real Property, Jurisprudence and the rest, while looking up all the amazing cases and judgements which have dotted our legal history. I had never heard of Real Property, which was all about land, inheritance, covenants, trustees, freehold and the like. It began to dawn on me that in some respects we had not yet left the Middle Ages. Someone must own all the estates without which Real Property would not have meant very much. Crime was always fascinating. What will people get up to next? Anything at all is the only answer. "Was a duck an animal within the meaning of the Act?" and similar related questions produced crude giggles in the Law Library, where we pored over Law Reports and scoured the dirty bits of Law Journals.

The fruit of the week's work, and of such lectures as one chose to go to, was the essay which then had to be discussed in front of the tutor. Tutors seemed to know by instinct when essays had only been completed one hour before the tutorial after some all-night party. Excuses for not producing essays varied with the imagination of the essayist. I once over-reached myself with the courteous and gentle Barry Nicholas, Roman Law expert and eventually Principal of Brasenose. The evening before, which was hot and summery, I thought the essay could wait just a little longer. I borrowed back my Royal Enfield from my friend Mike Shaw, to whom I had just sold it, and set off for the Trout, a lovely Thames-side pub in North Oxford. The evening wore on, with the essay still nagging me at the back of my mind. So, a bit beery, I started the return journey with a friend on the pillion. (This was pre-breath-test days.) At the last moment a female fellow student, much in demand, explained that she had missed her lift. So we put her between us and continued down the Woodstock Road. Half way down I thought the Third World War had started. Bells rang, lights flashed and something out of *Z Cars* shot in front of me. Police in numbers. I was nicked. First time in my life. Family disgrace. Criminal record. My two passengers disappeared fairly rapidly into the night, and I was left in the police station completing endless forms and trying to explain to impassive officers that I had not stolen the bike. This meant getting the new

48

owner out of bed. In some confusion, he was clearly willing to perjure himself in any way that would help me.

All this eventually resulted in a twelve-month loss of licence, but at least I had an excuse for not writing the essay. I explained to patient Barry the next morning that I had gone out to the Trout at tea-time but, having lied about the time, I laid the story on too thickly and eventually explained that amongst all the awful charges facing me was one for driving without proper lights. "At tea-time?" said Barry very gently. I blushed my way out of his room, since I could think of nothing else to say. My father's little jingle, "What a tangled web we weave when first we practise to deceive" came rapidly into my head. (Not that he used it again after an elderly aunt came down from Scotland one summer and told him, in front of us, "Kenneth – you always were an awful wee liar.")

It was not the police but the Bulldogs who were meant to see to student discipline in my day. The Bulldogs were bowler-hatted agents of the Proctors, and the Proctors administered the rules, of which there were a variety. Students who wanted to bring cars to Oxford had to ask for permission from the Proctors. It was usually given, but on condition that the car displayed a little green lamp in front. Proctors gave me no trouble, nor I them.

What to do in the future with my law was a problem. Not putting priesthood out of my mind – the idea which had so powerfully entered it three years before had always remained a background hope – I decided to back another horse as well and signed up with the Inner Temple. Motives are hard to sort out many years later, but I think that by taking steps towards the Bar I was trying to reassure my father that I was willing to look at other options. If I didn't become a priest then I would, at the Bar, surely be able to convince juries of the innocence of my clients, however bad the circumstantial evidence. The Inner Temple routine meant that one had to eat, at no small cost, a number of dinners each term in London. This absurd requirement seemed entirely normal to me then, but those were the days of not asking questions.

I wish I had been less conformist. International Law, which now seems to me to be so important as the bone-structure of a growing world community, was almost entirely a matter of international contracts, claims to territorial waters and the ownership of unoccupied territories. Perhaps there was more to it, because I do remember one case about liability for the sinking, by British mines, of a ship off the coast of Albania. Our distinguished law lecturer was also famous for an indelicate ditty which was meant to illustrate some point or other. It was all about a cabin boy, some broken glass and painful personal injury to the skipper. We thought it hilarious at the time. What International Law was *not* about, insofar as I remember, since memory can be very selective, was the Hague and Geneva Conventions, the laws of war and peace and the Charter of the United Nations, still in its early and hopeful days. International Law, as it affected conscientious objection, was certainly not on the agenda. Nor was Constitutional Law related to improving the democratic nature of British society. Criminal Law remained in the head. Never once did we visit a court or a prison, though a particularly unpleasant prison was immediately available in Oxford.

As the three years went past – and how rapidly that happened – exam fever began to stir. I knew I was no candidate for a First. But to get a Third would be an embarrassment. So the race was on for a Second. With a Second one might just have missed a First. With a Third that kind of explanation would not wash. The pressure in the last two terms was very considerable, and when Finals were actually in progress I and some others were not too far from hysteria. Physically it was an endurance test. Nine papers of three hours each had to be taken (and written) between a Thursday and the following Wednesday morning, in the big examination hall. With consequent semi-paralysis of the right hand, I never wanted to take any more exams ever again. At least I can now say that I just missed a First, not that anyone has ever asked.

Law, however, was only part of Oxford life. There was too much going on of interest. At the Oxford Union the great and the good made their mark as they moved effortlessly towards future political fame. Robin Day, Jeremy Thorpe and William Rees-Mogg could all be marvelled at from a distance. Rees Mogg was a bit of a disappointment. He was known to be Catholic, but he had not gone to a Catholic school and did not attend the Chaplaincy, and one had to wonder, therefore, if he was really one of us. I spoke once at the union – in defence of private education, I regret to say – but I had to stay up so late to get my profound thoughts aired in public that I never bothered again.

The Newman Society was more my cup of tea. When Catholics had finally been allowed to go to Oxford at the end of the nineteenth century, careful provision, in the form of chaplains and chaplaincies, was made to guard their faith from contamination or even loss. The Newman was the undergraduate Catholic society, affiliated, I now see from the Society's card, to the "OU Peace Society". What on earth was that? No one ever mentioned it. It was more comfortable to be a bigger fish in a smaller university pond, I suppose, and so many of us drifted to the Newman. The Chaplain of the day was the devoted, energetic and rather classy Mgr Valentine Elwes, a new broom but one who kept his links with the past. Once or twice a year his great predecessor Mgr Ronald Knox would come to preach in what was then a rococo Nissen hut tacked on to the back of the genuinely venerable Old Palace down the hill from Christchurch. Knox was always a winner – witty, pious and erudite – but he came from a different age. By Elwes' time women students mixed on equal terms with their male counterparts – a far cry from the segregated regime of the Knox days – a segregation which lasted very much longer at Cambridge under the velvet glove of Mgr Gilby. Not everyone went to Mass at the Chaplaincy. The posher products of Downside and Ampleforth removed themselves to the austere and intellectual Dominicans up at Blackfriars. Some didn't go to Mass at all, for that matter – something which was of grave concern to us, the faithful. I remember joining a prayer circle, the main aim of which was that each participant would "adopt" a lapsed Catholic and pray him or her back to the Church. I pursued my target for well over a year, but since he showed no sign of conversion I decided that this spiritual problem was just too big for me on my own.

If Newman and Chaplaincy life isolated us from other University interests, it did provide a circle and a centre where one could feel at home. These were not ecumenical days. I have no recollection of any effort to join in with the Nonconformist or the Anglican groups for any activity. Nearly every college had its chapel and its chaplain, and I often wondered what the latter actually did. Our chaplain at

Brasenose was a cultured man called Styler who helped the backward, like me, with the Latin necessary to cope with Roman Law. This was not a subject that gripped me. Roman Law seemed to be obsessed with the manumission of slaves. Roman furniture dealers seemed to have been endlessly selling tables which turned out, unknown to them, to have silver tops or legs. Thus they were always going on about the invalidity of contracts because of "substantial" error. Without an error of substance contracts remained valid. But slaves and silver-legged tables were not my current problems.

Leslie Styler seemed to understand such issues as well as Latin grammar, but I used to pity him as he flapped his way in his surplice on Sunday mornings to college chapel with a pair of altar cruets in his hands. Never once did I go in to see what he got up to or how many of his flock attended. Few, I was sure. It was not our job to support false religions, and so we centred ourselves around Mgr Elwes and the Old Palace.

As a social centre it was ideal. At the country dancing evenings and the cheese and wine parties one could meet others, especially girls. It was a difficult situation for young, rigorous Catholic men. Girls were warm and sympathetic. Proximity to them produced feelings of considerable pleasure. But at the same time the dangers of mortal sin were ever present, especially in what the catechism called "irregular motions of the flesh" or even "concupiscence". Moral life was therefore something of a minefield, and I do not thank those who taught me all about the trip-wires of the sixth and ninth commandments but so rarely mentioned that God made sex and it was rather a good idea. Not that sex was a constant preoccupation. Out of a mixture of prudence and principle it seems to me now that most of the students I knew lived very chaste lives.

The Newman Society was supposed to provide the intellectual back-up to Chaplaincy life, but what it actually meant was a group of very inexperienced students trying to get some great "name" down to speak under the misapprehension that any invitation from us would be honour enough. I remember one speaker who actually asked for a fee, which we thought was very vulgar. A dinner at the Mitre should have been reward enough for anyone. Most invitees were decent enough and went through the kind of routine with students which hasn't changed to this day. But there could be difficulties. In my term as Newman President I invited Gilbert Harding, who was always a great parental hero when he appeared on our wonderfully ancient TV which had actually survived the Second World War. The Harding invitation went sadly wrong. Billed to talk on "The Rambling Recollections of an Errant Convert" on 4th November 1951, he would certainly have packed the hall. Unhappily, in a last-minute note, I happened to mention that one of the female students would take the chair that night. The response was devastating and came in the form of a telegram. Those were the days of telegrams. The message in the yellow envelope was clear. I had not told him about this *woman*, and since there was to be a *woman* on the platform he would not come. I was less interested in his sexual hang-ups than I was in the thought of a packed hall and no speaker. Happily a lovely man called Professor d'Entrèves stood in and spoke, I think, on Natural Law, which gave some small satisfaction to the Harding-induced crowd which did actually turn up.

Evelyn Waugh gave me even more problems. To his neatly written postcard, bearing his agreement to speak on "Catholics and Novelists", he added as a PS: "Ask Lady X." I had never heard of Lady X and assumed this to be some sort of upper-class joke. It wasn't. When I went to call for him at a Woodstock Road manor he, surrounded by colleagues or friends or both, saw me and immediately wanted to know where Lady X was. This time lying oneself out of trouble worked. Without any idea of Lady X's interest or age I said, "She's gone to a dance." He seemed satisfied and said no more, though the evening got steadily more complicated. In the Mitre, when offered beer, he snorted, ran his finger down the wine list and chose the best. Then he ignored the male committee members – all, I am sure, awkward and spotty – and turned his full attention to lovely black-haired Pat, our Newman secretary from Somerville. Meanwhile more and more wine went down.

By the time I had got him away from an embarrassed Pat and down to the Old Palace and a packed hall he was in a difficult mood. I felt like the inexperienced trainer of a very experienced tiger. He gave a rather rambling speech and then proceeded to insult various questioners with a great pretence of being so deaf that he couldn't hear a word. The deafness had not been evident in his previous conversation with Pat. One student did throw him off balance by bellowing at full blast from a perch on a piano just behind him, "Mr Waugh, can you hear me?" I'm not sure that he even got an answer.

Time had come for more refreshment, and we all retired – I wishing that the ground would open up – to the Chaplain's room to drink whisky. At that stage a Belgian (or French, but certainly foreign) monk, about whose orthodoxy there were already enough suspicions, took Waugh over, and the two disappeared together, without a word to the rest of us, into the night, roaring with delight at their own jokes. For all this rudeness Waugh more than made up the next morning. A copy of his *When the Going Was Good* was delivered to my digs and in it he had written, "For Bruce Kent, with thanks for an entirely delightful evening at the Newman." From my point of view it hadn't been, but at least I still have the evidence of a very generous afterthought.

My most valued guest was a now almost forgotten scientist, Dr Sherwood Taylor, then curator of the Oxford Museum of the History of Science, and of course a convert to Catholicism. (In those days one counted converts as Iroquois counted scalps.) Sherwood Taylor was not only genuinely humble but was also the author of a little book entitled *The Fourfold Vision* which helped me to realize that truth comes in several layers, from measurement to poetry to mysticism. Absorbing the intellectual climate of the time, I had unthinkingly come to believe that knowledge was really only that which could be measured or weighed. Such knowledge was "science" and only science was true. Sherwood Taylor broke such narrow barriers for me. In a single evening meeting I think he did more to open up my mind to a broader concept of truth than anyone else in Oxford.

My mind was actually on the move. Somehow I had come across the writings of Dorothy Day and knew something of the American Catholic Worker movement. The Catholic Worker mixture of non-violence, social justice and personal involvement with the poor and disadvantaged was enormously attractive. I joined the Society of St Vincent de Paul along with others from the chaplaincy. The

54

members of the SVP, as it is better known, try in personal ways to meet Christ in the "least of his little ones". In a series of weekly visits to Oxford hospitals and old folks' homes, I started to learn a bit more about the lives of those born without silver spoons in their mouths. For most of my time as an undergraduate a print of Fritz Eichenberg's etching, *The Light* (produced for the *Catholic Worker* in 1940) hung on my wall. The light was the light of Christ (not himself seen in the picture), reflected in the faces of the poor, the confused and the crippled, looking up for the first time in hope.

That I was even President of the Newman at all was something of a miracle. The post was an elected one, and standing against me was the great Norman St John Stevas, ex-President of the Cambridge Union, who had come to do a year in Oxford. I and the Chaplaincy inner Mafia fought back, and Norman was just defeated. Foolishly, the election organizers left all the signed votes in a shoebox in a cupboard, and I was subsequently able to identify all those who had promised to vote for me but hadn't. Politics, I learned, was a pretty ruthless business.

Religion and its related activities were not my only interests. For one thing, in my first term I had joined the University Air Squadron. This was an enterprise that gathered up assorted enthusiasts from a variety of colleges, all keen to acquire a bit of glamour and to have some free flying lessons. Once a week an RAF truck picked us up and took us out to the grass airfield at RAF Kidlington. There were also RAF mid-week lectures which one was meant to attend but often didn't. Failure to do so meant that I had the pants scared off me one night when we were taken down to RAF Abingdon for night flying. I wandered about the sky, quite lost, hoping I wasn't going to run into anyone in front while trying hard to remember what all the various lights on the ground might mean.

We flew the Chipmunks which had just replaced the open Tiger Moths of earlier days. At least you could shut the lid on a Chipmunk and keep warm. Going in circles around Kidlington could be unexciting for us but no doubt annoying for the Duke of Marlborough, since Blenheim Palace was in direct line with the runway if the wind was in the right direction. The real joy of the Air Squadron was the summer camps. We were actually paid for spending two wonderful weeks in an RAF mess and doing as much flying as we could fit in. The summer camps were held each year at RAF Middle Wallop, and it made a nice little holiday. It was difficult to get really lost, because you could always ask for a radio bearing back to base. But you were not meant to get lost too often, and one misty day, having already asked for enough radio directions, I had to come down to find my way by reading a railway station notice-board. It turned out to be Andover. God knows what the passengers thought.

But the problems were small compared with the joys of looking at southern England spread out like a map below, of flying across the waves a few feet away from the Needles, off the Isle of Wight, of low flying over the hills and valleys of Dorset, Hampshire and Sussex, of playing games in and around beautiful white clouds, with your own shadow racing along the cloud-side to meet you – these are all wonderful memories. Just once, on a lovely sunny day, I saw a Spitfire shoot up between two clouds, roll over and disappear. Normally the sky was your own and you went where you liked. It was a paradise which you could not really share with anyone else. Travelling now on crowded Jumbos is no substitute.

There were other, very different holiday experiences. Once a notice went up explaining that there were fortunes to be made cutting up pit-props in a forest near Sidmouth. We worked out the sums involved, and it seemed that with minimum effort several of us could soon be very rich. There were, as ever in economics, unexpected snags. It was easy enough to cut the trees at the base. But it was extremely difficult to make them fall, since the softwood firs were so close and so dense at their tops that nothing would fall down. Dreams of an easy fortune vanished. The firm concerned eventually supplied us with a huge horse. The scheme was that we would tie a chain around the tree and also to the horse, so that horsepower would pull down the trees we couldn't shift. The idea was not a success. The horse was placid enough *en route* to the forest. However, once tied to the tree and urged on with cries of "Hup, boy!" and the like, it simply took off, vast and unstoppable, and would be found eating grass half a mile away, still chained to what was left of the tree. George Bull, fellow student labourer and subsequently editor of *The Director*, did his best to save us from this financial disaster, but even he could not manage the horse.

A major Oxford sporting outlet was the river. Our Brasenose boat was not very successful, though we practised hard and we all had, except the cox, hands with belts of callouses across the palms. For those not familiar with the Thames at Oxford, racing consists of chasing the boat in front of you until your bow crosses the line of their stern. We were told ancient stories of oncoming boats which had accidentally "speared" the cox of the boat in front. The process goes on for a week, and each day boats move up or down in line, according to the "bumps" of the day before. Brasenose Second Torpid of 1951 was not a matter of pride. Day after day the bow behind would sneak up yard by yard and overtake us, despite all our grunting and sweating. I even had the humiliation one day of getting my pants caught in the rails on which the seat moved, thus bringing disaster to the whole crew. Finally a strange ceremony took place. As the most bumped crew, we were marched off to the most successful college – Corpus, I think. There we had to sit in their hall while they feasted, and finally we had to watch while a boat was burnt in their quadrangle. It was all too Viking-like. Before they got any other ideas about the Vikings' treatment of prisoners I turned tail and went home. Our best days were spent during the Easter holidays at Henley, rowing up and down that lovely stretch of water, pursued by no one. It did not happen very often, but when a crew did get its act together and the oars all "chunked" in smoothly, there was something very beautiful about the whole experience. I did try riding as an alternative sport, but this I thought was not only expensive but also dangerous. One horse, which had to be prodded to get me down to the far end of Port Meadow, took off like an Olympic champion on the way back and did its best to decapitate me by galloping the whole length of the Meadow and through its stable door. From then on I stuck to rowing.

After one year in College I was more than lucky in the digs I found. For a term I lived on the Iffley Road in a house whose great merit was that it housed also the most beautiful girl in the University. She was Polish, very nice and worshipped by hundreds. One of my friends was so smitten that he was sick whenever he saw her, which made romance difficult and eventually impossible.

But I tired of the Iffley Road, not being among the hundreds smitten, and yearned to be with my friends. Another little personal miracle was arranged and half a dozen of us found a house which two New Zealand ladies with a Boxer dog were opening in Wellington Square. Could we find them some lodgers? Could we! Within a week every room was filled with our friends, and a very happy final year was spent by all. George Steiner, then of Balliol, later of Cambridge, and now of world literary fame, provided the intellectual centre of the establishment. Clyde Sanger, now author and *Guardian* correspondent from Canada, provided the wit. Not everyone could hold spellbound as he could an entire street while reciting the *Ballad of Dangerous Dan McGrew*.

It was Clyde's idea that he and I, both at Brasenose, should wander over and join in with the Wadham College formal photograph one summer. So we did, and colleges being what they are, no-one knew if we belonged or not or was rude enough to ask. The photograph came out very well, with both of us smiling in a dignified way in the back row. Some of the heavies from Wadham were none too pleased.

I shared rooms with a good school-friend, Alan O'Hea, who designed the most ingenious alarm clock ever invented. As the alarm went off there could be no escape. Two wires would, as the winder unwound, be joined together, thus setting off a battery-powered electric bell carefully placed on a vibrating tin tray. Not surprisingly, he went into engineering. One of the oddest episodes of a remarkable year was the arrival in Wellington Square of Mark Batten, distinguished artist and sculptor, who had come to cut some new stone heads to replace those that the weather had destroyed outside the Bodleian. He was also working at the time on a figure of Diogenes, the austere Greek philosopher alleged to have lived in a jar. Mark picked on me as a model and I spent several afternoons sitting nearly naked on a table while he got my legs and hips down on paper for posterity. Unfortunately my chest and arms he thought sub-standard, so above the waist I was replaced by another model. Those today who wish to examine my legs c.1952 can easily do so since "Diogenist" by Mark Batten still sits looking out towards Harrow in Golders Hill Park near the Old Bull and Bush in Hampstead.

But these lotus-eating years were drawing to an end. In a strange way time had stood still. It had been a good life – friends, sports, parties, dances and some study. I had for a time a girlfriend who was, and is, a good friend, but I still hadn't any certainty about what I ought to be doing with my life, and the water was running towards the rapids of Finals at a faster and faster speed. To Barry Nicholas I put my problem – quite unfairly, since who can sort out anyone else's direction? He kindly suggested a number of options, including that of being a District Commissioner in our rapidly diminishing British Empire. For a while the idea of being the Bwana of decency and justice in some remote outpost had its attractions, but the priestly pull of 1949 had far from gone and, the family truce still holding, I thought I ought at least to try my vocation as a priest. However far I had wandered in other directions there remained a conviction deep-down that God wanted something special from me. This time my father, though hardly delighted, put up no opposition. If the priesthood was still what I wanted after three Oxford years then he was willing to live with that choice. So at the very end of the academic year of 1952 I went to the University chaplain to find out how to apply. Mgr Elwes seemed slightly more cross than pleased, since I had left it too late for him to be able to get a place for me at the English College in Rome, which was the Roman Catholic clerical Sandhurst. He liked "his boys" to become bishops. It was said in those days that there were three qualifications for a would-be bishop. One had to be male, celibate and educated at the English College. The first two conditions could be dispensed with, but never the third. In clerical circles this is a very old joke, so my apologies, if necessary, for repeating it here. Early that summer, I had to see Cardinal Griffin in a gloomy room in Archbishop's House, Westminster. He asked a few unanswerable questions about why I wanted to be a priest, and then I thought he had been struck by palsy and St Vitus' dance. His right leg kept hopping about on the carpet in a very odd way. Only years later did I discover that under the carpet was an electric bell-push to signal to the waiting clerical secretary to come in and remove a visitor. But Griffin often had trouble finding the bell-push.

A medical report had also to be provided, and I wandered up Ambrosden Avenue to a dear old diocesan doctor who struck my knee several times with a rubber hammer and then asked me to pee into a small bottle. Both these tests I must have passed with flying colours because, by the autumn of 1952, I was on my way to St Edmund's College, Ware, rudely described by Pugin as "the priest factory". On high ground by the side of the A10 near Puckeridge, it looked just like one.

CHAPTER FIVE

The Priest Factory

Even the word "seminary" now sounds rather odd, foreign and Gilbert and Sullivanish. If it has foreign overtones, that is not surprising. It was in the seminaries in Valladolid, in Lisbon, in Douai and in Rome that young English boys, who went voluntarily into exile across the Channel, studied to become priests, to return at the end of their training to what was still, in my day, called the English Mission. For many years, to return under the Elizabethan settlement meant to be hunted down, arrested, probably tortured and then executed, often at Tyburn, now Marble Arch.

Towards the end of the seventeenth century, though the civil penalties remained, the worst barbarities were no longer practised. During the eighteenth century life got easier for the small Catholic minority, still centred around a few remaining old Catholic houses. Judges like Lord Mansfield made it more difficult for informers to earn a reward. They demanded that an informer not only have evidence that a priest had said Mass but also that he had actually been ordained in the first place. Anti-Catholicism had by no means exhausted itself. It burst out again in mob violence during the Gordon riots, and Kenwood House, as it is now called, Lord Mansfield's residence, was in danger of being burnt down as the mob from London made its way north. Happily, most of them got drunk at the Mother Shipton Inn, in what is now Chalk Farm, and got no further. Crass ignorance of history by the inn's present management has meant that it no longer bears the same name. May their beer go flat and may mildew settle on their roasted peanuts.

By the end of the eighteenth century the Catholic community was a small remnant which did its best to be inconspicuous. Only by accident did I see recently a plaque on St Joseph's church in

61

Philadelphia which said that in 1733 it was the only place "in the entire English speaking world where the public celebration of the holy sacrifice of the Mass was permitted by law". That tolerance was due only to the determination of the Quaker co-religionists of William Penn in resisting the demands of the Governor of the Province "that this church be outlawed".

By the end of the century attitudes had greatly changed. Catholics had, in England, kept their heads down during the 1745 rebellion and Stuart march on London, which petered out at Derby. The American War of Independence demanded much more religious tolerance if Scottish and Irish Catholics were to be recruited in numbers to fight for the Crown. Above all, the French Revolution drove scores of clergy across the Channel to safety, where they were welcomed and even given official government stipends. Many London Catholic churches today – Hampstead, Euston and Chelsea, for instance – owe their origins to the work of those who had fled the bloodier consequences of Liberty, Fraternity and Equality. How they all came to adapt to the great Irish Catholic influx of the early part of the nineteenth century is a story well told in *Catholic London A Century Ago*, written by Canon Bernard Ward in 1905. One man who forecast the future was Bishop Challoner, a faithful, scholarly pastor of the eighteenth century. The "new people", as he prophesied, came in the nineteenth century from both ends of the social scale: Irish labourers digging canals and building railways and the educated and upper-class converts of the Oxford Movement. A church which had nearly died out took on a new and vigorous lease of life. Buried first in the crypt of Milton Church (which is now under the shadow of Didcot Power station), Bishop Challoner's body was removed in this century and now lies in Westminster Cathedral.

All this may seem to be a rather long diversion and some distance from seminaries. It is not. As the climate of tolerance changed, so the colleges abroad belonging to religious orders and the secular clergy found that they could come home to England, and did so. All of which leads back to Pugin's "Priest Factory", St Edmund's College near Puckeridge. By the time I arrived in September 1952 there were three separate institutions on the same site, united under one

President. Allen Hall was the seminary: it had about a hundred students, aged from eighteen to fifty plus, who were placed there by a variety of dioceses to undertake six years of study before ordination. There was also a small private preparatory school called St Hugh's, and some of its boys would go on to St Edmund's School, which occupied the main Pugin block. St Edmund's was then a minor public boarding-school with a priest headmaster and some day boys, whose fees were paid by the Hertfordshire Education Authority on the grounds that there was no local Catholic secondary provision. A few pupils in the school were "Church boys" on their way to Allen Hall and priestly training in due course. Many of those changed their minds by the end of their school days. It is one thing to want to be a priest when aged twelve and full of altar-boy ideals, but rather a different matter when aged seventeen or more.

I knew almost nothing about this history when I arrived, though from my school days I knew that Stonyhurst had its roots in the Jesuit college at St Omer. As a pupil at a Jesuit school it had never occurred to me to wonder where diocesan priests came from or how they were trained. But the three years spent at University made me a little less enthusiastic about the rigours of Jesuit life. A two-year novitiate with total separation from friends and family was no longer my cup of tea. And I had met not a few friendly, reasonable secular priests since leaving school. Hence the visit to Cardinal Griffin of Westminster and the St Edmund's entry.

It was an entry into a mind-blowing new world. Eighteen of us started at the same time. Nine, six years later, were ordained. Only four of those are still active today as priests. There were amongst the eighteen some schoolboys, a plumber, a carpenter, a few university graduates, a senior Oxford Street department store manager, two railway clerks, three young Irishmen who had "tried their vocation" in religious orders, and me. Considering the culture-shock, we all got on very well indeed.

The shock was not so much the range of backgrounds but, granted my easy life, the awfulness of the regime. The seminary block faced east on a hill with nothing to interrupt the free flow of freezing wind across the North Sea, no doubt from Siberia. The central heating system was well past its best. Great pipes ran from room to room

63

and at times they became slightly warm. The east wind found its way through air vents, under the floor and up through cracks in the wooden boards. During the first term, while I was deciding whether this life could be endured any longer, I spent many a study hour plugging the cracks with large lumps of the *Guardian Weekly*, to which I had subscribed in the unrealized hope that I would still continue to be interested in the wider world scene. On the positive side, there was an excellent bath block with near-boiling water. If one got too cold it was always possible to nip down the corridor and poach oneself. The greatest shock was not the weather but the never-ending routine. Every minute of every day of every week was planned in advance. The contrast with Oxford could not have been more dramatic. There one worked up, at one's own pace, with whatever lectures seemed useful, to the Friday essay. After that, as proper reward for four or five days of work, came the weekend. The Oxford weekend was sacred. It was yours. Such blissful times were over. Nothing was yours. From the 6.30 a.m. bell to the 10 p.m. lights out it all belonged to someone else, and the programme just went on and on. Needless to say, survival meant adaptation, and there were ways around most obstacles. I soon found out what they were.

What we did not know, for the first few weeks, was that ours was the first intake of a new reformist regime. We arrived with a new President, a very kind, shy man called Mgr Butcher, whose mandate was to restore law and order. There had been, before we arrived in 1952, a possible scandal which certainly involved unusual relationships with rumours of homosexuality. The previous President had been very easy-going and the top-year Deacons were the rulers of the roost. Some had even adapted their wash-stands into primus stove cookers and were dishing up their own meals. What corruption! One, better funded than the rest, had been receiving hampers from Fortnum and Mason until a delivery fell into the hands of the new President, who soon put a stop to that.

So Operation Clean Up and Crack Down was on, and we were on the receiving end of it. Having spent two years in the Army and three in a public school, I knew the nature of male institutional life, however painful the transition from the softer life of Oxford. As in most all-male institutions, there was always an official fear that homosexuality would break out somewhere. Hence we inherited odd rules which were soon ignored. There was a box in the seminary hall into which one was supposed to put the names of those who were going out walking. There were meant to be no less than three of you in a walking party, lest "special friendships" flowered.

Another oddity was that we had to wear hats. The hat rule didn't last long, but it meant that I had to buy a strange black Homburg from which my ears stuck out each side. Cardinal Godfrey, who succeeded Cardinal Griffin in 1956, had an enthusiasm for such hats. He once found a student arriving at Archbishop's House on a motor-cycle, wearing overalls and a crash helmet. His disapproval was all too clear.

Seminary life involved both a packed weekly programme and an unusual annual calendar. The day started with half an hour of meditation and Mass in the chapel, followed by breakfast and lectures. Lectures were endless. Sometimes as many as four were crammed into one morning. For the first two years the main diet was Philosophy, with additional doses of Scripture, Church History and Canon Law. The Philosophy was divided up, in medieval style, into logic, ontology, cosmology and a few other ologies as well. Most of it was heavy stuff, as we ground through learned authors who set up logical positivists, agnostics and materialists, one after another, and then dealt them knock-out blows. The other side did not have many opportunities to answer back. The tedium was considerable. No-one can suffer four forty-five-minute lectures in sequence without getting a numbing of the soul. Most of the priest-lecturers were not exactly Ciceros when it came to delivery. Worst of all, it was not until well into three years of my seminary life that any opportunity for serious discussion was provided. The dogma professor, Fr Charles Davis (now married and a professor at Montreal), introduced what amounted to tutorial groups on Wednesday mornings, which livened up matters considerably. Our most brilliant philosophy lecturer was Father George Ekbury, a wonderful violinist and a devoted keeper of pigs. His lectures were usually delivered in Wellington boots, on his way to or from mucking out the pigs, who grunted away happily on the other side of the lecture hall. To

George I owe a debt of gratitude. Scholastic notions of substance and accidents were about as interesting to me as electrical differences between AC and DC. But he made reality come alive, and it occurred to me, for the first time, I suppose, that our sense-based knowledge is only the doorway to something far more mysterious. "Things" became much more interesting.

To Father Hubert Richards, Scripture scholar, guitarist, hymn writer and part-time local parish priest, I owe a new understanding of Scripture. I was waiting on arrival at the seminary for a collision between biblical inerrancy and scientific truth, but it never came. I started to take the various parts of the Bible apart with far greater interest than ever before, once I grasped that we were not required to believe that they were the products of some verbatim divine dictation machine. Church History had plenty of interesting by-ways – but those were the days when other Christian traditions were mentioned only in order to be put down. It was many years later that I started to realize that Henry VIII was not the last word to be said on the Church of England and that some of the sects, as they were dismissively called, had, like the Methodists, a spirituality, conviction and prayer life from which we could well learn – and subsequently did. Of non-Christian religions we learnt nothing at all that I can remember.

As the years went on the theology became more pastoral and we learned how to baptize plastic dolls, to give each other the Last Rites and to cope with the Confessional and moral direction. Homosexuality was grossly sinful, we were to say, though people couldn't be blamed for being homosexual. The best thing for such people was to urge them to join parish pastoral groups. They could then release their affections in acceptable ways by taking care of the poor or visiting the house-bound. At some stage in the proceedings a priest doctor turned up, with illustrations, to tell us all about the facts of life. He was a bit late in the day, as far as most of us were concerned. In a strong Scots accent he kept assuring us that sex was a "guid thing" but never managed to look entirely convinced himself. Finally we moved to practice confessions, ranging from "Bless me Father, I have struck the Pope" from the humorists to "Bless me Father, I have looked at dirty pictures or stolen office stamps" from the realists. We also learned to say Mass, which was a very precise operation indeed. There were rules for every movement – how high you held the chalice, how far apart your hands, how loud your voice, how many drops of water to pour into the wine. It could, like dismantling a Bren gun, have been done by numbers, but it wasn't. The aim – uniformity – was much the same. How horrified I was a few years later, after ordination, to see a French priest in Kensington holding his hands out like some Old Testament prophet as if to embrace the Almighty and turning around to face the congregation at moments when they had no right to be consulted.

From an academic point of view the seminary left much to be desired. As a place of personal formation it was very effective. In ways overt and covert it was dinned into us that we were the successors of those English martyrs who had kept the light of faith alive despite dungeon, fire and sword. Ours to comfort the desolate and to support the weak. Ours to add to the community of the Church by careful preaching and assiduous visiting. Ours to obey without question. You could make fun of bishops privately but they, via the Pope, were the successors of the apostles, and to them we were to promise absolute obedience. Weekly confession, regular spiritual direction, daily Mass and annual retreats were the foundation of a formation that went on all the time.

Students, of course, did from time to time leave. It was a strange process, not unlike the feared "Return to Unit" of Army days. It was even more secretive. Those with doubts about their vocation were told not to share them with other students, and they rarely did. So, almost in Orwellian fashion, people disappeared. I well remember one student with a room across from mine whom I saw washing in the bath block before meditation one morning; by breakfast an hour and a half later he had gone, with farewells to nobody. His room had been cleared of anything at all to do with him. Only the table, bed, bookcase, chair and table-lamp were left behind. It was as if he had never existed.

It sounds like a rather weird existence, and if such were the whole picture, so it would have been. But it was not. There were all sorts of diversions and entertainments, official and unofficial. The student refectorian, for instance, had considerable powers. For three weeks we sat in the same places on the same table. Then we were switched to another set of people for another three weeks on another table. One of my year, when refectorian, would amuse himself by putting all the redheads, or all the Scots, or all the teetotallers on the same table for a three-week spell. He, who enjoyed his drop, would place himself in with the teetotallers just before St Patrick's day or St George's day and collar all the rejected beer he wanted.

I had two areas of patronage. Quite early on I became both the seminary bee-keeper and the seminary infirmarian. The bees were a godsend, since they could get me out of almost anything. "I'm sorry Father, but I'll have to go – the bees are about to swarm." They also, thanks to a few good summers, made me quite popular as a dispenser of honey. Through the bees I gained access to local village gatherings of bee enthusiasts, so I reached parts of Hertford-shire life that were beyond other students. Retired colonels, the local bricklayer, the county librarian – it was astonishing how effective the freemasonry of bee enthusiasm could be. They also produced their own laughs. I recruited an assistant once who was not as careful as I was with net, boiler suit and smoke before opening the hives. One morning in meditation dear Peter, huddled in his cassock in a pos-ition which might have meant either sleep or deep spiritual transport, leapt to his feet with a scream. Several bees which had been asleep in his trouser turn-ups had crawled up his leg and stung him in a very personal way. The chapel was convulsed with sniggering as he fled in pain.

Being infirmarian also had its advantages. I was the gateway to the "long sleep" (an extra half an hour). I was the route to the "hot drink" (Ovaltine before bed). I was the mediator with the amazing Consolata nuns who ran the domestic side of the place, kept a bevy of Maltese and Italian girls out of trouble and nursed whoever was ill. The Consolata Superior was the motherly Sister Beatrice who, it was rumoured, had taken out her own appendix during the war. We did not like to ask for proof.

I don't think we ever had any really serious illnesses, mental or physical. Dr Harefield, the local GP, seemed to prescribe the same brown pills for most ailments. Many of them found their way out of the window on to the lawn below, which itself began to turn brown in sympathy. Dr Harefield was never too clear about his instructions. One youth with early piles was given a box of Anusol suppositories, God's gift to those so afflicted. But the doctor did not explain in detail what was to be done with them. I appeared just in time to stop this patient swallowing one. The worst disease was Locke's disease. Locke, a seminary student, had been sent off to Hertford Hospital for an appendix operation. There he fell for a nurse and never returned to the ranks of celibacy. For years thereafter, if anyone ever ran off with anyone, it was said that Locke's disease had struck again.

A great deal of outdoor sport went on, but since our numbers were never over a hundred and sank fairly steadily, most people played several games. The first rugby team looked very like the first football team or the first hockey team. We were regularly massacred at places like St Mary's Teacher Training College, Strawberry Hill, and just occasionally we massacred others at smaller institutions like St John's Seminary, Wonersh, south of the river. I don't think the attendant at the public conveniences in Putney ever really got used to the idea of a coach-load of young collared clerics pouring off a bus and into his toilets twice or three times a year.

Drama was also a popular activity, though it was difficult to find men-only scripts. *Morning Departure* was the only really satisfactory one, there being no women on a stricken submarine. So hysterical plays like *Charlie's Aunt* meant a great deal of transvestism and tennis balls down the front. I had a wonderful time as Sir Francis Chesney, Bart., with a pillow stuffed in my trousers. No pillow would be needed today. Sometimes we took plays on tour. *Ten Little Niggers*, as it was then called, was a wild success and much in demand by the Nuns of Pole's Convent School nearby, now a posh hotel. We had them transfixed. I well remember that as the villain crept up on the heroine from behind the stage sofa, a dear old nun leapt to her feet screaming in excitement, "Turn round, darlin' – he's right behind you!"

The nuns at Pole's were a wonderfully forgiving lot. One Easter two of us were sent down to act as servers for the Easter ceremonies. The chapel glistened, candles shone on brass, the sanctuary floor had been polished into mirror condition. In the sacristy, out of sight,

I swung the thurible with its burning charcoal with the greatest enthusiasm while waiting to go on to the sanctuary through the open door. The swinging was a bit too powerful. The lip of the thurible caught on the step from the sacristy, and the entire contents shot across the wonderful floor in front of the altar, sparking and smoking and hissing. From the body of the church it must have been a remarkable sight: all I could see, off stage, were nuns hopping about on charcoal as if on springs. I could only apologize, and they were very nice about it, despite an extremely messy sanctuary floor.

As the years went past the world beyond the seminary got more and more remote. It was not that we were locked up. On the contrary, on Wednesdays and Sundays we were encouraged to cycle off to hospitals, TB clinics and old people's homes and to give catechism instruction to children not in Catholic schools. I'm not sure that I was very good at the last. "I've just seen Jesus go past on his bicycle," said one little girl to her mother as I shot down Wadesmill Hill past her window. But how the world was being shaped and who was doing it was not our business. True, for the Coronation we hired a massive television set and, in rows as for a photograph, we watched the whole performance, much impressed when the Meteor jets, which had just been seen shooting over the procession, a few minutes later shot over us in Hertfordshire as well. Time for reading newspapers was minimal and interest soon flagged. When the invasion of Suez took place I have no doubt that three quarters of the students would have said, "About time too." If there was nationalist friction it was at a reasonably light-hearted level between the English and the Irish.

There were no black students for several years, until we were told that we would be receiving a couple of Ugandans. Very easy to get on with they were too, though the President was in desperate anxiety to make sure that no-one would put a foot wrong and that no bricks would be dropped when they arrived. That did not stop one of the students, very upset about some exam mix-up, saying in front of the Ugandans on their first day, "And more than that, I can tell you exactly who the nigger in the woodpile is . . ." They took that quietly, and we continued on in massive ignorance about the politics of Uganda and indeed of Africa generally.

Others knew about racism at first hand. On the A10 going north from Wadesmill is a small triangular monument. It was put there many years ago to commemorate one of Wilberforce's companions in the struggle against the slave trade. For as long as we knew it the monument was covered in moss and the dirt of ages. On it was the name Thomas Clarkson and the date June 1785. "On this spot," said the inscription, "he resolved to devote his life to bringing about the abolition of the slave trade." One day the monument stood there, clean, bright and fully restored. By whom? Two black soldiers from the US camp at Colliers End had come over one afternoon with sandpaper and soap to pay their own small mark of respect.

The local villages we did, of course, know well. Not only could we, on certain high days and holidays, go off for extended walks and cycle rides for tea in places like Buntingford, Hertford and Bishop's Stortford, but we were also often employed in building, or at least converting, local churches. Much Hadham today has a church which is a transformed Land Army hostel, and a lot of fun we had in the transformation as we bashed our way through breeze-block partitions and dripped paint over ourselves and each other. We were also in regular demand as local church functionaries of one sort or another. The parish priest of Buntingford caused us no small surprise by telling us, who were in apostolic pursuit of some lapsed Catholic, that he did not think it *his* job to throw pearls before swine. This was a new interpretation of "Go ye and teach all nations." But he was unusual. Most of the local clergy thought we were a godsend. I'm not sure what one bereaved family thought of us as, in large numbers, dressed in black cassocks and white cottas, we gathered in a very wet and rainy graveyard at Old Hall Green to say farewell to Mr Warner, a well-loved local parishioner. The coffin was still up on its cross-bars as the little undertaker, with his black suit and top hat, made his way down the side of the grave to get to the far end, stepping on the carpet of artificial grass as he went. Tragedy. The wet ground under the carpet gave way and the undertaker, hat and all, wrapped in green, disappeared into the hole. We, who had been dirging away with suitable gloom, collapsed in laughter. I think even the widow smiled. The undertaker did not as he was hauled out, covered in mud, trying to recover as much dignity as possible.

The structure of the seminary year was rather odd. From September to July our lives were ordered on an almost hourly basis. On Boxing Day we were allowed out to our families, which has meant that in my family at least Boxing Day has survived as the day of annual family reunion. At Easter there was a week's holiday spent at the College. But by the end of July we were free and entirely unsupervised for the best part of two months. Some students earned money in holiday jobs, as I did more than once. As a Walls ice-cream salesman at the Schoolboys Own Exhibition in Westminster I was quite successful. But there was more money in summer work on building sites. One summer was spent digging out the foundations of what is now a very expensive house on Hendon Lane, in the company of a one-eyed labourer known as Cyclops to his friends. I still look at a block of expensive flats in East Finchley near the vast St Pancras and Islington Cemetery and wonder if anyone has ever told the occupant of the first-floor flat at the front that his or her large living-room cupboard was once the lavatory for everyone on the site.

There were other summer activities more closely related to the role for which we were being trained. Twice we spent a late summer on the Belgian coast with groups from the Belgian Association for the Paralysed and acted as companions and helpers to large parties of wheelchair-bound people. Their courage was eye-opening. I do not forget a train driver from Brussels called Constance, who had lost both his legs but not his very active sense of humour. His kind of courage I have met sometimes since and especially at Lourdes. I don't know what experiences Constance had had, but as I tucked him into bed at our fourth-class out-of-season holiday hotel at Heyst sur Mer one night he told me not to worry about my impending celibate fate. Women, he assured me, were not really all they were cracked up to be.

Not long afterwards I visited a Dutch seminarian and realized how very lucky we in England were. This was before the days of the Second Vatican Council, and Dutch Catholicism was highly traditional. Far from digging on building sites, my Dutch host had to stay in his cassock all summer, help in so far as he could with his local parish and visit an endless series of admiring relations. His seminary made ours look like Butlins by comparison. In each dormitory, divided into single cubicles, a senior student slept. On one side of his cubicle was a mirror which enabled him to see right down the corridor, and above his head was set another at an angle to enable him to see over the tops of all the cubicles. This was a kind of surveillance happily unknown at St Edmund's.

Summers came and went – two at least spent in Essex at a boys' camp at Gosfield Lake (a wonderful place when it wasn't raining), run every year by the Society of St Vincent de Paul. It was a good camp with a lot of very lively small boys. Many, from London, had never spent a week in the country under canvas. The new intakes arrived on Saturdays, and having slept not at all in their bell-tents, used to get up at dawn on Sunday mornings, knock at the doors of local village sweet-shops and demand postcards from shopkeepers still fast asleep and very cross at being woken. This problem I cured quite rapidly. The Prize Route March was introduced on Saturday evenings. All new arrivals were sent on a very long walk around the lake and elsewhere in search of prizes. So long, indeed, that they were all exhausted and slept through till a decent hour on the Sunday. Why, I can't imagine, but eventually I was promoted to the position of Head Cook and learnt to mash potatoes with an old baseball bat and produce porridge with the weight and consistency of a good Christmas pudding. The boys ate nearly everything except fish, which they were inclined to bury in their tents under their straw mattresses, with unpleasant long-term results. I don't blame them. I wasn't very good at fish, though some of my experiments were quite inventive. Having run out of batter one day, I substituted custard powder and margarine. The result was a choice piece of fish, embedded in a rock-hard yellow casing which could be opened only with the greatest determination. My invention could well have been fired out of a cannon.

The most interesting summer job of all was certainly my spell as a temporary porter at Middlesex Hospital. The regular porters were delighted to have student assistants and let us do all the work and answer all the calls. This meant that we had an unrivalled run of the hospital and as good a view of real life as anyone else there. The Head Porter, highly distinguished in his green uniform and hat, also turned out to be the chief bookmaker. The route to the porters' sitting-room passed through the kitchen and the skilful would always manage to nick a pudding or two on the way past. The Chef burst in one day in fury to discover everyone tucking into one of his largest pies. But there is little justice in this life, and the old hands all pointed at once to an innocent theological student from Scotland who could not stop blushing and was promptly handed his cards. Many times I wondered if people in the large hospital lifts realized that the empty trolley which a porter would push in was often not empty at all. Underneath the flat surface was a large, long box covered in a sheet: the box and its occupant would be on their way to the morgue. Death became quite familiar to me, but not always to patients. I well remember one dear old lady in the cancer ward, without the slightest idea of what her real illness actually was, telling another that her poor husband was dying of cancer. "Such a nasty illness, my dear."

As the six years drifted past so the seminarians collected the various minor orders and moved on to subdiaconate, diaconate and priesthood. Sub-deacons and deacons really were people set apart. They were assumed to have made the irrevocable choices, especially of celibacy. The move to priestly ordination, despite sincere solemnity, had also a slight touch of pre-wedding fuss. Prayer cards were printed, chalices ordered, new cassocks measured and invitations to the First Mass and celebrations carefully printed and distributed. For five years others had come back to give us their "First Blessing". Now we would soon be in their position. I don't remember very much about the actual ordination at the end of May 1958 in Westminster Cathedral, except that it lasted a very long time indeed on a morning of great happiness. Cardinal Godfrey, a quiet, decent man, did the honours. He once only hit the headlines (and infuriated dog lovers) by referring in a pastoral letter to "pampered poodles". In another letter he wrote these memorable words about the wealthy: "Remember, there are no pockets in a dead man's shroud."

At the breakfast/lunch in Archbishop's House after the ordination ceremony he came out with a request for our prayers and the reminder that "The wind blows hardest at the top of the tree", which is where he felt fate had put him. On the table-mat in front of each new priest was a white envelope containing details of his first curacy. My envelope told me to report in a week's time to the Parish of Our Lady of Victories in Kensington.

I was more than willing to do so. If it had told me to report anywhere else I would also have obeyed just as willingly. True, I did not know much about the parishes of the diocese, but that did not matter. In fact the choice of Kensington was quite a clever one. With an English/Canadian public school background I would fit well enough into the Kensington and Earl's Court cosmopolitan atmosphere.

I was ready for the task which had taken six years of preparation. Christ, the light of the world, had to be known through his Church, the ultimate guarantor of truth. It was my job, in compassion, care and diligence to serve God's people in his Church. I was anxious to get to work, and said as much the next day during my First Mass in St Edward's Church, Golders Green, where I had been baptized and where my brother and sister had been married. Canon Thornton, the elderly parish priest, was more than pleased. His experience had been very different from mine. As a boy of twelve "with a vocation" he had left Ireland for the Lisbon College, to study at the junior seminary. Aged twenty-two, with no sight of parents or friends in the meanwhile, he had returned as a priest to say his First Mass in Ireland before moving to Westminster diocese. I was a success story for his parish of Golders Green. My father was proud in his own way, and so certainly was my mother, whose dreams had come true. I had no idea that only a few weeks before thousands had marched to Aldermaston or that Golders Green was the home of Gertrude Fishwick, one of the most inspiring of the pre-CND anti-nuclear test campaigners. I was living in a different world.

CHAPTER SIX

Curate's Eggs in Kensington

The envelope with the instructions about reporting to Our Lady of Victories in Kensington did not tell me how to get there. So, getting on to the wrong train at Earl's Court, I managed to be late for lunch. Late or not, the welcome was just as warm from the very kindly, highly traditional and remarkably structured parish priest, Canon Bagshawe. His structure was the first thing I noticed. Quite small, he had nevertheless, over the years, acquired an enormous stomach which was almost self-supporting. It sloped away gently from his chin down to the mountain around his navel. Moving this way and that under a cassock it seemed to have a life of its own. Inevitably, he was nicknamed "Baggy". He was the gentlest of parish priests, ever anxious to avoid a row, and always willing to delegate work to the curates. Very rarely was he angry though he did have his moments. The existence in the parish of the large but non-parochial church of the Carmelites on Church Street did cause him certain irritation. Late one night, one of the wealthier families from the Carmelite area phoned to ask him to come and anoint a dying parent. "Why not one of the Carmelites?" asked Baggy, in his pyjamas. "Much too late to wake dear Father X," was the reply. There followed a controlled explosion.

He and his Fulham neighbour and friend, Canon Shaw, made weekly outings either to the Old Ship in Brighton or to their club in Pall Mall and returned late in the afternoon, rosy and cheerful, for a good sleep. There were four curates, a housekeeper, a maid, various cleaners and a large fat cat. The housekeeper and Baggy ran the house between them. Food was plentiful, drink flowed at least on Sundays and the smooth lino on the corridors shone with polish. Chasing the cat on the lino was the nearest thing we had to blood sports.

Someone had clearly designed the house as a model presbytery on pre-Vatican II lines. Inside the front door was the beggars' parlour – a small room with nothing in it except a chair which was itself firmly screwed to the floor. Into that parlour went any tramp who had managed to get through the front door. A shilling or a sandwich, and they counted their blessings. Along the corridor were two further parlours, each with a desk, two chairs on one side, one on the other. All other visitors – and there was an endless stream of them – found their way into one of these parlours. In the desks were forms galore: marriage documents, funeral lists, convert instruction sheets, dispensation applications and even instructions about fees. It was not cheap to get married at Our Lady of Victories if organist and flowers and red carpet were included. Those living in the parish – a vast block of London extending from Holland Park Avenue down to Brompton Road, and from Holland Road to Kensington Gardens, could of course marry without a fee. But "outsiders" had to pay for the privilege of our classy operation.

Between the parlours and the rest of the house was a frosted-glass door through which the laity did not, except in most unusual circumstances, pass. The parish was benignly run by the clergy. No Parish Council existed to interfere with the decisions of the parish priest or his senior curate. There were plenty of parish organizations, but they all depended on our good will and they did not exceed their proper functions as laid down by us.

The church itself was very large and grand – a late Gilbert Scott production in faced sandstone with a crypt below. Bombed out during the war, when I arrived it was in the process of reconstruction. For the first year or so all liturgical activity took place in the crypt, and plenty of that there was too. It was a very good church for a new curate. Every Sunday there were ten Masses, starting at 6.30 a.m. with the nurses from St Mary Abbot's Hospital, a few insomniacs and early risers. The church was full for the ten o'clock Mass, and the High Mass (deacons and plenty of incense) at eleven and the Noon Mass were always packed. The Church of God was very much a going concern in Kensington, as hundreds poured in and out every Sunday from all parts of the world and from every class of society. The Earl's Court Overseas Visitors' Club meant a regular mixture of young Australians and New Zealanders who had great smiles and painfully crushing handshakes. There were diplomats from various Embassies, au pair girls doing their stint in the larger family houses, new arrivals from Ireland looking for digs, public school families into insurance or the City, students from India, Africa and the Philippines. God knows who they all were or where they all came from, but they filled the church time and time again. They were amazingly generous, delighted to meet an English priest and happy to have an ear available for their various problems.

In no time at all I was plunged into activity which never seemed to stop and which I much enjoyed. Marriage was a major industry. Looking back, I wish I had taken a more personal interest in the many, many couples I helped to marry, but the sheer numbers made that kind of concern quite difficult. The routine was all laid out. Prenuptial inquiry forms to be filled out and signed, mixed marriage dispensations to be applied for (a considerable waste of paper, I now realize), registrars to be notified and fees to be collected. I soon learned once more how to bend the rules. There were endless searches to be made for evidence of baptism, and this posed real problems for many of our extremely international community. More than once I ran out of patience with the paperwork, took the victims into the church and baptized them on the spot with the formula, "If you are not baptized I now baptize you . . ." This, it seemed to me, covered all eventualities. It could certainly do no harm and enabled me to produce a certificate.

Non-Catholics all signed up for the Catholic education of their children, and everyone agreed in writing that they would observe Catholic moral teaching, which meant no contraception. That I had the right to make such demands was my unhesitating conviction. The family of the Church was just that: if people didn't like its family discipline, then they could go elsewhere. One or two recipients of this cheery news gritted their teeth and looked less than amused, but there was not much they could do about it if they wanted to get in front of our altar. All those weddings! How many hundreds I have helped to launch on life together. Just occasionally in some far part of the world someone will even now come up and say that I married them years before at OLV. My best wedding memory is of the couple from Hong Kong. They knew no-one in London and explained that they couldn't even produce friends to act as witnesses. No problem, I assured them. OLV was never empty. Someone could always be found at their prayers. I would find the witnesses. But when the day came it was an empty church until almost the last moment. Then in came two Sisters of Charity wearing those large, white, folded head-dresses which used to look like oversized school-boys' paper darts. I wandered down the church and explained to Sister A that she would make an excellent Best Man and to Sister B that, as the Bride's Father, she would be first-class. So, not for the first time, nuns saved the day, and there is still a photo somewhere of my five-foot Chinese couple flanked and overshadowed on the steps by their two tall sisterly witnesses, all four of them with smiles from ear to ear.

Not all weddings were quite so happy. On one occasion an angry non-Catholic father stood at the back of the church and bellowed outrage at his daughter about her betrayal, whenever he managed to get free from the sacristan, a small man who was doing his best to control him. What a dreadful start to a marriage. Sometimes weddings did not start at all. One day our then crypt church was packed with what was clearly going to be a very elegant affair. But time went on and there was no sign of the bridegroom. Then into the sacristy through the back car park door he slipped, unshaven, miserable and alone. "I can't go on with this," he whispered, and that was quite clear. I gave him as much brief comfort as I could and told him to push off at once down a side-street. He did, leaving me to the rage of the bride's mother, with which I could cope, and the shock and tears of the bride, with which I could not. That was the worst wedding morning I have ever experienced, and very untypical.

Most were happy affairs, and I always did my best to turn up when invited to the subsequent receptions. Many an ancient aunt I have sat next to while playing with cold chicken and hoping for the rapid return of the wine waiter. As a rule of thumb it was quite easy to distinguish between working-class, especially Irish, weddings and the public school ones. The Irish would always come up with a pile of pound notes or fivers in their hands and push them into your pockets. Public school boys would be equally grateful but, with cheque-book in hand, would come up and say, "How much do we owe you, Father?"

Easter was the time when marriages really multiplied. It was not unusual for there to be six or seven weddings on the one afternoon. Thus I met CND for the first time. The wedding programme on Easter Monday, 1959 was going badly wrong. Taxis and brides were ·turning up late, and I couldn't understand why until I saw a long column of people winding their way along the High Street with banners and prams and police. This was the cause of the traffic-jam that was wrecking our carefully timed wedding timetable. Someone said they were the CND. I had no interest whatever in who they were. I just wished they would go somewhere else if they wanted to block the traffic. No doubt the *Daily Telegraph*, which arrived in the presbytery every morning, had something similar to say.

The Sisters of Charity were no strangers to OLV. We had one of our own – the remarkable Sister Angela, whose life was given to the poor of the parish, of whom, despite all the West London luxury, there were plenty. I do not forget the first time I saw a whole family – parents and three children – living in one Holland Road room, with the baby asleep in the pulled-out top drawer of a very second-hand chest of drawers. All such families were Sister Angela's special preserve. She collected old clothes and bits of furniture, like a religious magpie. She was not above scouring the refuse-bins of West End hotels. She also had a round of bridge clubs where she would gather up cigarette butts, remove their tobacco, pack it into tins and take it round to her large army of old men living on their own or in various homes. In those days Sisters of Charity were not supposed to be seen eating. One of the worst crimes for a junior curate was to knock on the door of her room at the back of the church at lunch-time. There would be a clanking and a banging and a rattling of cutlery. Eventually the door would open and beyond Angela, wiping her lips and not too pleased, would be a table without the slightest evidence of food. She had a great devotion to a particular picture of the Virgin Mary and, when the new church was finally opened, lobbied with all the energy of a Parliamentary professional to get "her" picture installed in a prominent place with a decent rack of candles in front of it.

Converts were, after marriages, the second major industry. It is hard, today, to convey the sense of the exclusive certainty of those years, but so it was. Against pagans and Protestants we were clearly winning. Not only were our parishes and our schools full, but people were queuing up to join. I never had less than a dozen converts on my books at one time and, granted an hour-long session every week for three or four months with each one, there was plenty to do. They came in all shapes and sizes, few from real unbelief, most from other Christian denominations. Once I thought I had fished in a young Japanese banker, brought up as a Buddhist. He sat through four or five of my non-stop sessions before inviting me out to a marvellous Japanese dinner. After that I never heard from him again. That was his inscrutable way of saying "Enough is enough", I don't doubt. But Mr Watts was the best convert I ever had. As I droned on and on he would nod happily, saying, "Yes, Father. Yes, Father." There came a point at which I thought there ought to be some small sign of intellectual movement. I asked him if there was no single point in the new faith which he was about to swallow entire which caused him problems. None at all, I was assured. "Why not?" I asked. The answer was that he had lived with Mrs Watts for fifty years over a garage in some Kensington mews and she, an Irish Catholic, was convincing enough. Indeed she was. Not long after he joined the Church she contracted lung cancer and died in my presence after a long night's vigil in their little bedroom. I did not even know if she had died, so gentle was the ending of her breathing. He went to live afterwards in Nazareth House, Hammersmith, where there is much kindness behind high walls. Now they both lie in Kensal Catholic Cemetery.

The youth club was my other major responsibility. I'm not quite sure now why we ran it. To start with I thought it might even produce its harvest of converts – a forlorn hope. It certainly allowed young Catholics to meet other young Catholics, and all concerned had a good time. On Bank Holiday coach outings to Hastings or Southend they seemed to snog just as enthusiastically as non-Catholics, so denominational differences were not always obvious.

They liked me and I liked them, even though cleaning up the hall afterwards was not their strong point. From time to time we would be raided by gangs from elsewhere. World's End, in Chelsea, seemed to be a safe haven for raiding parties who would break our windows, pull our lavatories off the floor and slash cycle tyres. I was not then much into Gandhi and, if not so outnumbered, I would gladly have taken to extreme violence. We ran a football team and a netball team and I eventually found myself on the Kensington Youth Committee as a serious local person. It dawned on me that there were other churches and that they also ran youth clubs. Ecumenism started with table-tennis in my case.

The other great place for growing up fast was the hospital. With a large collection of Irish nurses and sisters we, the Catholic chaplains, were in a strong position. As long as we did our pastoral work with the patients, we were welcome visitors in Sister's office. At night tea and toast would be rustled up rapidly from somewhere. At Christmas-time there had to be defensive measures taken against the flow of alcohol on offer. I remember pouring many a double port surreptitiously into the pot of the large ward cactus in the hope that it would do as compost. We were welcome not only for cultural reasons but, in simply being with people and sharing some of their problems, we were also part of the cure. In those days new mothers stayed in hospital for over a week with their babies, so we saw a lot of joy. But we also shared a lot of tears with those whose babies had come to them dead.

Many questions ran through my head in those days. One of my fellow curates took me one day to see Mrs Jones. The curtains around her bed were drawn and he gave me no warning of what to expect, except to say that Mrs Jones was very ill. The floor went round when I saw her. Her entire lower jaw had been removed, tongue and all. All she could live on was fluid given through some sort of drip. The astonishing thing, never forgotten, was that when my friend started on the "Our Father" and held her hand, her other one moved upwards and made the sign of the Cross. What a cross she had to bear, I thought, as eventually I buried her in an Ealing cemetery.

Inexplicable to any honest person is the suffering of young children. Of that I saw enough too. In the children's ward one day I was called to a couple whose little baby was in a transparent box, lying on some sort of very soft cradle. The little boy had a bone condition which meant that, as he moved, his bones were so fragile that very often they would fracture. I couldn't explain that one away and nor could all my theological books. What answer could I give to the beautiful twenty-year-old girl who fell from a car in Iverna Gardens and broke her neck against the pavement? She died two years later because she, paralysed, simply did not want to live. The more time I spent in the hospital the more I came to appreciate the dialogue in Camus' *The Plague* between Paneloux the priest who thought, to start with, that he had all the answers, and Rieux the doctor who knew that he had very few. "Perhaps we should love what we cannot understand . . ." says Paneloux, having watched a child die. To which the doctor replies, "until my dying day I shall refuse to love a scheme of things in which children are put to torture". The hospital certainly taught me that anyone with easy answers to the problem of innocent suffering has no answers at all.

One night in Casualty, a couple of Indians were brought in, covered in blood. It was the time of the Notting Hill race riots and I was seeing the effects at first hand. The two victims had been walking up Warwick Road at about ten in the evening when a car drew up with four white youths on board. Each had a brick. They got out and hammered the two men down to the pavement, got back in their car and drove off. The race hatred of that hot summer taught me many lessons that had never come my way in the leafy streets of Hampstead Garden Suburb. From time to time the hospital also provided its embarrassing moments. Once I had to deal with a very ill and crabby old man who said he had given up his faith years before because of the hypocrisy of the Church, the riches of Rome, the rudeness of Father Murphy, etc., etc. Some wonderful Irish nurses coaxed him out of all that, so one day shortly before he died I was able to give him Communion and help him on the road he knew he was on.

As I was leaving he reached out, in gratitude, for a large purse which spilled pound notes all over his bed. I tried to gather them up for him. At exactly that moment the Matron, and she was a formidable one, appeared around the corner, took one look at me and my handful of notes, and exuded disapproval. My explanation sounded feeble so I blushed and moved on.

Life's problems became very real in the confessional. Those were the days of long lines of penitents waiting outside the boxes. At Christmas and Easter they came in their hundreds. Ours were nice modern boxes. When the penitent knelt down behind the grille the light outside the box went red. Our four boxes would be alternating, red and green, for hours on end at major feasts. Much, of course, was routine, but sometimes on the other side of the grille there was a voice that needed help, described problems unthinkable, listed cruelties endured, asked for a sign of sympathy, at least. People now pay £50 an hour for the chance to discuss their problems. Behind the red and green lights I tried sometimes to give the same service for free. "My yoke is easy", I remembered from the New Testament, and I never saw any reason to make anyone else's more difficult.

The confessional, or the No. 28 bus, nearly caused my first row with our Baggy. One Christmas Eve I set off for home in Golders Green by bus at an early hour to deliver presents, in the confidence that I would get back in time for my two hour confessional stint. The traffic was bad and the bus was late. Baggy, whom I was supposed to be relieving, had to cope with nearly an extra hour of Kensington sins, and it did nothing for his temper.

Only once did he really have me in the dock. Baptisms in Latin had always been something of a curse, especially when perhaps eight or ten babies were being baptized at once, most of them howling, relations chattering and flash bulbs popping, until we put an end to that. Worse, baptisms were on Sunday afternoons after lunch, and Sunday lunch was the time when the wine flowed fairly freely. I once had to tell someone, who turned out to be the Philippines Ambassador, to shut up, and he did look rather surprised. So it was a great relief when I saw some *Catholic Herald* headline which said that baptisms were to be conducted in English. A nod was as good as a wink to me and that Sunday I swung into English with improved results. Then came the news that this was premature. The second curate told me to say nothing – no one would ever know of my grievous liturgical sin. Not so. Months later one of the families, treated to my dose of English, met Bishop Parker of Northampton and told him how wonderful this Kensington reform had been. He was not amused. He waited until the next bishops' meeting to tell his old and traditional friend Cardinal Godfrey what way-out things were going on in his diocese. Cardinal Godfrey swung into action and had our Baggy up on the carpet. Our Baggy rushed – not in his case an easy thing to do – back to the parish and put to all his curates the awful question – "Who has used English in the Liturgy?" Since by now six months had elapsed I had nearly forgotten one Sunday's weakness so long ago. I was let off with a very solemn warning. Never again English, until authorized, not by the *Catholic Herald*, but by the Pope in Rome. But I think even Baggy smiled. He was not one to go in for the heavy hand.

In our turn we had often to forgive him. One of his infuriating habits was to appear in church just as one started to preach. Then, like a part-time policeman he would, back to the pulpit, move up and down the centre aisle finding empty seats and gesturing to individuals standing at the back to move up. His arms waved as if he was giving racing tips. Eventually some unfortunate was forced up the aisle to be properly seated. It was not easy to get the congregation to give full attention to my crafted and inspiring words coming from the pulpit when all these manoeuvres were going on immediately below. His other little weakness was to over-sleep. This would mean that when he was supposed to be doing the 6.30 a.m. Mass, the sacristan would often have to wake him at 6.35. Baggy would then toddle down the corridor in pyjamas to the nearest curate at 6.40 and wake him. The nearest curate was usually me, and however much I threw my clothes in the air and leapt into them I couldn't get into vestments and ready for action until 6.50. To arrive twenty minutes late for the 6.30 Mass was not popular. The nurses, who had to go on early duty, were decent enough but some of our dear old ladies could look very frosty indeed. Out of Boy Scout spirit one couldn't really blame the parish priest in public.

If he was a character, so were many of his parishioners. Who could forget Miss Bleaden, for many years a contemplative nun, who lived in a little sparse Earl's Court room with a foot on each side of the world's dividing veil? When a German man named Podola, who had murdered someone near Gloucester Road, was due to be hanged, Miss Bleaden prayed for him as if he had been a brother. Which in her eyes he was. On the morning of the execution she, kneeling alone at the back of the church, wept and wept and wept. There were so many wonderful characters, like the Goddard brothers, real old Kensington natives, who Sunday after Sunday counted the collection after every Mass, bagged it up for the Monday morning banking and never took a penny of reward. They loved the parish and counting was their work for the church. Today they would have been deacons. Mrs Barker of the primary school endlessly astonished me. With a class of forty-six or forty-seven she was still utterly and amazingly in control. "Good morning, Father," they would all pipe up as one when I arrived. I, who could not keep children in order for more than five minutes, was more than impressed. Not that I ever managed to imitate her. Some of her infants knew exactly what they wanted. One day, behind the statue of the Sacred Heart I found a little note which I still have. It reads, "Dear Jesus, I would like a baby sister with your help please Ann." I hope she got one.

Thanks to an enthusiastic Catholic teacher in Holland Park Comprehensive School I had from time to time to go up there to give "Catholic" instruction. This meant that seventy or eighty Catholics of various degrees of lack of enthusiasm aged from eleven to seventeen would be handed over to me for twenty minutes on my own. I would sooner have been in the Coliseum facing the lions. Actually it was the Coliseum that solved my problems. Nothing gained the attention of the whole group as rapidly as stories of martyrdom, the bloodier the better. There was no shortage of Christian martyrs over the centuries. From Stephen's stoning to the lengthy and painful deaths of the French Jesuit missionaries to the Hurons, I gave Holland Park all the blood it wanted. All the same I rather doubted if this was exactly Catholic instruction of the sort the bishops had in mind.

Not that Kensington and Earl's Court with their ex-soldiers and refugees from many countries were themselves short of contemporary heroism. On one occasion I was called to the death-bed of an old Polish officer. He was propped up on pillows in a basement flat on a large bed. His breathing was very heavy. But he also knew his liturgy. He treated me like one of his lance corporals. "Anoint me. Say the prayers for the dying. Give me absolution." He knew exactly what he wanted, but his timetable for dying was going wrong, since I had run out of prayers. "Say the Memorare again" was his last instruction. Before I got to the end he was dead.

There was also the courage of the living. One night, in one of the hundreds of hotels in Earl's Court, a man stepped on to the court-yard parapet to adjust his TV aerial seven floors up. He slipped and crashed through two sets of glass roofing before he hit the ground. Amazingly, he was still just alive when brought to St Mary Abbot's but died in Casualty. I was asked to tell his wife, still waiting in the hotel. She knew at once from my face and it was she who comforted me. We talked for so long that the police, who had brought me, began to wonder if all was well and knocked on the door to find out.

In all this welter of pastoral activity were any seeds of radicalism beginning to grow? A few, perhaps. One of our less happy duties was to prepare the initial papers for marriage nullity cases. It came my way to deal with an application made by a woman on the grounds of her husband's permanent impotence. But when I had done my part and had the dossier ready, I found a brick wall at the Diocesan level. The old Canon in charge of such matters may have been wonderful with widows and orphans but obstruction was his special-ity when dealing with fresh young uppity curates. I could not get a date out of him, or any other indication that he was in any way interested in this very human problem, spelt out so clearly to me in frustration and tears in the presbytery parlour. I got very fed up and decided on unilateral and immediate action. Off I went to the Earl's Court Post Office and sent a telegram to the Roman Rota at the Vatican requesting them to ask the Westminster authorities to take up the case. Whether it was the result of my telegram or not I have no way of knowing, but a month later Rome did exactly what I had asked. It still took another couple of years to sort out, but she did in the end get her nullity. There will be a specially heated sub-department of purgatory for the clerical bureaucrats of those days with Canon Law degrees who regularly made life impossible for so many people.

My other brush with authority came with a couple of adoption cases. A young Irish girl from Dublin, eight weeks pregnant, turned up in tears in our presbytery parlour. What should she do? With many good wishes I sent her up to the Catholic Crusade of Rescue in North Kensington to discuss adoption. The next day she was back in near hysterics. They had been very nice to her but wanted to know where the child had been conceived. The answer was Dublin, so they had provided her with a return ticket and the address of a mother and baby convent *in Dublin*. She was, in short, being sent back to face the risk of shame which had made her flee to England in the first place. I got on the phone and was politely told that Westminster Diocese could not cope with the numbers of unmarried Irish girls coming over and, by agreement with the Archdiocese of Dublin, they were to be returned to a secure convent. Not by me, I said to myself. The next day I took her to a British adoption society and introduced her to a lovely Irish couple in the parish. They made her their daughter for the next few months and saw her through the birth and adoption, which she still wanted.

Adoption nearly brought me into mild collision with the police. A Scots nurse had come to London, taken a room in South Kensington and had a baby in St Mary Abbot's. She told me that her parents would kill her if they found out. She was desperate to get her baby girl adopted. I knew a family equally desperate to adopt. So I introduced them. It seemed a sensible thing to do. It all worked out happily in the end, but apparently I had committed various crimes by making the introduction and had to listen patiently to a lecture from a very righteous local official. I had to explain that I was not actually in the business of selling babies, which he seemed to think was my sideline.

It was being introduced to the Catholic peace movement Pax Christi ("Peace of Christ") which started me on the road to CND. My first contact with the organization was very simple. Two young New Zealand girls who had turned up at the youth club asked for some suggestions for a good European summer holiday. I had noticed in the *Catholic Herald* that this organization with the odd name, about which I knew nothing, ran international summer "Routes". On these routes hundreds of young people would go walking through different countries in smallish groups, living with families, discussing a different theme each year and ending up after ten days with a great collective celebration. It sounded a good idea to me and to the girls as well. They came back delighted, having had a cheap and very different holiday. A few weeks later a Pax Christi representative appeared in the youth club and asked if I would mind being chaplain to the very small British section of the Pax Christi movement. It had started after the war with the aim of reconciling the French and the Germans and was now a general international peace movement aimed at reconciling anyone who needed reconciling. I could not imagine that such aims could actually be against my religion, and since the members were a nice lot and did not expect too much from their chaplain I signed up. Frankly, for the first year or so it seemed all rather boring. Much discussion of Papal Encyclicals and not too much action. Little did I know on what a slippery path I had ventured in a church world where "peace" was assumed to be a Communist trick and where those who advocated it, even if they wore cassocks, were thought to be a threat to God, private property and the Western Way of Life. But Pax Christi was still a minor part of my world for several years.

Major change came with a summons in 1961 to Archbishop's House to see the Vicar General. This ancient gentleman with very large bushy eyebrows sat behind a roll-top desk, with a lamp casting some light on a gloomy room. Archbishop's House itself was not exactly a fun-fair. Women had hardly yet penetrated the place. On each side of the main staircase were separate washrooms and lavatories. The signs, as might have been expected, did not say Men and Women. They divided the ordinary priests from the Canons and Monsignors. The Higher Clergy went to pee on the right. Lower ones to the left. Where women went I only found out much later.

The Vicar General had news for me. I was to go to North Kensington, double as curate there and as part-time assistant to the Financial Secretary, who was the centre of most of the power in the diocese at the time. He appointed the architects who built the churches. He negotiated with local authorities for new schools. He held the cheque-book, and the hand that holds the cheque-book is even more important than the one that rocks the cradle.

Orders were orders, and off I went to St Pius X church in St Charles Square and a much simpler regime. Dear old Father Hathway ran the show, counted the cash himself, watched telly with Elsie, the housekeeper, and specialized in gruff generosity. One winter he found me with a heavy cold, took a look at my rather thin dressing gown, snorted with indignation, took the bus to Whiteley's, returned with a garment so thick that it would have coped with a Russian winter and made me put it on at once. Long years later I went to baptize a child at the same church. Hathway charged into the church holding several sections of hoover piping in front of him like a lance. "I'll get the blighter", were his first words to me after many years. The "blighter" was a pigeon that had got into the church and was perched above the altar dropping its business on the sanctuary. Only after persuading the pigeon to leave did he return to greet me. He was, and happily still is, a good and much-loved man without ambition or pretensions. His was a much smaller parish than Our Lady of Victories and was almost entirely working class. The gentrification of North Kensington was only still a glint in some property developer's eye. Granted that the senior curate kept a small crocodile in a tank in his room, and had a mynah bird which was not toilet trained, we all got on well enough together. Over the dining room table looking at the interminable telly one afternoon with Elsie, I learned that John Kennedy had been shot. It could not be true. I had, on the corner of Marloes Road not so long before, cheered as this hope of a new world had waved from an open car. Delighted crowds waved back as he, with his beautiful wife by his side, drove along Cromwell Road from the airport. As his skull, in slow motion, flew apart on TV, it seemed that the world was doing the same thing. Soon there were Irish prayer cards with Kennedy on one side and Pope John XXIII on the other – the two great hopes of the early 1960s.

I was myself on my way to acquiring another hero. The Methodists in the area were doing great work for the homeless and against racism. In schism or heresy though they certainly were in

religious matters, I could only admire what they were trying to do
– parallel in part to the work which I was attempting, on a much
smaller scale, with the Young Christian Workers. Better known as
the YCW, this was a movement for social justice and the application
of gospel principles to workplace situations. It had been founded in
Belgium in the late 1920s. I had helped to form a North Kensington
group which met weekly in the home of a generous Anglican convert.
The Methodists asked me one day if I could get someone called
Archbishop Roberts, a Jesuit, to chair some meeting they were
organizing. I had never heard of Archbishop Roberts but popped
over to Farm Street on my bike to ask him – a small man in a
sweater – if he would oblige. He would, but he wanted to know
where I was working. At Archbishop's House, I replied. He was
amazed. I did not know that at the time he was threatening to take
the Apostolic Delegate, Archbishop O'Hara, to Court for defamation, which is an unusual way of dealing with Apostolic Delegates.
This determined, unpretentious person was soon to have a great
influence on me.

His views on nuclear deterrence were entirely convincing. It was
wicked, so he said, to threaten to do what it would be wicked to do.
Never a pacifist, he patiently explained in endless articles that the
Church had never supported the idea that non-combatants could
be directly attacked, even in a "just" war. The English bishops of
the day were desperate to find ways of squaring what was meant to
be their moral position with the political and military facts of nuclear
deterrence. Roberts, who had retired as Archbishop of Bombay to
make way for an Indian, was never given an official position as a
bishop on his return to this country. He remained an endless irritant
to the Hierarchy, since he had to be invited to official bishops'
functions, even though his support for CND went entirely against
all episcopal grain. He was ordered once not to appear and lead
prayers at some Trafalgar Square Christian CND rally, on the nonsensical grounds that somehow he would compromise the true faith.
He impressed me deeply, thorn in the official side though he certainly was.

I myself had no idea of being a thorn. Three times a week I
cycled around Marble Arch and Hyde Park Corner on my way to

Archbishop's House, where I sat on one side of an enormous desk and tried to work out sums for "displaced pupils" grants. In those days there was no general denominational school building grant, except for some categories of new secondary schools or primary replacement places. I met architects, listened to curial gossip, dealt with complaints and hammered out envelopes for the clergy on an addressograph machine which, even in those days, must have been ready for the Victoria and Albert Museum. Little did I know it, but the power of Canon Rivers, the Financial Secretary, was already being threatened and I was part of the operation designed to clip his wings.

A new Schools Commission and a Finance Commission were formed and I, under the entirely amiable Bishop Cashman, was to be the secretary of the former. Never has anyone been thrown so rapidly into the deep end. I hardly knew an All Age school from an ESN one. Within days I had to cope with County Hall phone calls about the lavatories at St Joseph's or the playground repairs at St Mary's. By dint of verbal flannel and the ability to keep the conversation going with one half of my mind while reading the file with the other, it took me about six months to become an expert on school administration. This has made me doubtful about all experts ever since.

CHAPTER SEVEN

Bishop's Batman

In January 1963 Cardinal Godfrey, the kindly, very formal man with the large, round face, died. An era had come to an end. We, the lesser clergy, hoped and prayed that a new broom would arrive in Westminster to do some badly needed cleaning up. Too few people with too much power had run the place for a long time, and it was the moment for a change. Those priests who felt as I did soon had their prayers answered. Archbishop John Heenan was on his way to Westminster from Liverpool, and it was a popular choice with the rank and file. He had laid a reforming trail from Brentwood to Leeds and from Leeds to Liverpool. In Liverpool he had even managed to sort out the problem of what to do with Archbishop Downey's pre-war would-be St Peter's-style cathedral, of which only the crypt had been built. There was, thanks to Heenan, an architectural competition and the result was the unusual structure with wonderful stained glass at the other end of Hope Street from the Anglican cathedral. It is known now as Paddy's Wigwam. In view of its subsequent history of rain and roofing problems it should perhaps have been called Paddy's Sieve.

Anyway, Heenan was on his way and his arrival meant another bit of re-routing for me. As secretary of the Schools Commission I had, I am sure, upset the steady ways of the Old Guard. At least I, with the able help of a clerical golfing genius, John McCoy, whose energy and vision were well ahead of mine, had some successes to chalk up. For one thing, we managed to reorganize most of the diocesan secondary schools into a comprehensive pattern, which meant a great deal of coaxing of the existing grammar schools, not all of which were very happy with these new ideas. Ours was not a reorganization motivated by some high theory of education: it was

93

simply a matter of survival. It was quite clear that many of the smaller Catholic secondary modern schools would simply go down the drain if there was a general Local Authority pattern of comprehensive schools, unless they could be enlarged and become schools which offered parents chances of "O" and "A" levels and even university places for their children.

Bishop Challoner Boys' School in the East End was the awful advance warning. Creamed off by a Catholic grammar school, a Catholic central school and a four-form entry Catholic secondary modern school which was almost comprehensive, Bishop Challoner Boys, despite a staff who really cared, was already doomed. Supposed to take sixty new pupils every year, it could barely manage forty. There were never any higher bands amongst the forty. It was perfectly clear to McCoy and me, and to most of the Schools Commission, that if we did not go with the comprehensive tide all that would eventually be left of Catholic secondary education would be some isolated élite grammar schools. The predicament of the Challoner Boys even reached the level of the Cardinal when an irate parent complained that some of the demoralized, angry and frustrated pupils had found out that one of their mates had actually been to parish Benediction. For this act of piety his head was put in the lavatory pan and flushed for most of the school break. Cardinal Godfrey was not into the niceties of comprehensive school theory, but he knew a religious problem when he saw one.

It was also quite clear that the previous Diocesan schools planning regime had actually held back the building of Catholic primary schools. Parishes were endlessly being told that their schools could not go ahead until they found a place in a government building programme. Since no public grant was available anyway at the time from the government for new, as opposed to replacement, schools, McCoy and I could not understand why they had to be "in programme". The answer was that they didn't. As a result, with the full co-operation of the Hertfordshire, Middlesex and London Education Authorities, who were as keen as we were on new schools, we went ahead with the job of persuading parishes and religious orders to start on new primary schools. Large sums of money were involved but parishes take on debts more easily when they know they are going to get the new school they want.

To have enough land was, of course, essential, and hard to get. Often enough sites were too small, and I learned the art of hard bargaining and the value of democratic muscle. Many times we were told how impossible it would be to get a site for a primary school in the White City area of London, with its hundreds of Catholic families. Just nothing available, the County Hall planners assured us sympathetically. However, when we announced that we would be bussing children, at our expense, down to a primary school in Kensington where there were places, the planners quickly thought again. Parental wishes expressed through a private bus service were not going to look good at County Hall committee meetings. In the end the White City parish gave up a bit of land and the Authority arranged not only for a road closure but for the area of the road to be dedicated to the new school. Where there is a will there is often a way, and the White City Catholic Primary flourishes still.

I suppose I also learned something about the power of information. Many parents and indeed many parish priests and teachers did not have half the information that we had at our disposal. Consultations with parents and parishioners could be very unfair events, since we, the administrators, were the ones who could always claim to know "the facts", and could block other proposals on the grounds that we knew best. Parents could and did get very angry about what they perceived as high-handed behaviour from those "at the Schools Commission". I well remember a furious letter arriving from Waltham Cross where a school was long overdue for rebuilding. It was directed to Bishop Cashman, the titular head of the Schools Commission. "Dear Bishop," wrote the angry Italian, "if your children, like my children, had to put up with our school outdoor toilets you would feel as I do."

Sometimes, despite detailed planning and attempts at democratic decision making, important choices could easily be made between cup and stirrup. One day Cashman visited the office in the company of Mr Ferguson, a senior and sympathetic London County Hall officer. Gins and tonics were produced. The two were on their way to a jolly lunch and its foundations were being laid. Before they went Ferguson explained to the Bishop that though the rebuilding of the London Oratory secondary school had been included in the government programme for the year, the new site was not available. Unless we could come up with an alternative proposal the programme allocation would lapse. The Bishop turned to me, expecting a rabbit out of a hat. It may have been the gin and tonic but I managed to produce one. Swap the allocation over to La Sainte Union school in Highgate, where a site was immediately available, I suggested. Grunts of agreement all round and the deed was done. I have never moved £250,000 around so rapidly in my life and never will again.

But all this wheeling and dealing, which I much enjoyed and the purpose of which – more Catholic school places – I never doubted, came to an end with the arrival of Archbishop Heenan. Shortly after he arrived in Westminster I was asked over to lunch, which I later realized was for a vetting. The upshot of the vetting was that I went to Archbishop's House, initially as second secretary, and after six months or so as principal secretary to the Cardinal. I lasted less than two years, which I learned later was actually about par for the course for secretaries to John Heenan.

Perhaps he never really realized how much I admired the way in which he took on the Augean stables of Westminster. Reforms of all sorts, from pension schemes for housekeepers to retirement homes for elderly priests, were introduced. He tackled awkward and obstructive clergy with supreme courage. If they wouldn't change their ways then out they went. His programme of parish visitations was always packed. He would sweep into a parish with perhaps a late-morning school visit and then run a non-stop programme through hospitals, convents, prisons, old folks' homes and the like till most parish priests were themselves exhausted. The day would conclude with a parish Confirmation Mass and supper in the presbytery. Before supper the curates went to their rooms and would be asked privately if they had any adverse comments about the parish. Some comments were quite colourful.

As a batman and visitation planner I do not think I was really in the top league. Major liturgical ceremonies always brought on panic.

What on earth comes next? Were the altar boys in the right place? Who's got the mitre? Heenan rarely made mistakes, unlike his fellow Bishop George Craven, who forgot to adapt his regular little "thank you" speech one night and, at the end of the list, thanked a parish choir for their wonderful singing which had made the ceremony such a success. The problem was that there was no choir and there had been no singing.

An intermittent line of dropped liturgical bricks marked my passage as secretary. The worst of them happened in Finchley where I managed to leave the chrism oil case in the official car. I only discovered the nature of this disaster when the Cardinal was ready to confirm. Persuading the choir to add a generous number of extra verses to whatever they were singing, I wandered down the aisle, as if this little personal procession was all part of the rubrics, up the street, found the car, got the oils and returned. Heenan had turned bright red but, as instructed, the choir were going through their hymn for the third time.

The amount of work he could get through was astonishing, but one weakness was his conviction that all problems could be sorted out in fifteen-minute slices. We secretaries were to fill his diary every weekday morning with interviews which started at ten thirty and ended after twelve. Perhaps eight interviews in all. No matter if a Provincial was coming to sort out the future of a private school, an old lady to get a blessing, an Ambassador to pay his respects – they were all down for fifteen minutes. One of my self-appointed extra-curricular activities was to coach interviewees. It was vital, I told them, to state the case, whatever it was, in five minutes and to pose a question to which the Cardinal could say "Yes". After seven minutes he invariably would be summing up the situation and pronouncing his own judgement. Of course, this is partly untrue – longer sessions did take place. But it is much more true than untrue.

His generosity and compassion were, it must be said, outstanding. Many a missionary priest would come out of an interview with an unsought cheque for hundreds of pounds. He gave uncritical support even to unauthorized initiatives. Once I was phoned by a nun in tears. Her mother was very ill in South Africa. But it was the rule of her order that the Sisters did not make long journeys even to the possible death-bed of parents. I took it on myself, the Cardinal being away, to phone the Provincial and tell her that the Cardinal wished Sister X to be allowed to go to South Africa at once. So she did, and when I confessed this usurpation of authority, Heenan simply said, "Well done." Priests "with problems" were carefully looked after – unless, of course, they did not accept that they had problems. He could smell a priest with "woman" problems miles away. In fact he suspected that most so-called theological problems had a woman behind them somewhere. Not that he was always wrong.

For many months this dizzy existence went on. The great and the good turned up to bend the Cardinal's ear and the poor and very ordinary turned up to get his advice, a word of encouragement and probably a miraculous medal. Once I was sent, long before the mantraps and fortifications of today, along to 10 Downing Street to deliver a rosary to Harold Wilson's maid. Those were good touches and certainly outflanked anything the Church of England could manage. Not that we liked the Church of England much, despite the many bravely ecumenical speeches that were made. For Heenan there was only one True Church and it was not based at Lambeth. Indeed Lambeth was no-one's favourite on our side of the fence – much too established, much too precious and much too self-righteous. It was our conviction that *we* were the Church of the ordinary people, and I don't think we were far wrong, especially if the ordinary people were Irish people. One lovely Sunday morning, on our way to the great Irish Catholic parish church of Quex Road in Kilburn, Heenan got out of his limousine in the Edgware Road, unfurled his long red *Cappa Magna* or train which flowed for yards behind him and walked up Quex Road, surrounded by thousands of his own under green banners reading, "God Bless our Pope" and "God Bless Cardinal Heenan". This was really his kind of church. It was God's and it was winning.

Sadly, he was born out of due time. His reforming instinct would have been the greatest of gifts in the 1950s but in the age of the Second Vatican Council it was just not enough. His task, as he saw it, was to defend the Church, not to water it down or to explain it away, as he feared the Council might be doing. It was a shock to me to discover that ordinary truth could get a severe denting from him if it came into conflict with The Truth. I do not forget that poor Spanish journalist who interviewed the Cardinal on his own one day. The first we knew of the interview was a headline, picked up from a Spanish newspaper and plastered in the British press, which said that the Cardinal assured Spaniards that the British people did not give tuppence for Gibraltar. Probably quite true, but I was told to issue a press statement to the effect that the Spanish reporter did not understand English very well and had misunderstood the Cardinal. A couple of days later the unfortunate man sent me a tape. There, as clear as a bell, was the Cardinal saying everything he had been reported as saying. There was nothing I could do except to put the tape recorder on the Cardinal's desk, set it going and leave the room. Never did we discuss that episode again.

His conservatism was very clear both during the Birth Control debate which started in England and in the subsequent Vatican Council. My friend Archbishop Roberts had started the Birth Control controversy in April 1964 in the radical Catholic magazine, *Search*, by saying simply that he would accept on faith whatever the Church explicitly taught, but that did not mean that he could defend it on what was supposed to be Natural Law principles of reason. That was enough. The Cardinal penned a ferocious assault on such heresy and sent it off to the press, in May 1964, in the name of the Hierarchy. To his credit Archbishop Dwyer of Birmingham, a wilier old bird, asked Heenan, during a phone call from Lourdes, to delay his blast, but one might as well have asked Vesuvius to postpone an eruption. Letters poured into Archbishop's House from hundreds of Catholics in vigorous protest. Angry husbands even rang me up to tell me how nonsensical they thought the whole business was. Without any matrimonial or sexual experience I was supposed to tell them how wrong they were. It was not easy.

An even larger personal difficulty faced me. "My" Church had always been a top-down Church in the sense that the whole pyramid of belief depended on the inerrancy, indeed infallibility of the Church and above all of the Pope. In one sense, therefore, all propositions had the same value – they depended on the authority of a Church which could teach without error. Now I was faced with an impossible situation. That which clearly had been taught with complete conviction – that artificial methods of birth control were gravely wrong – was being challenged by all sorts of good Catholics, good priests and even good bishops, at least in other countries. My pyramid of belief was starting to fall down. I had to come to terms with this and find a better basis for belief. That process still goes on today, and the result is, I hope, a more solid, personal Christianity than the one with which I started. But the process of change caused every kind of pain, especially to so many who had turned to the Church as the solid rock of absolute conviction on all matters, only to find that the rock was not as solid as they had hoped.

The controversy was raging during the Vatican Council (1962–65), during which Heenan clearly saw himself as the bastion of orthodoxy facing the modernism of the Dutch and even the Germans. I spent only a few days in Rome during the 1964 session, since my job was to take the Cardinal on to Bombay and the Eucharistic Congress which Pope Paul VI was due to visit. They were, however, packed days. Outside St Peter's I watched the hundreds of bishops flowing out of the great doors, a river of purple and scarlet pouring over St Peter's Square. The base for the English Hierarchy was, of course, the Venerable English College just across the Tiber. There Cardinal Heenan would gather his forces – the Indians, the Asians and the Irish, for instance – to fend off all those of Küng-like mentality who threatened his Church. I was more interested in the College itself. Excavations were still going on deep in the basement, which centuries before had been the site of the barracks of a Roman regiment. The workmen had just come down to the level of what had been the regimental latrines. Down there they found a pair of dice, buried for centuries. I imagined two soldiers attending to nature and spending the time gambling.

When I had been told about the Bombay Congress I could hardly believe my luck. We flew from Rome to spend, first of all, a few days in the Lebanon. In Beirut at the Phoenicia Hotel, facing that wonderful sea, we put up in luxury. There were visits to refugee camps, but they were places apart. Beirut was a beautiful, busy, active city and there were still no shadows on the wall. We went on to Karachi to an Apostolic Delegate's residence which outdid Hollywood. An air-conditioned car met us and we sped out past camels and rickshaws to a Papal palace of white stone and marble out on the sea front. I woke to the piercing prayers from a minaret nearby and said Mass looking out through a vast window at sea and sand shimmering together in the sunshine. It was a tonic to get back from this fantasy luxury to the much more down-to-earth residence of Archbishop (now Cardinal) Cordeiro of Karachi. Poverty in Karachi was on the scale I was to meet later in Calcutta. Everything was there, from open sewers in the middle of narrow streets to families living in what looked like enlarged tea-chests. To balance the Apostolic Delegate's establishment we visited a Belgian priest living in a one-room hut with no running water or sanitation of his own. On a shelf in the place of honour was the Bible with a candle burning. The local Muslims, also people of a Book, had made him their friend.

Bombay was another new world. There was something about the brilliant morning light I had never experienced before, nor indeed had I ever seen so many people. Everywhere there were people. We stayed in a comfortable flat in the Malabar Hills provided by an hospitable English lady. Laundry disappeared and returned a few hours later, clean and beautifully ironed. A car and chauffeur were always there when we wanted. A little altar was set up in the drawing room. There the Cardinal would say "his" Mass and I would follow on with "mine". No concelebration nonsense. Down in the town, on the Midan, a great altar had been erected for the celebrations when the Pope arrived, and all around the town Catholic events had been organized. The presiding genius was Cardinal Gracias, the man for whom Archbishop Roberts had moved over some years before. Roberts had been determined, despite centuries of Portuguese and British control, that the See of Bombay should be headed by an Indian bishop. Not that Roberts got many rewards for his pains. The Indian Hierarchy was as conservative as the English one, and though Roberts came to the Congress he was shamefully frozen out. It was painful to see him at the airport when the Pope arrived, not part of the Episcopal welcoming party but in a large pen with hundreds of other ordinary clergy watching from a distance. One who had done so much for Bombay deserved more generous treatment, I thought to myself.

The Papal visit itself was a bit of a miracle. The night before the arrival we were having dinner with some British official or other and the Cardinal asked if the road to the airport would be clear. "Of course," was the reply. "These Indians haven't got a clue about the Pope. Crowds will be very small." I don't know where that official was the next day but I know where we were – stuck in the middle of the largest possible traffic jam as thousands of ordinary Indians made their way out on foot to greet the Pope. Eventually Cardinal Conway, Cardinal Heenan and I left the car and by dint of weight and size heaved our way to the Terminal building. As we got there a tall telegraph pole with Indians perched on every cross-bar gave way and toppled slowly into the crowd below. When the big Alitalia jet finally touched down the fence in front of the tarmac gave way and thousands rushed across to greet the Pope. The plane did a quick turn and taxied to the far end of the runway while police with bamboo sticks drove the crowd back to safety. It took hours to get him finally into Bombay, and his car passed under flowered arches bearing the words, "Welcome Pope Paul." So much for British advance intelligence.

The next day, touring the vegetable market with our hostess, I noticed on the shelves of our usual trader a picture of the Pope. "Who," he was asked, "is that?" The man explained that a new god had arrived to take his place with the pictures of Vishnu and Shiva, which looked out over the piles of fruit and greenery. My own opinion of Pope Paul was steadily rising. Not only was he taking the Birth Control issue rather more gently than my immediate master, since he was setting up a commission to study the matter, but he also made in Bombay an excellent speech about world poverty in which he underlined the contrast between poverty and military spending. Specifically, he suggested a percentage reduction in the second to enable countries to spend more on relieving the first. This was music to my ears. My many evenings spent listening to the enthusiasts of Pax Christi were paying off.

The best bits of Bombay were the off-the-record moments. I wish I had had a tape recorder so that I could hand over to history the "good crack" which went on when Heenan, Conway and Patrick

O'Donovan of the *Observer* all met in some seedy country club bedroom before going on their separate ways. The fan creaked round and round, there was a crate of beer under the bed, they all were in their shirt-sleeves and braces and the jokes went much faster than the fan.

The next day we set off, flying over Goa, down to Kerala where we were to be the guests of the Bishop of Ernakulam. It was not a happy visit, despite the good will of our host, who spent a long time explaining why his Christians did not get along too well with those of the Syrian variety. We had two difficulties. My Cardinal, who had frequent problems with his throat, was in the process of losing his voice and could hardly be heard, even with microphones, as he tried to address a large banquet organized for him. I went to bed feeling rather odd and woke up with food poisoning in the middle of the night. Never have I felt so helpless. Vomiting at one end and with uncontrollable diarrhoea at the other, I crawled on all fours around the room, trying to find a bell somewhere which would summon help. I will never forget that room. I kept passing a plaque which said that it was in this room that Gracias had heard of his appointment as Cardinal. That was the least interesting fact in the world to me in my then condition. Eventually a lovely, quiet Indian brother turned up, took me in his arms, put me on the bed, washed me down and eventually produced doctors with needles, who took charge. For a couple of days I was entirely out of action. The Bishop was very nice, but between Cardinal Heenan's throat and my bowels we had rather wrecked his carefully planned programme. And that was the farewell to India.

Via Delhi we flew up and over the Himalayas and across to Moscow in a line which took us straight across the Aral Sea, which I suppose I will never see again. But there it was, four or five miles below us, the same shape as the bit of blue on the airline map. The Cardinal had much wanted to return via Moscow. He had visited the Soviet Union before the war under false pretences, since as a Catholic priest he would never have got in. How he squared this with his conscience I never asked. His political perspectives had not changed. He hated Communism and Communists with a deep passion. There was no other evil to compare. These were still the days when every Mass ended with prayers for the conversion of Russia.

On the Easter Monday of 1964 we had together driven around Trafalgar Square on the way to the Westminster Diocesan country house at Hare Street. As we passed the Square we had to wait for the CND marchers to pass. Some carried the red banners of the Labour Party and some the red banners of the Communist Party. There were Christian crosses as well. I asked him what he thought about the Bomb. This was no time for moral theology. "Better dead than red" was his only answer. It was not an answer that I could accept. Under the influence of Archbishop Roberts in particular I no longer found arguments for nuclear deterrence convincing. They seemed to me to have little to do with loving one's enemies and doctrines of non-combatant immunity. But from the look on Heenan's face it seemed wiser to postpone such reflections.

When Cardinal Heenan returned to Moscow in 1964 it was without any subterfuge. He was an honoured guest of the Ambassador, Sir Humphrey Trevelyan, at the British Embassy just across the river from the Kremlin and its red stars. I had a large panelled bedroom, a large bathroom and every comfort. The atmosphere was very cold-warish. We mixed with diplomats and their families for the few days we were there and everyone thought they were being spied on, which was probably the case. In one family the husband would write down, on one of those children's plastic slates, anything he thought to be important, show the slate to his wife in silence and carefully wipe out his words. The same spirit existed in the little chapel run by American Assumptionists. A police guard on the door meant that everyone going in or out was noted down. Heenan, in a very Heenanesque move, demanded to go to the Catholic parish church of St Louis (the only one open in Moscow), and after Mass visited the sacristy. Then he asked the elderly Lithuanian priest in French if his movements were very restricted. The old boy rolled his eyes and avoided an answer, wondering no doubt who had been sent to trap him into some indiscretion.

It was deep winter. Snow was on the ground everywhere and the main roads slushy and impossible. Our stay was short and much of it was devoted to discussions between the Cardinal and leathery old

Sir Humphrey on their own. But there was one excellent party, full of interesting youngish diplomats, all of a slightly hawkish disposition, which I greatly enjoyed. So much so that the Cardinal personally told me to stay on while he returned to the Embassy in the official car.

I was to remember that party. It was not long after our return that I experienced one of the most unexpected and unpleasant evenings of my life. We were watching the nine o'clock news, after which Heenan usually retired to his room and some roaring music which billowed up the long corridors with just once in a while the smell of a cigar. On this particular evening he was very restless and hardly was the news over when he turned to me and said abruptly, "You will have to go." I thought he meant on an errand until I realized that I was getting the sack. I had apparently, when in India, laughed at an anti-Irish joke and in Moscow I had left him to find his own way home after that party. In short I was disloyal. Incompetent perhaps, a liturgical disaster no doubt. But disloyal? I couldn't believe what I was hearing. I, who had defended his every reforming move within the Diocese. The next morning he half apologized and said he wanted me to stay and that there had been misunderstandings. But from then on I could not wait to get out of Archbishop's House. For all his personal kindness to me, and indeed to my parents, of whom he had made a great fuss, I felt that the ground was no longer solid under my feet.

So we soldiered on together for a few months until he found his opportunity. Bishop Cashman had been promoted to the new Diocese of Arundel and Brighton and I was asked to take over as chairman of the Diocesan Schools Commission. So my less-than-two-year span of High Life in the Church was over, and it was quite a relief. I had suffered a Royal Garden Party dressed up like a Moss Bros dummy, with a size 7 top hat stuck on my size 7¾ head. I had attended Churchill's funeral in St Paul's Cathedral because the Cardinal had insisted that he would not attend without his personal chaplain and secretary. I had met Julius Nyerere, who was sent by Harold Wilson one morning to see the Cardinal on some Commonwealth mission. His Tanzanian security men had flooded into Archbishop's House for the visit, and each of his security men had one of "ours" in tow. Eventually I explained that there were few dangers in Archbishop's House, except the carpet rods, and got them all to sit down and relax together with coffee and biscuits.

I had even become a Monsignor, which meant the impossible future task of trying to explain what on earth a Monsignor was to well-meaning non-Catholics. Initially I was quite proud of this amazing distinction and even had a small square of pink sewn on to my black shirt front. Tom Driberg MP did me a lot of good at some Fleet Street party when he spotted the modest patch of pink, walked up to me, tickled my chest and said, "Who's this, then? Robin Redbreast?"

The manner of our parting aside, I still think that I always got on pretty well with Cardinal Heenan – a man for whom I had considerable admiration, despite the fact that he had some rather odd ways. We certainly had quite a lot of fun. Nothing pleased him more than to slip down the back stairs of Archbishop's House in shorts and jumper, pop into my venerable green Morris 1000 and head off for Battersea Park for a game of tennis on the public courts. Never was he recognized, even by passing nuns, and more than once he won his game. He had a mean serve and knew how to get his opponent well into the sun.

It was actually after I had stopped being his private secretary and was well into school work again that I had my most remarkable Archbishop's House experience. Whenever we proposed a new school or a school extension public notices (rightly) had to be issued and, from time to time, there would be objections. Up in Finchley the Marie Auxiliatrice nuns ran a successful old-style private girls' secondary school, and part of their property consisted of a field, which was hardly used and was more or less surrounded by private houses. The nuns were persuaded to build – with some help from the Diocese, I think and hope – a one-form-entry aided primary school. Protests poured in from the surrounding houses – misguided, I thought, since a school is used for only part of the day and only during term-time, and the site is protected from being the location of anything much noisier or nastier. The usual ding-dong took place in the press and finally I had a call from the secretary of the Finchley MP. The MP wanted to visit me to discuss the project and to see the supporting evidence which would justify a new school. So into one of our Westminster offices one morning popped a brisk, blonde woman, of less than average height, as I remember. She had no time for gossip. The planning permission? Titles to the site? Evidence of baptismal rolls? Details of parental demands? Approval of Local Educational Authority? Bang, bang, bang – I had the uneasy feeling that traffic police always induce. If I wasn't guilty then I ought to have been. The interrogation took little more than fifteen minutes. Every question was satisfactorily answered, and away went my interrogator, at last perfectly satisfied. Thus passed my one and only meeting with Margaret Thatcher, and St Teresa's Primary School, Finchley, stands today as its memorial.

Many years afterwards I wrote to remind her that once I had shown her conclusively that there was a need for a new Finchley school. I suggested that she should in turn write to me to answer the same sort of questions about Trident nuclear submarines. What, for instance, were they actually for? I felt rather cheated when she did not reply herself, but gave the task over to one of her more devious supporters who seemed convinced that threatening to blow up the world was actually quite an intelligent way of ensuring our national security.

1965 turned into 1966, and the Pope appealed for volunteers to go, on temporary secondment, to countries in Africa and Asia with a priest shortage. This sounded more interesting than a lifetime devoted to school planning permissions and grant negotiations, so without too much premeditation I put down my name. The Cardinal arranged for a solemn send-off for the ten or fifteen in the first batch, which was to include me. A couple of days before the deadline my marching orders were reversed and I was asked to take on the job of chaplain to London University, so that the existing chaplain, John Coonan, an older man than I, could do his spell in Africa first. So it happened that he went off to become bursar and fund-raiser for a bush school and I appeared at St Patrick's, Soho. It was then both a local parish church and the chaplaincy base for the vast spread of London University (one of whose colleges, Wye in Kent, was actually closer to Calais than it was to Senate House).

CHAPTER EIGHT

A Landlord in Gower Street

My initiation as a university chaplain consisted of being thrown into the deep end in the hope that I could swim. Just as I had started on school planning and development work by dint of living on my wits, in much the same way I was launched, not at all unwillingly, into the world of university chaplains and chaplaincies. I was expected to learn the trade on the hoof, and the only way of doing it seemed to be by copying the best of what had gone before. In the 1960s the fortress days of Catholic flock-protection were beginning to go, but no-one was quite sure what came next. The really active and successful chaplains, like Fr "Benjy" Winterborn, SJ, in Manchester, believed in having a large physical base in the centre of university life and a mission which extended *de facto* to everyone, of whatever faith or non-faith, who wanted to be involved, and explicitly to Catholics be they students, academics, administrative staff or domestic workers.

Once I learned I was heading for London University I made a point of visiting the Manchester set-up, full of admiration for all that Benjy and his team had managed. It is symbolic of something or other that a large part of what was once the pride of Catholic chaplaincy building is now let to a bank, while less than half a mile away the Anglicans and others have created their own separate spiritual plant.

London was quite another matter. It was hardly a single university at all, with colleges and medical schools spread out all over the place and more than 40,000 students dotted around the invisible campus somewhere. But I knew almost nothing of the size of the new job when I turned up at St Patrick's Church, Soho, in late May 1966 as both chaplain and parish priest. I suppose that if they had said,

"Would you mind being diocesan archivist and convent chaplain as well?" I would probably have agreed to do it.

Soho was an experience not to be repeated. To start with, I was scared of students. Such brains, such theological depth! Getting my first sermon ready, I sat up in a parish library room on a lovely Saturday afternoon and swotted up St Thomas on original sin, which happened to be on the preaching menu for my first week. It was a disaster. In the first place not many students came. In the second place neither they, and still less most of the parishioners on whom the students had been dumped, were in any way interested in semi-erudite sermons delivered from some lengthy text (especially on original sin). I gave up such pretensions and wondered how on earth I would make anything of this new job.

Insomnia was also setting in. Soho Square is a lovely place on a quiet Sunday morning as Chinese families play on the green grass and Charles II looks rather sadly towards Oxford Street (his view is now interrupted by one of those modern, ten-pence-in-the-slot, automatic, tip-up-seat loos). But Soho Square was not a place for sleep. Car doors banged till the early hours, a kind of truce set in between three and five a.m., after which the refuse lorries crashed their way around the rubbish bins.

Moreover, my predecessor was much loved by the gang of students who did use the house and I, seen correctly as a hit man sent from Archbishop's House to retake student high ground from modernist influences, was not an immediate hero. It did not strike me as very helpful, for instance, that a visiting Dominican priest, Fr Laurence Bright – in Archbishop's House's opinion a notorious doctrinal trouble-maker – was both much admired by the student committee and had been given his own front-door key and thus easy access to the presbytery. This was not the kind of presbytery life for which Our Lady of Victories had trained me, and I felt considerably threatened and a little jealous.

I rather liked the parish, which had an interesting history – a small part of which I was there to witness. On the wall to the right of the altar inside the church was a memorial to the Connaught Rangers, an Irish regiment with a famous history, tarnished to some extent in English eyes by involvement in the 1920s mutinies in

India. Every year the few survivors came to pay their respects at the memorial and every year there were fewer and fewer of them. In 1966 the previous parish priest forgot the date and three old Irishmen turned up to find the church taken over by a very noisy Italian wedding. They sadly left, and that was the end of Connaught Rangers' Day at St Patrick's, Soho.

The church itself boasted a large bell up in the tower. One afternoon I climbed the tower and swung the clapper in the very unused bell to see if everything was in working order. It was. A heavy boom shook the pigeons of Soho and I ended up covered in showers of rust, which my curiosity had earned.

Worries about the future increased. To my dismay, there was actually a proposal, well advanced, for erecting another massive chaplaincy building on the site of a school in Great Chapel Street. This new building would be even further away from anything that might be described as the centre of London University. Worse, an architect was already at work on the scheme and the student in-group were actively involved. I had no idea how to go about averting what I was sure was an expensive planning disaster which would result in a diocesan white elephant south of Oxford Street.

If not a miracle or an answer to prayer, I do not know how to describe what happened next. In mid-July 1966 I was asked by Dr Audrey Donnithorne to a drinks party in University College to meet other Catholic staff. Audrey was both a very traditionalist Catholic and one of the few staff members who took a keen interest in student welfare. As we walked out on to Gower Street she pointed across the road at a block of four houses and said, "What a pity the Church has just sold those four to the University – they would have made an excellent chaplaincy." I was looking, I discovered, at St Teresa's hostel, run by the Sisters of Charity for working girls. It must have been the sherry rolling about inside me, but I crossed the road, rang the bell and asked to see the Superior. Monsignors still had clout in those days and the Superior, instead of telling me to get lost in a polite way, gave me the name of their solicitor and told me that after four years of negotiations the deal with the University was within days of completion.

The next morning, lacking all authority, I phoned the solicitor and told him to proceed no further until he had heard from the Cardinal. Cardinal Heenan had flu but that, typically, was not enough to keep him in bed. Wrapped in a blanket, he was driven at once to Gower Street, had a quick look round, decided that the place would be ideal as a student centre and told the Sister Superior that the Diocese would pay the nuns whatever the University offered plus any of their expenses. The four interconnected houses had been priced at £30,000 a piece so, for a bit more than £120,000 the Diocese acquired a large property in the centre of the University area, now worth well over a million.

All this wheeling and dealing proceeded at such a merry pace that the University authorities took some time to catch up. When they did they were not pleased. Dr Creed, the Vice Chancellor, had, weeks before, been invited to have dinner with Cardinal Heenan, and I, with many others, was on the guest list. It was a jolly evening with many Heenan stories well told. (He had a ready wit, as the cliché goes. During his wartime experience in the East End he had one night been helping an old lady towards a shelter. Suddenly she stopped and said she had forgotten her teeth and wanted to go back for them. "You won't need them, dear," Heenan was reported to have said, "the Germans aren't dropping sandwiches.")

The Creed dinner proceeded from one joke to another until the University car arrived and I showed the Vice Chancellor down the front steps. At the last moment he turned to me and said that he had forgotten to bring a message to the Cardinal. And what was that, I asked? Creed explained that some Monsignor Kent had been interfering with University property deals and would the Cardinal please stop him. I asked him if he knew who I was. He did not. When I told him that I was the Kent concerned he looked less than happy, got into his car and drove off. Good relations were soon re-established. The University actually wanted the property to guarantee space for the future expansion of the University College Medical School. That was a long-term prospect. When the Cardinal assured them that, should a capital allocation ever be made to allow that to happen, he would give up the Gower Street premises if they would find some alternative, smaller base for chaplaincy work in the

University area, everyone was happy. Except, I am sure, the solicitors involved. And perhaps the original architect.

So, by the beginning of August St Patrick's, Soho, lost its students and returned to being a normal parish church. I was the proprietor of a large Gower Street establishment with accommodation for some sixty residents and the employer of several domestic staff, some of whom had been with the Sisters of Charity since the 1930s. More than that, I was a chaplain who knew very little of what that job might involve, with only a few weeks to go before the student term started. The building itself required some attention since the nuns, in expectation of a sale, had done little to it for some time. My simple faith in Divine Providence was much encouraged when I found hanging from everything – from the boilers to the lift control gear, from the main fuse-boxes to the arms of lavatory cisterns – little blue-stringed Miraculous Medals. Since none of the machinery so decorated had actually broken down, who was to say that Our Lady was not watching over the safety of 111 Gower Street?

The medals, however, did not satisfy various GLC and Camden Borough officers, who brought more secular eyes to the proceedings and required a great deal of money to be spent. An excellent firm got on with the job at amazing speed. George was one of their best workmen and a great conversationalist. He told me one day that his wife had just had twins and that he was not too pleased about this. "I know what went wrong," he told me solemnly. "Twice in one night, Father. I'll never make that mistake again." It took me a while to work out what he meant, my biology being better on frogs than human reproduction. Even so, mine was evidently more advanced than his.

In the middle of that chaotic summer Providence shone again and the Marist Sisters, who were in the process of leaving the French Hospital in Shaftesbury Avenue, agreed to come to the new Chaplaincy, promising not only to take care of the domestic side of the establishment but also to provide a nun to act as chaplain. Whatever sexist mistakes I may have made since, let me claim to be the first to have introduced chaplains, other than male priests, into the English Roman Catholic student world. The Marist nuns brought more than their labours to the project. They provided a solid community base and a spiritual backbone to the establishment, without which it would have been a much much poorer place.

When term did start there was no problem whatever in finding enough residents. The word went round rapidly and anxious students were soon queuing to get in. £3.15.0. a week was then the price of a single room with breakfast, so no-one could claim that I was a Rachman at work. Such was the demand for student accommodation and the pressure on me to keep rents low while getting in enough revenue to pay for the place, that I was endlessly finding places to put more beds. Thanks to a generous C. & A. Modes donation, not only did we eventually manage to stick various new rooms on to the back of the premises, but I also exploited the attics, never used since the houses were built over a hundred and fifty years before. The dust came out in bagfuls.

During one of our extension operations the builders found an old well in what had once been the garden of one of the houses. I had myself lowered down it on a rope in the hope of finding something wonderful, but all there was at the bottom was mud and a few pieces of old clay smoking pipes. The next morning history disappeared as the builders filled it with concrete.

I was not unaware of the dangers of fire in an old building full of wood and old wiring. But our usual fire-drills were indifferently supported until I got more realistic and crafty. My brilliant scheme was to light paper in a tin bucket by the main staircase, get plenty of smoke going, let it circulate the house and *then* ring the fire alarm. The sniff of smoke produced rapid results as pyjama-clad students poured downstairs. Only once did a fire warden have to report that a room was empty which should have had one occupant, while another found two occupants in a room meant for one. A *very* embarrassed couple came downstairs, red in the face, to greet all the rest of the house, assembled on the pavement.

To start with I admitted only men, convinced that if I had set out on the revolutionary road of a mixed hostel someone somewhere in the church world would have decided that I had gone too far. I need not have worried. Testing the waters, I let a few rooms on the corridor occupied by the nuns to women students, and no-one seemed to notice. By the second year we made no bones about being mixed, and a change for the better it certainly was. The Saturday night phenomenon of half-sloshed male students charging around the corridors was much reduced.

Even in our single-sex days we had someone who could deal with the most excitable male. Miss Tout, previously housekeeper at Soho, had come with me to the chaplaincy, and a great asset she was. Tall, motherly and firm, she soon had the measure of eighteen- and nineteen-year-old male undergraduates. Unruly ones returned to their rooms rapidly when her feet were heard on the corridors. But contact with Miss Tout opened my eyes to unsuspected injustice. I did not know much about the working conditions of clergy house-keepers and was very surprised to discover that it was quite "normal" for an incoming parish priest to bring "his" housekeeper along with him. Mgr Coonan, Soho parish priest and university chaplain when I arrived, had gone to Africa, and it was made clear to Miss Tout by the priest appointed to run the parish after me that another regime was now going to run St Patrick's and it would be as well if she moved on. This outrageously unjust principle got well under my skin. Things are better today, though when finally I became a "proper" parish priest in 1977 I discovered how much injustice still went on, and what unreasonable hours housekeepers were often expected to work for inadequate wages, little security and minimal pension rights.

Rooms in the Chaplaincy were sought after by students from all over London. The problem was not to forget that the residence was only a convenient base. If some kind of Christian/Catholic witness was to be provided, it had to be to the whole University. Too much concentration on one building and the seventy or eighty students living there could actually get in the way of wider aims. I tried for as broad a spread of colleges as possible and as wide a spread of faiths, too, amongst our residents. Parents would look rather con-fused when I explained that those with the least possible chance of getting a room with us were lapsed, Catholic, white, male students from University College across the road. We were not out to run an ecclesiastical bed and breakfast establishment. And we did not. Not only did students from all over the University drop in whenever they felt like it, but we also had a string of amiable eccentrics who made our lounge their home for years. Alex, a brilliant mathematician who had never found a rut in which he could roll, was an honoured guest. His only unsociable characteristic was a weakness for eating raw fish out of newspaper in the library, which did not improve the atmosphere. He began to enjoy our Liturgy, in which he found so many echoes of his own Jewish childhood and, when encouraged to read the lessons, did so in a way of which Olivier or Guinness would have been proud.

We – and that means an excellent team of priests, nuns and lay staff and a lot of very supportive students – turned 111 Gower Street over the years into an open and interesting place buzzing with activity. The core team all got on remarkably well, with hardly a row. Our Marist Sister, Mary Magdalen, soon better known as Maggie, was not only an artistic genius and a great support to the musicians but she also had a big heart for all the problem cases. Her room was one of the centres of the house. Our Dominican, Sister Jacinta, who had to be Jackie, could make any piece of electronic equipment work and determinedly brought in students from the previously neglected non-University colleges. Brendan Soane, now a Rome lecturer in Moral Theology, had the kind of analytical mind and gentle disposition which made him an ideal chaplain. He never seemed to run out of time. Philip Carpenter, once an Anglican priest, was our touch of civilization. Older than the rest of us, he put up with student antics with good grace and helped them to understand that history didn't begin yesterday. He was also more than tolerant of my excesses. Once, one summer, when he was away, without any authority I let his room to two stranded French girls. By the time he came back we thought we had successfully removed all the evidence until he turned up at coffee one morning and calmly handed over a pair of black knickers found behind the radiator. Over the years there were many, many more who helped to make Gower Street work.

For the majority of students the Chaplaincy provided as a minimum, through the bar, socials and various outings, a chance to meet other students in what could too often be, in such a dispersed University, a rather lonely life. It was our aim, however, to make it much more than a social centre and to some extent we succeeded.

My eight years of chaplaincy life were not only very enjoyable, if exhausting, but they also transformed me. With a substantial blush I remember my early conservatism and caution. In the style I had learnt from Baggy years before, I was convinced that the notice-board was mine. Notices going up without my permission came down again quite rapidly. When good friends married in the nearby Anglican church of Christ the King I told them that I could not read a lesson at an Anglican eucharistic wedding. The supposed modernism of the Student Christian Movement, our near neigh-bours, I examined with the deepest suspicion.

So it was to start with, but so it certainly was not eight years later. When I began the job in 1966 I might even myself have made Opus Dei material. By the time I ended in 1974 I wanted nothing to do with the Opus Dei rigid moral theology and sexual hang-ups. One exile from a Bayswater Opus hostel who came to live with us had been amazed to discover that, at the Opus hostel, her father was not even allowed to carry her trunk up to her room: no men above the ground floor. Another, just eighteen, who joined the Opus as a would-be member, was told that she was not to admit her member-ship to her parents: they were not ready to understand. No wonder she later left. It is incredible to me now that the Opus Dei founder, Mgr Escrivà de Balaguer, Marques de Peralta, a man who once said that celibacy is for the officers of God's army, marriage for its other ranks, is now at breakneck speed heading for canonization.

Inside the house we had the usual range of socials and lectures but at the centre of activity were the Sunday Masses, which always involved a very overcrowded chapel. I doubt if we kept all the liturgi-cal rules, but certainly we kept some of them. Rarely did something truly experimental happen, and when it did it was not always wildly popular with the students. A gifted and creative chaplain experi-mented one Sunday by covering the chapel floor with mattresses, under the impression, I think, that a semi-prone position would somehow create a better Last Supper atmosphere. I don't think it did. The mattresses were dirty and our women students in particular were not entirely amused, this being the age of mini-skirts. This was exceptional, though. With his liturgy group, Fr Adrian Walker

Right: My mother's parents, Thomas Marion and Mary Bonfield, on their wedding day.

Above: My parents, Kenneth Kent and Molly Marion.

My father's parents, William George Kent and Margaret MacIver.

Above: Bruce and George, Littlehampton 1930.

Left: Learning to drive, 1931.

Opposite page, top: Stonyhurst leavers, 1946. Paul Johnson is standing on the right. *Bottom*: Ending my French tour, 1947.

Below: An early threesome: Rosemary, Bruce and George.

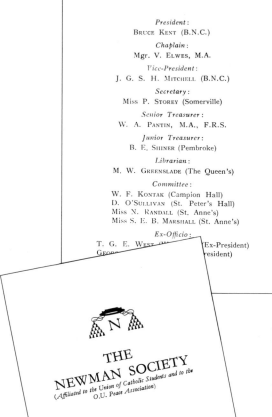

President:
BRUCE KENT (B.N.C.)

Chaplain:
Mgr. V. ELWES, M.A.

Vice-President:
J. G. S. H. MITCHELL (B.N.C.)

Secretary:
Miss P. STOREY (Somerville)

Senior Treasurer:
W. A. PANTIN, M.A., F.R.S.

Junior Treasurer:
B. E. SHINER (Pembroke)

Librarian:
M. W. GREENSLADE (The Queen's)

Committee:
W. F. KONTAK (Campion Hall)
D. O'SULLIVAN (St. Peter's Hall)
Miss N. RANDALL (St. Anne's)
Miss S. E. B. MARSHALL (St. Anne's)

Ex-Officio:
T. G. E. WEST ... (Ex-President)
GEOR... ...resident)

MEETINGS

IN THE SOCIETY'S ROOMS
ROSE PLACE

October 14th   8.15
Visit of SENOR AURELIO VALLS (First Secretary
     Spanish Embassy, London):
     ' Spain, To-day and Yesterday '
October 21st   8.00—11.00
          NEWMAN TERMINAL PARTY
October 28th   8.15
          MATRIMONIAL BRAINS TRUST
               See Chaplaincy Card
November 4th   8.15
     Visit of Mr. GILBERT HARDING:
     ' Rambling Recollections of an errant Convert '
November 11th   8.15
     Visit of Dr. SHERWOOD TAYLOR, M.A., Ph.D.
     (Director of the Science Museum, London):
     ' Evolutionary Theory and Catholic Thought '
November 18th   8.15
     Visit of Mr. EVELYN WAUGH:
          ' Catholics and Novelists '
November 25th
               See Chaplaincy Card
December 2nd   8.00
               A DEBATE
     with London University Catholic Society
     Visit of Mr. CHRISTOPHER HOLLIS, M.P.

THE NEWMAN SOCIETY
(*Affiliated to the Union of Catholic Students and to the
O.U. Peace Association*)

MICHAELMAS TERM, 1951

Above and left: Newman Society term card, Michaelmas 1951.

Opposite page, top: Brasenose Ball, 1952.
Bottom: First year Philosophy, St Edmund's College, 1952.

Below: Brasenose College, Second Torpid 1951: a doomed crew.

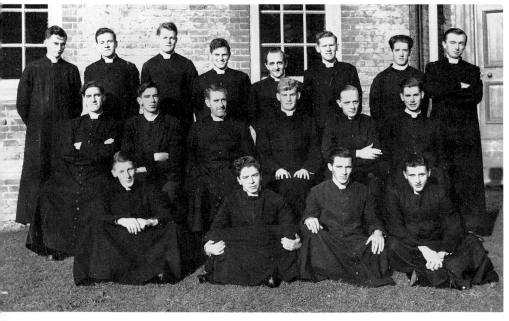

Holiday with Belgia
group, 1957.

My lovely family, C
1963. On left, Rose
Dick Meakins with
On right, George ar
Kent with children.
and Molly seated.

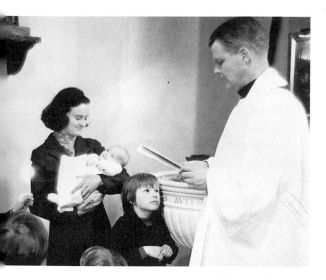

Baptising Mark Grayson, 1968 *(Jeremy Grayson)*

Right: On visitation with Cardinal Heenan.

Below: The new chaplain with Pat Millen, subsequently secretary to the New Zealand Cabinet.

Above: Biafra, 1969.

Left: 'Food not Guns' protest with hired armoured car.

Below: British Council of Churches and Commission for Justice and Peace reception for Archbishop Helder Camara, London 1969. (*Universal*)

"Wrong loch monsignor!!"

The *Catholic Herald*'s cartoon comment by John Ryan.

The Faslane Exorcism, 1973. (*Frank Melvin*)

With Cardinal Alfrink and Brian Wicker, Pax Christi International Council Meeting, Dublin 1977. (*Pax Christi*)

CND Office, 1980. A space problem. (*Radio Times*)

"Now we know why priests wear a dog collar!"

Cartoon warfare from *The Sun* (*News International*)
...and *The Star*. (*Star Newspapers Ltd*)

"Monsignor Kent is out but he asked me to take a message"

CND's 25th birthday party in 1983, Westminster Central Hall. I hold the cake with (from left) Michael Foot, Pat Arrowsmith, Annajoy David, Olive Gibbs, Joan Ruddock, Sir Richard Acland. (*CND*)

Greater London Council, Nuclear Free Nagasaki Day 1984, with Donald Soper and Illtyd Harrington. (*Greater London Council*)

CND rally 1985 with Meg Beresford (next CND General Secretary), Alf Dubs and Glenys Kinnock. (*Melanie Friend*).

Arrest at Sculthorpe, January 1986.

Above: With Jesse Jackson, Geneva press conference 1985. (*Samuel F. Yette*)

Left: Sean MacBride and Bishop Tutu, Roebuck Castle, Dublin 1984.

Below: Ron Todd explains the way forward *en route* to Burghfield, 1986. (*David Rumsey*)

Arriving at Burghfield, Hiroshima Day 1986, George Galloway (later MP) on right. (*Press Association*)

Keeping the Battleship Iowa out of Portsmouth 1989. (*Peter Blunt*)

Valerie learns to paddle,
Ottawa River 1991.

Below:With Lord Soper
after a Gulf War protest
at Downing Street
1991.(*Nigel Tanburn*)

brought out the best in some students. Worship was well prepared and very moving. The music students in particular worked very hard, composing new settings for the Mass and leading the singing. Not often did we suffer old chestnuts like "We shall overcome". Unfortunately we used that one Sunday when Cardinal Heenan was present. Liturgical platitudes were red rag to his bull and he snorted, not very *sotto voce*, "Haven't they overcome *yet?*"

Sermons varied. I had a large white labrador who would often attend Mass, always sleeping through the sermon and occasionally walking out. When he left, it was time to stop. Arthur was as good a chaplain as any of us. When some student came to me in real distress, after doing my best with an open ear, I would often ask them to walk Arthur around Regent's Park by way of therapy. We also had a black cat called Guinevere who gave birth one day under the altar to Faith, Hope and Charity. Father unknown.

My Finals walks were very popular. If students had exams at 9.30 a.m. I would get them all to drop their books, meet at 8.30 a.m. and follow me and Arthur on a brisk walk around the park with a brief pause for duck feeding. The walk would end up at the examination halls. I had never forgotten my own pre-exam hysteria nearly twenty years before. I still believe that fresh air is the best form of revision.

Intellectual input on the chaplaincy programme was quite consistent. "Great" speakers came and did their stuff. We had ethics days for would-be doctors and lawyers, marriage days for anyone who wanted to turn up, Scripture evenings, history evenings, musical evenings. A very useful innovation were the sixth-formers' days, which would introduce those still at school to University life, with its future pleasures and pains. Such pre-university days were always overbooked. Some events were wild successes. A young German philosopher from University College, Hans Sluga, now a professor at Berkeley, California, packed them in week after week. People wanted to know what philosophy was and how it fitted in with their growing ideas about their Christian faith. It was my conviction that chaplaincies were not just first-aid stations for personal problems, important though that work was. It was just as important that chaplaincies should help students to think critically about the values of society in the light of what ought to be Christianity. The more they noticed the contradictions in advance, the better.

We also had disastrous evenings. Once I produced some distinguished speaker who knew all there was to know about Gregorian chant. Having given him sherry I went, a few minutes before the meeting, to see how the hall was filling up. It wasn't – there was no-one there. In desperation I rounded up students, promising them a free drink if they would attend the lecture. With such corruption ten or fifteen were mustered. But they all left when it was time for questions: they had contracted, they said afterwards, for the lecture only. Could they now please have the drink?

More prestigious events were also organized. A Shrove Tuesday dinner was arranged on an annual basis and famous names were induced to speak. Butter did not melt in Auberon Waugh's mouth when he spoke at a Bedford College Dinner (tickets, including wine, £1.50!). I'm not sure whether I told him of the evening with his father twenty years before. Shirley Williams was warmly received, I think at Imperial College. Dear old Patrick O'Donovan was a great success. Rather more formal grandeur centred around the Academic Mass, which was much harder to organize. Senior academics were not too keen to stay on in town for an evening Mass and still less on returning to London for a Sunday. But enough came to give tone to the affair as they processed up the aisle of Westminster Cathedral in their gowns.

The grandest annual event was the Royal Albert Hall presentation organized by Senate House staff with Brigade of Guards precision. Thousands attended, and proud mums and dads clicked away with their cameras for a long time afterwards. The Queen Mother often made the awards with great charm and a tireless right hand. There was only one electric moment that I ever remember. A student, in front of the Queen Mother, opened his jacket and put his hand into an inner pocket. It all went into slow motion as his hand came out with something in it. It was a rolled-up scroll of some award which he proceeded to tear up in protest at something or other. I'm sure I wasn't the only one who thought we had a lunatic with a gun on our hands.

Most of the activities took place not in the Albert Hall or Westminster Cathedral but in the prefabricated building which I had managed to put up in what had been the gardens of two of our Gower Street houses. It could seat a couple of hundred, which was more than most meetings would attract. It even sheltered Lord Chalfont one evening, during his disarmament days before he turned into the Scourge of the Left.

The building, known to me as St Dominic's Hall, and to our Yorkshire Bursar as "that bloody 'ut", was also a means of turning an honest penny. RADA in particular were regular tenants and, since my office looked directly into it, I was alternately entertained by Shakespearian love scenes and practice sword fights, which seemed to be critical to dramatic training. Too much country dancing finished the floor of the bloody 'ut eventually, and there now stands in its place an attractive permanent building put up by a chaplain long after me. Its most interesting feature is a spiral staircase leading straight to the bar. Though I was brought up in the Chesterton-Belloc tradition, I had never thought of that.

Believing that the place where the community meets, worships and socializes is also its parish, I eventually got the place licensed for marriages and baptisms. Some wonderful marriages took place under our roof. Where now are the two barefoot New Zealand postgraduate students who pronounced their vows with the greatest seriousness as they bound their arms together with garlands of flowers? Once two Japanese Buddhists turned up wanting to get married. I had seen them often enough at Mass and assumed that one of them was a Catholic, but it turned out that neither was. They liked the worship, the music and the friendship, which seemed to me to be more than enough to qualify them for a wedding in our chapel. The registrar, when they unwisely told him that they weren't Catholics, refused to turn up, rather primly telling me that I was only licensed for Catholic marriages. Another small collision between Church and State.

One of our most popular big-name speakers was Archbishop Ramsey of the wonderful eyebrows and the total lack of small talk. He was always generous with his time, never hesitated to answer student questions and never used put-downs or evasions. He was a difficult man to entertain because of his nervousness and the small talk problem. In fact one evening he even managed to pour sherry right down his generous purple front, which looked rather odd afterwards in the photographs. But the students loved him. They had, and I'm sure have, the ability to get with devastating innocence right to the point.

Once Archbishop Cardinale, the Apostolic Delegate and a cheery, open man, gave a very good explanation of all the things expected of Apostolic Delegates. They report to the Pope, deal with governments, recommend new bishops, etc., etc., etc. The list was a long and interesting one. But a student took his middle wicket without even meaning to. "Why do you have to be a priest or a bishop to be able to do all these things?" was the question. It was a googly. Poor Cardinale floundered around and finally said that if he wasn't a bishop he wouldn't be able to open and bless new schools, would he? Since that activity had not even figured on the previous list of activities the question really went unanswered. Its implications for so much other "priestly" activity just hung in the air.

Catholic life in the colleges varied with the size and location of the college. Once a term I would make my way down to the Agricultural College at Wye, say Mass for the students, have a discussion about something or other, enjoy a meal in a hall that might have come from Oxford or Cambridge, and make my way home. The same sort of missionary enterprise went on in that extraordinary place, Royal Holloway College at Egham, whose architect must have mixed up plans for a Tudor fortress and a Carmelite convent. My work in the larger, more central colleges, however, consisted mostly of the weekly Mass and bread-and-cheese lunch. Five weekdays of bread and cheese lunches during most of those term-times will get me off a few centuries of purgatory. Always a faithful few would turn up, perhaps ten, perhaps twenty: students, postgraduates, sometimes missionary priests or nuns, sometimes secretaries from the administration block, sometimes – but not too often – academics.

One of my own particular responsibilities was University College which involved a trip past the stuffed corpse of Jeremy Bentham in his glass box. Very odd, I thought it, that this home of rationality went in for a larger and more exposed "relic" than any I had ever seen in a Catholic church. All that was lacking were candles and a few old ladies saying their prayers in front of Blessed Jeremy. It was University College that nearly caused me a mild collision with the police. We said Mass on the top floor of a new building facing Gordon Street. There were no sinks on the floor, or taps, so in preparation for Mass a cruet was filled with water from the floor below. Always lazy, I got into the habit of chucking what was left of the water out of the window after Mass, convinced that by the time it fell five floors only an agreeable mist would hit the street. One day a policeman, quite cross, appeared at our door, saw who I was and said apologetically, "I'm sorry to bother you, Father, but have you seen any students who might have been throwing water on to our men on the pavement?" "No," I said firmly, "not one." The students were kind enough not to laugh.

Much Christian activity was on an inter-church basis, except for that of the Christian Union, who outdid old-time Catholics for confidence and exclusiveness. One of the women students drifted off in their direction one summer, and in the autumn a Christian Union enthusiast asked me if I knew that Mary Moriarty or Bridget Murphy or whatever her name was had become a Christian. No, I did not know, and, I asked him, what had she been before? A Roman Catholic, was the answer.

Relations between the denominations were on a warmer footing. Once I had discovered that Methodists existed, were concerned with social change and had an impressive prayer life, I took them very seriously. They also, as we did, felt rather overwhelmed by the size and power of the official Anglican organization and the automatic Anglican assumption that even in a very secular University they, first of all, represented official Christianity. But I must say that I experienced nothing but kindness from the senior Anglican chaplains that I knew and was particularly fond of Prebendary Gordon Philips, who went out of his way to welcome his "Roman" friends to Gower Street.

A final endeavour before I left chaplaincy work in 1974 was to try to set up a single chaplaincy centre in which all denominations could find their home. But it is no good getting bright ideas six months before you are due to leave a job. My germ of an idea did not survive my departure. I had begun to feel that we had all become too tied to our separate properties and that some fresh thinking was needed.

On one side there had been a great growth. The Canonesses of St Augustine had, by making available their Cromwell Road property, provided a chaplaincy base for West London as large as the one on Gower Street. It was presided over in my time by a wonderful Benedictine monk from Worth Abbey, Fr Edward Cruise, OSB, who would always conclude chaplains' meetings in his room by throwing open his cupboard door with a cry of "Drinks, everyone!"

He had turned his cupboard into an excellent bar. We enjoyed meeting in his room. Out at Brunel University, in Uxbridge, the Diocese had built another student centre. We had become chaplains also to the City University. In fact the work seemed to expand in direct relation to the numbers made available to do it. Almost as an afterthought we had asked our Dominican sister to "take on" the non-University colleges in the London area, and in no time at all she was producing totals of well over 100,000 full- and part-time students for whom, at least from the Catholic side, there was no direct pastoral provision at all.

However, as the years went past, I was not only getting tired but I was also becoming preoccupied with many other issues. Getting tired was not difficult. In term-time "being available" was a full-time occupation, day and night. For a period, with the famous Simon Community, I lost sleep one night a week on soup runs which took students into the other side of London life to meet alcoholics crouched over fires under Waterloo Bridge or dossers sleeping in cardboard boxes outside the Casual Labour Exchange in Mortimer Street. I think we did some good, certainly to ourselves, and perhaps to others on these expeditions – though more than once, after waking up some old cardboard box-dweller at 2 a.m. to ask if he would like some soup, I was told angrily to "Fuck off!" Not the polite way to react to such well-meant endeavours as ours, but then Jesus might well have heard exactly the same sort of language from the outraged owners of the Gadarene swine as they went over the cliff.

The soup night was a certain no-sleep night. There were others unplanned. A favourite friendly local drunk, when bored in the early hours, would always manage to get some student, working late in the library, to let him into the house. Once in he knew exactly how to get to my room, and then my light would go on and he would be sitting on the end of my bed, ready for an extended monologue confession. The Pope, I often thought, does not have to put up with this. Perhaps I needed Swiss Guards.

Nor did University vacations mean much more leisure. With no other income of any substantial sort except that coming from room lettings, the summer vacation was economic harvest time. Even with doubled rents we were still cheaper than the local hotels and never had empty rooms. One old Indian gentleman was a particular favourite. Only after a second or third visit did I discover that he was running a commercial meditation clinic in one of our front rooms.

One Christmas a lovely crowd of Sudanese turned up, and I went to some effort to point them in the direction of Mecca when it came to the time for prayers. In return they joined us for midnight Mass, all presented themselves for Holy Communion (Jesus will understand, I assured myself) and took to the Kiss of Peace with enthusiasm. Too much enthusiasm, as a matter of fact. So much so that Sister Mary Ita, the Superior, watching as her third nun had been very warmly seized and embraced, shouted "Stop!" They probably thought that that command was part of our liturgy as well.

Every summer we had flocks of wealthy, beautiful, Lebanese girls, sent to language schools to improve their English. Money was no object for them. One, on impulse, bought a kitten in Harrods for her sister and had it flown home. There must have been cheaper ways of acquiring kittens in Lebanon. Where now have all those flowers gone in the chaos of their sad country?

One flower I never want to see again was the Italian Bishop with a job in the Vatican who arrived one summer with the request that I find him a student who would help him with his English. I found a large husky lad called John who was very willing to do so for a modest fee. But large husky lads were not quite what the Bishop wanted. After a few days he asked me if I could find a suitable woman student – dear John was a little too uncouth to be a useful teacher. So, stupidly, or innocently, I produced Denise, a good-looking young medic. She came to me in some shock and tears a day or two later. The Bishop's interests went well beyond English and his advances were crude and to the point. After a major row, I learned that he had spent several summer holidays away from the Vatican pursuing his interests in different universities. It will be a long time before he returns to London.

The freedom of the Chaplaincy meant also greater and greater strain for those of us tied in different ways to a still very conservative Church which relied as much on authority as persuasion. Students were never short of questions, about birth control, about Catholic schools, about inter-Communion and about clericalism, and we chaplains were too often supposed by some bishops and parents to be able to deliver certainty when there was no certainty. If the students did not fall into line, then we chaplains must somehow be at fault. From time to time I arranged dialogues between bishops and students. They were rarely a success since students were not much inclined to accept answers based on authority.

I did not sign the famous open letter of 1968 from clergy to the bishops about birth control because I thought that private letters were better than open letters, at least as a first step. Then I watched as one after another of the 155 priest signatories of that letter either left or were forced out.

But I did write to Cardinal Heenan after his uncompromising views on priestly celibacy, expressed in 1969 when he was in South America, were made known. I said, "It seems to me to be vital that the official mind and the actual mind of the Church should not become as widely separated on the celibacy issue as they were, and are, over birth control." Bishop Butler, the respected Benedictine and auxiliary bishop, had a copy of that letter and thanked me warmly for it. "I am glad that you had the courage to send it to him," were his words. To Heenan it was another sign of insubordination.

To be honest, the celibacy issue was not for me simply an academic concern. No normal person, plunged into friendly close relationships with people of both sexes as I was, could possibly fail to wonder why, in reality, as opposed to textbook theory, he (or she) should not have the warmth, sympathy and companionship of interest which marked the lives of many other Christians. In short, it was not surprising that people, including me, who were not meant to fall in love did fall in love, with sometimes painful and even damaging consequences for themselves and others. Of my failures in that department I am not proud. Today I believe that the automatic and compulsory linkage between priesthood and celibacy does more harm than good and makes the priest more important than the Church. Perhaps I should, in honesty, have taken then the path trodden by many of my friends in the 1960s and 1970s and departed – but I did not, since I was determined to try to reform from within and conscious that in some small way I had become a reason for hope for many with shaken faith.

After eight years it had, anyway, become time to move on. A variety of other interests were claiming time that ought to have been student time, and my relations with the Cardinal were getting progressively worse. Part of the problem was, of course, Pax Christi and CND, with which I had also become involved because I was convinced that someone had to support these decent, ordinary people who knew a wicked intention when they saw one. As a consequence various public appearances of mine were very ill received indeed. Priests who got newspaper coverage were clearly egotists, neglecting their spiritual duties. Coverage I certainly did get as a result of a letter I wrote to *The Times* in October 1967. The influence of Archbishop Roberts had grown over the years and with it my concern about the nuclear issue. It seemed to me and others that the Second Vatican Council's condemnation of indiscriminate acts of war was highly relevant to the morality of nuclear deterrence. When it was reported that the launch of the first Polaris submarine had been honoured with a religious ceremony at which the Senior Roman Catholic Chaplain to the Fleet was present, I put pen to paper in the following way:

FROM MGR BRUCE KENT

7th October

Sir, There must be many Roman Catholics like myself who find the presence of the Senior Roman Catholic chaplain to the Fleet at the religious service connected with the commissioning of HMS *Resolution* very strange.

The Pastoral Constitution on the Church in the Modern World of the Second Vatican Council says (para. 80), "Any act of war aimed indiscriminately at the destruction of entire cities or of extensive areas along with their populations is a crime against God and man himself. It merits unequivocal and unhesitating condemnation."

Is it that the use of Polaris missiles is thought not to involve such an act of war or that the crew of HMS *Resolution* do not really intend to use them even if ordered to do so?

Yours faithfully

Bruce Kent

Roman Catholic Chaplain to the University of London,
111 Gower Street, WC1, Oct. 5.

This effort fired off an extensive correspondence which put me, unblushingly, into the limelight. This was not where Cardinal Heenan thought youngish priests should be – certainly not on issues where he was in profound disagreement. It also provoked an interesting comment from the Bishop-in-Ordinary to HM Forces of those days, who said, "May I reassure Monsignor Kent that certainly as far as the British forces are concerned, there will be no indiscriminate use of nuclear weapons." How there could be any discriminate use of a Polaris missile, with its two or three warheads, each with about ten times the power of the Hiroshima bomb, devastating a circle of about twenty miles in diameter and inevitably releasing unknown quantities of radioactive fall-out, was not explained.

In any event, I rapidly became a sought-out speaker by CND and other peace groups and involved myself in a variety of other activities which were looked on rather doubtfully. Pax Christi, of which I was by then an enthusiastic member, was engaged in a range of hopefully peace-making initiatives directed at the conflict in Ireland, and since some of the proposals we made, in relation to British Government behaviour and to church attitudes to "mixed" schooling, touched sensitive nerves, our interventions were not always welcomed. Still less was it appreciated when, under the inspiration of an active Australian postgraduate student, now Dr Joseph Camilleri of Monash University, Pax Christi started to bring pressure to bear on the Hierarchy, in the hope of changing policies in relation to South Africa and its apartheid rule.

There were other outdoor events which certainly did not enhance my Westminster status. I well remember a walk one Easter from Salisbury up to Porton, the germ and chemical warfare establishment. There couldn't have been more than a hundred of us – a few odd vicars, a platoon of prams, wonderful Simon Blake the irrepressible Dominican, assorted Quakers and the like. The military over-reacted obligingly. A helicopter watched our dangerous progress. Troops were seen behind bushes. A large green van was drawn up at the main gate, sideways to our little march, and out of its quarter-opened window a long camera snout kept appearing. We all took turns to pose before getting on to the business of the day – the medieval plague dance on the "ring a ring of roses" theme, with its concluding words, "all fall down". That we did. A small piece of theatre outside a rather sinister place. Thanks to the over-reaction by the security services, who saw some threat in our little group, *The Times* covered our march generously on its front page with an excellent photograph.

The question marks were accumulating on my files, ecclesiastical and civil. My worst sin was certainly the exorcism at Faslane, the Scottish nuclear submarine base, in 1973. Equipped with a brass bucket full of water and a paintbrush, we advanced down the lane that leads to the Polaris gate, explaining to the police that we were going to conduct a service of exorcism. So we did, with a long litany about driving out the spirit of evil: "From the willingness to murder, deliver us, O Lord," we prayed. With the help of the paintbrush and God's unblessed water, the sign of the cross was made on the Navy entrance board.

Correspondence columns in Catholic papers were afterwards peppered with angry letters complaining that we were not taking religion seriously. On the contrary, we were taking it very seriously indeed. As the American Jesuit, Richard McSorley, once said, "The taproot of violence in our society today is our intent to use nuclear weapons. Once we have agreed to that, all other evil is minor in comparison. Until we squarely face the question of our consent to use nuclear weapons any hope of large scale improvement of public morality is doomed to failure." Our Faslane ceremony was not in the style of the unction of *Thought for the Day* but it was sincere religion none the less, though not of the sort that gets much official approval.

Faslane came after two astonishing, unexpected and formative experiences – Biafra and Bangladesh.

The Nigerian civil war broke out in 1966 and through Pax Christi I became involved in a coalition of peace groups attempting to stop the flow of arms to both sides. As I learned later, Her Majesty's Government was only interested in stopping the flow of arms to one side, in the hope that the Federals would be able to make what was described in Parliament as a "quick kill". Our coalition was a small enough affair and, granted that the Labour Party and the Conservatives had what amounted to a common policy, our real hope of actually changing it was limited. But we met, wrote letters, had meetings, went on marches – and were told that we were misguided, muddle-headed and pro-Biafran, but not, this time, Communist. That would have been difficult, since the Soviet Union was also selling arms to the Federals and indeed providing the bombers which made landing at Uli, the Biafran airstrip, a more exciting experience than it would otherwise have been. We also raised funds for the famine victims of that war, in which task our London students very willingly joined.

Then a bit more Providence appeared. A young Marist brother walked into my Gower Street office in the early summer of 1969 and said that he was engaged in relief work in Biafra, or what was left of it, and would I like to come and have a look for myself? It seemed to me that I might just as well have been asked if I wanted to go to Mars.

Actually, it was rather less complicated than Mars. A Joint Church Aid plane left Amsterdam several times a week, bound for the little Portuguese colonial island of Sao Tomé. From there a night flight could be organized for Uli. Within a week I was on my way, flying over an Africa I had never seen before, in a plane with half its seats missing and the spare space filled with seed, tractor tyres and medical supplies. Thus we arrived on the tiny palm-tree island, just cutting the equator, which had become a hive of international activity.

Someone else will have to write the history of the Joint Church Aid operation. The courage of those who took part needs to be recorded. Several transport planes had crashed or been shot down as they made their night flights over Nigerian guns and under Nigerian bombers. The international organization and funding was meticulous and very generous. The chief administrator on Sao Tomé was an Irish priest who presided over a massive warehouse of food and medical supplies. I think that most of the financial support came from the German and Nordic churches. Churches have usually been well to the fore in relief work, but this one was different. It could not have been more directly political in that its whole operation was in defiance of the limitations imposed by "national sovereignty". Church flights even continued after the International Red Cross, having lost a plane and its crew to a Nigerian fighter, felt that it had to discontinue its work.

After a day or two spent in a very simple Portuguese presbytery or wandering along the sea front, with its seedy cafés, past the Presidential Palace, feeling like someone who has got into a Graham Greene novel by accident, I was told to appear at the airport that night. The three-man crew on the large transport plane were Canadian. It was full of bales of dried fish, long strips of it. For several hours I sat on the bales, and those trousers smelt of dried fish long after I got back to London. It was a dark night as we crossed the Bay of Biafra and headed over the forests to the long strip of tarmac road which had been turned into Uli airport. Sitting directly behind the pilot, I could see the altimeter dropping steadily until it got down to something like 500 feet, with the trees clearly visible below. Suddenly a long line of blue lights appeared and seconds afterwards the plane made a reasonable landing, at which the lights all promptly went out. The pilot seemed to know where he was going, nevertheless, as he rolled along and soon I was welcomed by a group of Holy Ghost Fathers and taken to Bishop Shanahan College in Orlu, which was to be my base for two weeks. Plays by Sheridan in the classrooms and cricket caps hanging on hooks left behind in the hall were signs of Western culture. The College compound had become the Biafran Sandhurst, and each morning there was much Aldershot-type shouting as skinny men, often without boots, pretended that bamboo sticks were rifles and went through their drill. At that stage in the war only Owerri was still in Biafran hands and its half-built cathedral was full of ex-soldiers, demented with shell fire, wandering about aimlessly and sometimes howling.

In Owerri I was greeted by Bishop Whelan as if he were quietly at home in Sligo or Wexford or Cork. The oddest experience of the whole venture was to cross a river by boat, since the bridge on the road to Aba had been blown up, and to be welcomed into a convent by two American nuns within three or four miles of the front line. "Do have a beer," they said and opened a fridge still working thanks to their little generator. Holy Child nuns they said they were, and they could not have been more hospitable. The war might have been a thousand miles away and not just beyond the village on the other side of the valley.

There were few places in what was left of Biafra that I did not visit by car or up on an ancient lorry loaded with airlift food. Ours had the hopeful message painted on both sides: "One with God is a majority."

My two weeks were spent in hospitals, feeding-stations and parishes, and I saw enough of war in those two weeks to disgust me with it for ever more. It was not just wounded soldiers I saw but starving civilians – thousands of them – nearly all Ibos, who had been driven into what was left of their territory. To see hutfuls of children, twenty or thirty in each, lying on little wooden beds with their ribs sticking out, waiting for death, was to meet the real victims of that war. This was a starvation war and everyone knew it.

In Parliament lies were told by respectable men about British arms deliveries to the Federal Government. *Peace News* exposed them time and time again. The official line was that arms supplies were proportionate to the quantities supplied in 1966, before the war began. In fact millions of pounds' worth were delivered. After the war ended *Peace News* was able to discover the exact totals, but no-one was interested then. Uli, a Minister assured the House, had only a grass runway and could not take transports. Having walked on its tarmac, I knew how untrue that was. General Ojukwu, it was said, would hand over any food to his soldiers first of all. I saw the civilian food compounds and I knew how careful the Irish priests were to make sure that Joint Church Aid relief went only to civilian victims.

Not long after I returned to England, I was put through the reprocessing machinery. The Foreign Office organized a lunch for me with Maurice Foley and the Nigerian High Commissioner and other guests. I was told, at length, how anxious everyone was to avoid civilian casualties and how desperate they were to avoid civilian starvation. "Very well," I suggested, "why don't you just load dried fish on to Nigerian bombers and drop it in sacks along the dirt roads leading from village to village? No one could stop you: you command the air by day. Nothing would do more to encourage the Ibos to have confidence in your good intentions. Why not?" Even the lady from the *Financial Times* had no answer to that one. There wasn't one.

I also learned something, which was new to me, about Government manipulation of the media. Francis Wyndham, then a *Sunday Times* journalist, who took an anti-war line and recorded doubts about some British claims, told me that oddly enough his invitations to the Foreign Office briefings then began to get lost, so that when there were stories he was too late for them.

No other event in my life has ever sharpened my ideas more rapidly than the Nigerian civil war. I began to understand how ruthlessly those with power can behave if major interests like oil and trade are at stake. I also began to realize that to talk seriously about relieving poverty without facing up to the issues of militarization is to delude oneself and others. It also became my conviction that no-one, especially the innocent, wins wars. I wonder whatever happened to Colonel Adabayo, Military Governor of the Western Region, who said in May 1967, "I need not tell you what horror, what devastation, and what extreme human suffering will attend the use of force. When it is all over and the smoke and dust have lifted and the dead are buried, we shall find, as other people have found, that it has all been futile, entirely futile, in solving the problems we set out to solve." We could have done with that Colonel in the run-up to the Gulf War.

If such experiences took my mind away from direct chaplaincy concerns, so also did the visit in 1970 to Calcutta on behalf of War on Want, on whose Council I served. I went to act as administrator to a small medical team which the organization was sending out to help with the endless flow of miserable refugees from what was East Bengal and was about to become Bangladesh. This was very different from the Biafran experience, though the suffering was just as dreadful. Millions were fleeing from the Pakistani army, and they came with nothing along the roads from the border, hungry and sick, drenched in the heavy rains.

I hope we did some good, though I had to wonder at the end of three months if we were not as much a hindrance as a help to the Indian Government. India is not without doctors and capable administrators of its own, and some of the rivalries for media attention by the relief agencies were not very edifying. I even remember one Danish pastor flying in with a load of plastic sheeting and telling the Indian relief coordinator that if he could not take it to his own Danish hospital he would fly it out of the country at once. I myself had to wander around Calcutta on a three-ton lorry with a load of serum which badly needed a freezer. This meant bribing policemen at most crossroads since heavy lorries were not allowed into the centre of town by day. The agency which had access to a freezer was not prepared to give me information about it. Sad to say, much of this nonsense was motivated by the need to look good on TV and to enhance the brand image with donors. "Not being political" also meant in fact being very political. It was only War on Want, and members of a much more radical group called Operation Omega, who were determined to cross the border without permission to distribute their aid, who were prepared to use the name Bangladesh. Until, that is, it became clear that Bangladesh was going to survive!

What good we did was largely due to Mother Teresa, who found the site for our little War on Want field hospital and cut her way through red tape to get us permission to stay. An angry and egotistical War on Want doctor was once stupid enough to say to her, in a room full of Bengali administrators, that she had no monopoly on charity. Fatal words for him. From then on every official door was closed. He had insulted a woman for whom everyone had enormous respect.

Those three months were not without their bizarre moments. Amongst us was, as we discovered, an active philanderer whose main object in coming to Calcutta was to develop an intimate association, unknown to his wife, with another journalist. Six of us were sleeping in one large hotel bedroom when a call came through in the middle of the night from the wife, full of the deepest suspicions, based on his silence. From our end the philanderer had to shout endlessly, the line being poor, "But I do love you, darling!" Liar, thought the rest of us, pretending to be asleep.

In Calcutta I also met for the first time a thin, wiry little journalist called James Cameron, sitting on his own at a table in the Grand Hotel. He looked a little poorly, which was understandable, since he had just been driven into a major traffic accident which involved at least one death and considerable injury to himself. His Grand Hotel dinner was his last there for some time. The next day he went, critically ill, to hospital. It was years before I realized what an honest man I had met and what an entertaining and courageous writer. I myself did not go in for dinners in Calcutta. After my previous experience in India in 1964, I lasted for nearly three months on hard-boiled eggs.

In short, between War on Want and Pax Christi, Biafra and Calcutta, time for chaplaincy work was certainly running out. In any event, I was more than inspired by the remarkable document on the Church and justice issued after the Bishops' Synod in Rome in 1971. In its popular form it was called *Our World and You* and it drew together all the threads which had seemed to be unconnected and a jumble in my mind. Its introduction linked problems which many seemed to want to keep separate. It said: "*This Gospel has a power to set us free, not just from sin but from what sin has done to our society.*" "What sin has done to our society"! That striking phrase rolled around inside my head. My six years in a seminary had not taught me much about the sinfulness of our society. Birth control and abortion were sinful, of course. The refusal to give voluntary aided schools the grants to which they were due in justice certainly was. But that the light of the Gospel should play over the world of power, property, privilege and national self-interest was a new idea, at least in these words.

The same Synod document put into words much of my previous disquiet about educational content:

> But all too often education simply teaches us how to get on in the world. Much of the human race has been steeped in that mentality which glorifies in possessions. Schools and the mass media tend to be so much taken up with the established order of things that all they manage to produce is a carbon copy man whom that order wants, produced in its own image – a far cry from the "new man" of the Gospel.

The language today is sexist. The ideas then were potent and I wanted to promote them through the educational work of Pax Christi on a full-time basis.

The Cardinal, to my face and behind my back, poured scorn on such naivety. I was profoundly shaken when two students came back one day from a diocesan meeting to tell me that they were amazed at how openly hostile the Cardinal had been about me. It was a bad time, and I suppose if I had had a label to hand I would have called what happened to me a semi-contained nervous breakdown, brought on also by family worries. My father had died in October 1972, compassionately cared for by the nuns of St Joseph's Hospice in Hackney. He who had started life in bitter anti-Catholicism ended it under an oxygen hood with a nun holding each hand while they said in turns softly, time and again, "Jesus and Mary help me". They must have done so, since with a smile and a sigh he just gave up breathing.

It was, for a variety of reasons, a difficult time and, such were the pressures, I felt it was Providence again that put me in touch with a kindly non-Catholic doctor who could not take the problems of the Catholic world as seriously as I did but knew when it was a good idea to prescribe quantities of valium. It had a gin-and-tonic effect on me and straightened me out enough to face the problems of 1973. The Cardinal wanted me, post-Chaplaincy, to go to a parish and stop trying to solve the world's problems. I wanted to work full time for Pax Christi, with some parish work to keep my hand in. Rather legalistically, I said that if he wanted me to give up Pax Christi work then he, who had appointed me as its chaplain years before, should now appoint someone else. This he had no intention of doing. With such dings and dongs 1973 passed into 1974, and I got ready to leave. My University friends gave me a wonderful send-off and a cheque so large that I could purchase a United States unlimited mileage Greyhound bus ticket. The University Principal, Dr Douglas Logan – no softie – wrote a very touching farewell letter, which was more than decent of him, since it was under his nose that I had pinched 111 Gower Street eight years before.

The Diocese did exactly what they had done eight years previously – they appointed a priest to succeed me without any training and threw him in at the deep end. He also turned out to be an excellent swimmer. But I was finally outflanked in a minor war by dear Norman St John Stevas, against whose acquisitive designs I had protected for years the one piece of antiquity that the Chaplaincy possessed – a marble bust of Cardinal Manning as a youngish man – and a bald one as well, if I remember correctly. Between my departure and my successor's arrival our Norman did a deal with Heenan, and away went the bust to the Stevas collection. Perhaps it was just as well. If I had ever had to choose between paying the gas bill and keeping the bust, the gas bill would certainly have won.

Despite all the heart-warming farewell parties at the Chaplaincy, it was not difficult to leave student work in the summer of 1974. I was running out of fresh ideas and my sermons had started to go around in predictable circles. Progressively students tended to get only whatever time was left over from a range of my other preoccupations. It had also dawned on me that I was not getting any younger as I began to meet parents of students who were themselves younger than I was. Students, up and down in three years, stay the same age. Chaplains get steadily older. It was time to go.

So we had the parties and the presentations – amongst them a lovely pair of silver candlesticks which had to wait twenty years before getting into history. They were seized years later by bailiffs in Islington as a consequence of my nuclear weapon tax refusal, only to be bought back by Brian Bethell (an active CND supporter and an entertaining author) at an auction and re-presented to me. The largest farewell gift came in cash which I invested in a return flight to New York and that US Greyhound bus ticket.

CHAPTER NINE

The Anchor Starts to Drag

Greyhound buses made no profit out of me. I ran through three booklets of their tickets in about six weeks and travelled in a great circle which included Montreal, Vancouver, San Diego and New Orleans, with detours to St Louis and Memphis on the way. In Vancouver the whole tour nearly came to an abrupt end when I put a shirt into a washing machine with the bus ticket still in the breast-pocket. This turned the ticket into a ping-pong ball of boiled paper, which I steamed and ironed as best I could. I only just succeeded in persuading a kindly Greyhound agent that this tatty mess was actually one of their wonderful unlimited tickets.

For a while I could not understand why people in front of me on buses were putting their feet not just on empty seats, but right up above the headrests of the seats in front. When my ankles began to swell to elephantine proportions I started to understand one of the effects of long-distance bus journeys. The trip turned out to be a great way to meet a wide range of people, and since most of the bus stations were located in the poorest part of town I soon heard some awful warnings about what can happen to visitors who leave the security of Greyhound Terminals late at night. Mostly I slept on the buses and stopped off with old friends who had been unwise enough to have invited me to drop in if I were ever to travel in their direction.

One of my most unusual stays was in Washington, where I landed myself on a group called the Centre for Creative Non-Violence, whose work for the hungry and homeless was known world-wide. Immediately below my window was a set of traffic lights and there, every night, black prostitutes with dresses more pelmet than mini would work their trade. Within sight, not many blocks away, stood the floodlit White House.

Over in Los Angeles I stayed in a Catholic Worker house and was filled with admiration, there as elsewhere, for the numerous young people, mostly Catholic Christians, who were devoted both to radical politics and to the relief of the worst symptoms of a sick society in which rich and poor were so widely divided. Those were the days when it was still possible to sell blood, and it was not unusual for the tramps in the soup line, if their blood was refused because of low iron content, to beg the cost of a bottle of iron tonic, swig it all down and try again.

It was an America of incredible beauty, especially in the mountains and on the West Coast. It was also one of most generous hospitality. I was taken into people's homes as if I had always belonged there. It was a frightening America too, as any stranger to the New York subway will agree. In church terms it was an amazing America. English Catholicism was almost suffocating by comparison. This was the Catholic America of Dorothy Day, the late Thomas Merton, the Berrigan Brothers and Vietnam trauma. In Washington, just before I arrived, a priest had undertaken a long fast aimed at stopping his Archbishop from buying a mansion in the suburbs and getting him to give the money instead to poverty-relief projects. I could not imagine Cardinal Heenan wanting a mansion in the suburbs in the first place, and I also couldn't imagine one of his clergy fasting against him even if he did. But it was also an America of the most awful cloying religion paraded on one TV channel after another by an endless series of comfortable evangelists who all claimed to have found Jesus.

The American idyll ended with a trip to the very tip of Long Island, from the hell-hole of Pennsylvania Station in the rush-hour out to a place called Montauk, surrounded by ocean and sand. It must have been left over from the Garden of Eden. Old friends, John and Elizabeth O'Donnell, were waiting there. They were in the first place friends of my dog Arthur. Arthur had introduced himself, on the top of a No. 73 bus in London the summer before, to Elizabeth, who just happened to be looking for a priest to help organize her daughter Maureen's wedding. The wedding worked wonderfully, and I made and kept my Montauk friends. I spent some good days with them before heading down to JFK and home.

The problem with home was where exactly to go. If the Diocese of Westminster was not going to stop me working for Pax Christi it was also clear that it had no intention of actively assisting. I did persuade the Diocesan finance officer to pay my health and insurance stamps to establish that I "belonged", but that was the limit of official concern of a practical nature for almost three years until Bishop Guazzelli took a personal interest. Where I lived or how I supported myself were not questions anyone asked.

But more Providence arrived. Fr Peter Edgar, the kindly and wise Prior of St Dominic's Priory in Hampstead, had heard of my predicament before I left for the States and had said I could have the use, for Pax Christi, of some rooms which had been the premises of the parish licensed social club. That the place had been closed down rapidly was very clear. It was a social club Marie Celeste. Beer glasses still stood on tables, the sink was half full and various biscuits and crisps were mouldering in the cupboards. No matter – it was home, and very soon it became a real one. The largest room became a dormitory where I slept in the company of two young Spanish seminarians on their way eventually to South America. They thought all Monsignors were Bishops and could not believe that one was sleeping in a dormitory. Another room became the Pax Christi office, in which abandoned ping-pong tables became large if slightly wobbly desks. What had been the bar area was ideal for socials and discussion groups and was well used for that purpose. We had teach-ins, weekend conferences and Bible study groups. We were able to host other peace groups which were less well provided for. It was not unusual to find someone from far away in a sleeping-bag in a corner of the place. Up on one of the walls was an elegant period print which had been presented at Easter 1911 to a Miss Ada Ballard by her Bible Class. It carried the text, "Underneath are the Everlasting Arms". This was entirely appropriate: Someone, with arms open wide, seemed to be keeping the Pax Christi show on the road.

Underneath our rooms was the parish hall and there, every week-day lunch-time, was the old folks' lunch club. This was just within walking range for my mother, now in a flat on Haverstock Hill, and on her good days she would trot across and join in, exuding a slight air of Garden Suburb grandeur, with the old ladies of the NW5 neighbourhood and then have coffee upstairs with us. On her not-so-good days, if the mist was coming up over her mind, she would call a taxi or get on a bus and end up God knows where in North London, from whence, called by the patient police, I would have to fetch her. Those who have had wandering mothers will know exactly what I mean. Those who have not have missed out on a hard chunk of real life. To the end – which came several years later and, like my father's, in the loving care of St Joseph's Hospice, Mare Street – she refused to admit that her memory had almost entirely gone, and her blue eyes would twinkle at the chance of a laugh. Once, when finally out of her flat and into St Joseph's, she persuaded her grandson Stuart to take her for a drive "to see her aunt". Around and around Hackney they went, turning left and right according to a long series of directions. "Where, Moo [Grandparents were known as Moo and Poo], does your aunt actually live?" said poor Stuart finally in desperation. He only got his answer later from my brother, who explained that the aunt in question had lived in Montreal but had been dead for some time.

Looking after my mother, a task well shared with my brother and sister, was the backdrop to those years. Front stage was endless activity. There were many invitations to preach, organize study days, speak at Pax Christi fund-raising events and encourage parish groups to get started. Post Vatican II, there was a new interest in nonviolence, social justice, disarmament and peace. All this was not my job alone. As well as volunteers and two hard-working nuns "lent" by their Orders, there were two full-time lay members of staff. One was a young graduate from Bedford College named Valerie Flessati – she was quiet, well organized and exceptionally efficient. The other was Mark James, a volcano of enthusiasm, the centre of our work with young people and a pioneer in promoting practical reconciliation schemes in Northern Ireland and the building of Irish–British bridges. Both gave up any idea of a career ladder when they came to Pax Christi to work for peanuts, without any of the security enjoyed by priests or religious.

Pax Christi broke a lot of new ground and in so doing did not always endear itself to Church authorities. The idea of investment responsibility, old hat now, was new then and financial secretaries of dioceses did not appreciate what they too often saw as interference. To do Cardinal Heenan full justice, just before he died in 1975 much of his hostility towards what he would earlier have called "political" activity began to diminish and I actually got his permission to represent the Diocese at the 1975 AGM of Consolidated Gold Fields, since in that firm the Diocese held some shares. Even to attend the AGM was an awesome experience, as the world of powerful money paraded itself and the platform filled with twenty or more comfortable, well-groomed men with a woman to run the secretarial side of things. My direct questions about the minimum wages paid by the Company in South Africa and the conditions of migrant workers were smoothly if unsatisfactorily answered, and the meeting came to an end.

Not long afterwards, the Cardinal died and Bishop Butler stood in during the interregnum before the arrival of Abbot Hume. I soon began to understand the workings of the Church old boy network. Bishop Butler, fully supportive of Pax Christi's work, kindly showed me a letter from one of the Catholic CGF directors, whom he had once taught at school. The letter started "Dear Fr Christopher" and went on to explain how the imprudent behaviour of Mgr Kent was putting at risk the social improvements that the Company had made. Progress in matters such as apartheid was better made slowly, quietly and prudently, etc. etc. and could dear Fr Christopher do anything to get Mgr Kent returned to more parochial work? How many letters of that sort there must have been over the years which I never saw. I had not been surprised when, several years before, Cardinal Heenan had shown me a letter from a Foreign Office future mandarin, complaining on a Catholic-to-Bishop basis about me. Heenan had covered over the signature, but having spent years at Oxford with the complainant, I knew exactly who he was from his familiar neat script.

The investment saga, however, came in the end to a dead stop. We actually persuaded the Bishops to fund research into the possibility of establishing an ethical advisory centre on the model of the American National Catholic Coalition for Responsible

Investment, but the final report was side-tracked and, incredibly, listed as a confidential document not to be released by the Church's official Justice and Peace Commission. I don't think that many Bishops saw the investment issue as more than a concern to get rid of shares in undesirable enterprises, especially relating to South Africa.

The investment issue did not go away. My own pittance I have entrusted for a long time to the Midland Bank. Some anonymous humorist inside the Midland must have entered my name in the computer as a suitable recipient for details of the Midland "Defence Equipment Finance Department". Did I need help with financing my overseas defence sales, the accompanying letter wanted to know? If so, the glossy brochure made it clear that Messrs Cormack, Kock and Head, supported by Brigadier Shrimpton ("last appointment was as the senior Army officer in the Defence Sales Organisation where he established close links with many defence equipment exporters, trade associations, overseas customers and government departments"), were only too keen to help. There was nothing they could actually do to help me, so I passed the revealing little proposal on to the Diocese, which had Midland connections. Whether any action followed I was never told.

As I write in 1992, there is an ethical investment organization in the United Kingdom called the Ethical Investment Research Service, but it has too little official Church support. Perhaps it will have more now that Bishop Richard Harries of Oxford has bravely taken on the Church Commissioners. My own interest in investment as carrying with it positive opportunities came both from a commitment to nonviolent social change and from the awareness that my association with War on Want had given me. In 1974 War on Want had published its famous report on the milk powder industry with the chilling title *The Baby Killer*. It was the first of several such reports on the social effects of major companies. In this case it was clear that several of the large companies, Nestlé's in particular, were actually increasing infant mortality by promoting milk powders in countries of great poverty. This they were doing, not only by spreading the idea that breast-feeding was unfashionable, but also by using girls dressed up to look like nurses to advertize the products. The consequence was that bottle-feeding was taken up by those who could perfectly well, in many cases, breast-feed and by those who did not have the facilities to sterilize bottles or the financial strength to keep on paying for milk preparations. Unhappily, the investment question came to be understood within the Church only in terms of disinvestment, not in terms of using moral and economic clout to change company policy.

The years at Pax Christi were not only concerned with such questions of high-flown morality. Pax Christi's hostels and Summer Routes were the bread-and-butter stuff of increased Christian awareness. The hostels met a very real need, especially in London. In the summer of 1967 we opened our first hostel in the empty school in Soho which might once have been turned into the London University Chaplaincy. London was full of young people from all over the world, humping rucksacks, with little money and few places to stay. As a last-minute initiative we bought forty or fifty of those canvas beds with three folding legs much loved by scouts, explorers, celibate hermits and the like. It is just possible to sleep on them, but if you roll too far to one side or the other, instant ejection results. Anyway, up went our beds, a team of volunteers was collected, a week's supply of breakfast cornflakes and toilet paper was purchased and we were in business. The place was full from the day we opened the doors, and so it has been for many summers in different schools during the tourist season, until London prices frightened off young people and London Catholic schools became more cautious about the use of their facilities.

Saying Mass in one of the hostels was always a good experience. Almost everyone can sing more interestingly than the English, and bidding prayers came in many languages, not only European ones. Every summer we collected Kenyans and others who were studying at Moscow University and couldn't get over to the West quickly enough when the long holidays came. The Kiss of Peace was genuine and friendships made in the hostels have lasted. So have marriages. In the course of fund-raising sermons, I always told the tale of an evening at the Pax Christi hostel in a Tower Hill primary school. Both young Palestinians and young Israelis had booked in. It could have meant trouble but it didn't. By the end of the evening, after a few trips to the off-licence, a lot of stories were exchanged and the whole thing ended with a great circular dance in which everyone joined. Peace work at a very basic level!

So also was, and is, the peace work of the Pax Christi Summer Routes. They were obviously a Continental invention. No one on this side of the Channel would think of getting several hundred young people together, dividing them into groups and sending them off through the countryside to walk ten or fifteen miles a day while discussing "community" or "democracy" or "Europe" or "the future of the Church".

When I first went on a Route in 1965 in Spain, I already knew from my New Zealand youth club girls of some years before that it would be a lot of fun. But I also had a sense of duty. I was determined that orthodoxy would be maintained and that none of those dangerous Dutch priests would, under the guise of being chaplains, be able to dilute the true faith of the participants. Our group of thirty or so wandered from village to village, from Valladolid to Burgos. Much more time was spent singing, organizing village entertainment, drinking wine and sleeping than was ever spent on "community" or "democracy" or whatever was the theme for the year. The whole affair ended with a grand reunion of all the different groups into which the route had been broken, over in Compostella. All three hundred stayed in a massive seminary and a gathering of two or three on the stairs meant an instant rousing sing-song. Farewells meant much kissing and hugging and nostalgia, into which the Brits, by that time much unfrozen, put their full weight.

My most astonishing memory of Compostella is, however, that of the thurible, not the people. In the Cathedral, the final point of that long pilgrimage across Europe in honour of St James which thousands of our medieval predecessors undertook, there stood a thurible (or incense burner, for the benefit of non-Catholics or post-Vatican II Catholics). It was no ordinary thurible. It must have been at least two feet high, perhaps more. As crowds gathered to watch, its attendants stoked it up with charcoal and then bunged on a shovelful of incense. It was then hoisted on long ropes a foot or two off the floor and, by clever pulling on the rope, it began to swing, faster and faster, with an arc that took it higher and higher.

At the end it was, streaming smoke, hurtling almost from the level of one transept window down through the crowd, wisely parted, and up to the other. It was, granted some very smelly pilgrims, a kind of medieval air freshener. If the ropes had broken, it would certainly have shot through one window or the other, a very unguided missile indeed.

My second Route, in Ireland in 1972, did not have quite such a dramatic conclusion. Though Irish village hospitality was every bit as good as Spanish, the weather was not. We crossed the pass over the Knockmealdown Mountains on our way from Youghal to Kilkenny in a downpour with more wet days than dry ones. Bishop Birch, who welcomed us at Kilkenny, was a man way ahead of his time, and he decided to confront these well-meaning Continental peaceniks with some reality. As we walked into the Castle grounds, we found ourselves alongside several platoons of the Irish Army and, in their company, we listened to the final speeches. His message was the entirely reasonable one that peace is no-one's private patch.

In Spain there had been no great fuss about who was and who was not a priest. When it came to accommodation in very basic villages the priests had to muck in on the same basis as everyone else. Ireland was very different. Almost always, as we drew near the village where we were to stay, someone would come out to meet us with two questions: "Which of you is the priest?" and "What time would you like to say Mass, Father?" (Accommodation was usually in a presbytery or a convent.) When that priority had been sorted out the rest of the party would get their warm welcome. The Dutch in particular thought that the priestly focus was rather funny.

No one thought funny the end of that Route. Quite a large group took the train from Dublin to Belfast and to a very different world, where troops were on the streets and armoured Land-Rovers rolled past. The entire party was stopped and searched, to their considerable surprise, while on their way to the Lisburn Road Friends' Meeting House, where a group of Quakers did their best to condense hundreds of years of history into a couple of hours as they tried to give a framework to what was going on in the province.

In 1974 our small British Pax Christi section offered to host the international Summer Route. These being Common Market days, the chosen theme was "Europe for itself or for others?" Our hundreds of young visitors gathered at Westminster Cathedral and were then dropped by coach at starting-points ranging from Canterbury to Winchester, with Brighton as the final meeting-place a week later. It was an experiment which worked very well. Most churches gave a great deal of support, and if the Home Counties were not quite as unsophisticated as rural Spain there was a lot of interest. Much of the time I spent in my Renault 4 dashing ahead of groups and improvising with barns and church halls where there were gaps in the accommodation chain. In Brighton, I'm not sure how, we ended up in the Dome with a Methodist Church Choir of women all dressed in blue gowns. Not quite the cutting edge of British Christian radicalism. After the usual party the several hundred who had taken part in the Route gathered at Brighton Station the next day for connections to Gatwick and the Victoria boat-trains. It was good to hear the Brighton Station staff over the loudspeaker system rising to the occasion and wishing all their foreign guests a good trip.

The visit to Belfast in 1972 had not just been political voyeurism on the part of Pax Christi. For some years we had been engaged in various schemes which we hoped would contribute in some small way to peace and understanding in Ireland. There had been children's holiday play schemes, lecture tours to enable Northern Ireland residents to speak to groups in Britain, fund-raising projects for inter-community schemes in Belfast and visits to the Home Office about prison conditions. There had also been criticism, at least implied, of Church policies, especially in relation to education. We also learned a few lessons about ourselves. One group of women from the Falls Road did a London tour in the early 1970s and gave a minority community perspective on what was going on. We all clucked in sympathy until they turned on us and asked about our minorities. "Which minorities?" we wanted to know. They explained that on Essex Road and Euston Road and Oxford Street there had been many black and brown faces, but not once at any meeting we had organized for them had there been anything but white faces. Their question left us with plenty to think about and few answers. The honest fact of the matter is that most social change organizations were and still are white and middle-class.

I was becoming more aware of how easy it was to deal with symptoms rather than causes. This problem came home to me when in 1974 a group of organizations, including Pax Christi, set about the creation of that small but excellent body, the Campaign Against the Arms Trade. When we asked the Catholic Fund for Overseas Development, amongst other "charities", for support, very little was forthcoming. We were told that such campaigning would be "political" and that the function of such organizations was only to be of a "Good Samaritan" nature. I have never forgotten the phrase. It was, we were told, up to others to deal with the political roots of poverty, amongst which the endless commercial supply of weapons is certainly one. Charities, including CAFOD, have taken many more risks with their status as time has moved on, but the problem still remains. One of the consequences of legal charity status, an entirely self-imposed restriction, accepted for financial reasons, is to make it difficult to expose not just the symptoms, but the real causes of poverty.

The Campaign Against the Arms Trade was one that ordinary people could easily identify with and it gave me a new understanding of the scale of the problem we were facing. At a vigil outside Stuart House in Soho Square, which was then the home of the Labour Government-created "Defence Sales Organisation", my eyes were opened. It was Denis Healey who had said that, regrettable though the Arms Trade was, while it existed we must secure our share in "this valuable commercial market". As we waited, watched by police across the road, a man in his fifties came out of the DSO office and crossed over to talk to us. He said he worked for Westland on the design of helicopters. At the end of the war he had left bomber design because he wanted to work on aircraft with peaceful purposes. But helicopters had now become a major instrument in the kind of war going on in Vietnam and were sought after by oppressive regimes all around the world for policing operations. He was married and he had several children and a large mortgage. Just what did I expect him to do? I hope I told him to join the United Nations Association and to press for research into arms conversion through his union, but I probably didn't. Those were the thoughts of the 1980s.

A campaign which did not have such immediate attraction was the one Pax Christi helped to launch for conscientious objectors. This was not a British problem, since we had no military conscription in operation, except what the Americans have come to call economic conscription or the volunteering of the unemployed. But it was a world-wide problem about which, both at the Vatican Council and at the 1971 Synod on Justice, our Church now had something positive to say: "every country should give legal recognition to Conscientious Objection".

For years in Spain a few small groups like the Jehovah's Witnesses had refused military service on religious grounds. They faced a cat-and-mouse game. They went to prison for the period of their service, were then released, called up again, and again sent back to prison. Some young Catholics now also began to challenge the system and we started to campaign on behalf of one of them, Pepe Beunza by name. We were civilly received in the Spanish Embassy, but I have never forgotten what the young diplomat said to us in conclusion: "What you do not understand, Father, is that to be a Spaniard and a Catholic is to be a soldier."

Problems relating to the refusal to undertake military service are experienced in many countries. Through Pax Christi we were able to give some small support to the growing numbers of young South Africans who would not join in the apartheid wars of their government. We could give no direct help to those who refused in Eastern Europe, but there was never a time when we did not raise their rights of conscience with visiting official delegations. There was, in fact, a curious parallel between the attitudes of Catholic governments, particularly Spain and Portugal, and the attitudes of Communist governments. Under both kinds of regime refusal meant punishment.

At one inter-church gathering at the Grail Centre in Pinner, organized by Pax Christi International, I remember walking up and down the lawn with an Archbishop of the Russian Orthodox Church. On issues of democracy, human rights and Communism he gave guarded answers with the air of a man who had not come to the West to be put on the spot by people like me. But when I asked about conscientious objection in the Soviet Union he was clear and spontaneous. Of course a young man must be ready to die for his country, was his answer. He and the Spanish diplomat had much in common. Through all these experiences, the powerful grip of militarism on world thinking was being underlined for me. Its cultural, economic and political roots ran as deep in the West as in the East.

Since those days, not only has conscientious objection been given official recognition as a human right by the United Nations, but in 1983, in a memorable speech to the Pontifical Academy of Sciences, Pope John Paul gave his encouragement to civilian scientists who refuse to work on weapons of mass destruction: "By refusing certain fields of research, inevitably destined, in the concrete historical circumstances, for deadly purposes, the scientists of the whole world ought to be united in a common readiness to disarm science and to form a providential force for peace."

I suppose it was because I both attacked British nuclear weapon policies and promoted ideas of conscientious objection that my rather devious application to join the United Services Catholic Association, a Catholic military organization, was rejected after an unprecedented intervention by the Bishop to the Forces. As an ex-services Catholic priest, officially in good standing and ready to pay the subscription, I should have been eligible. No doubt the Bishop suspected a Trojan Horse and decided to bend the rules to keep it out at the gates. I was not too downcast and much appreciated several kindly letters from ex-officer committee members who wrote to say that though they didn't agree with my views, they nevertheless thought I had the right to express them.

However, I doubt if many Bishops were too enthusiastic about a regular series of articles which I contributed to the *Catholic Herald*. I turned them into platforms for promoting various causes, from Church financial accountability and democracy to women's rights, inter-communion and non-nuclear policies. St Bingo's and its parish priest, Canon McGroggin, were an early invention. McGroggin was particularly good at neutering parish councils, pouring water on charismatic revival and seeing off ecumenical stirrings. There were many real-life McGroggins. St Bingminster served very well as a double for Westminster Cathedral. Canoness Gladys McEverite would appear occasionally on the scene, saying things like, "If Our Lady had wanted male priests she would surely have made such an extraordinary wish clear from the very beginning." My favourite was the Neo-Coptic Patriarch Mars Bar II who had to justify the Doctrine of the Just Adultery despite the sexual chaos it had produced in later centuries: "The civilised world would have collapsed if, under highly restricted circumstances adultery had not been permitted for the consolation of matrimonial partners separated as a result of a national crisis."

A small fan club laughed with me, but I'm quite sure that there were many who did not. In fact the Westminster Canon whose displacement had meant my promotion to the work of school administration years before was heard to say sadly as he pulled his fur cape around himself at some seminary function, "That boy is just not thinking about his career." Which was quite true.

That Pax Christi ever became deeply involved in work for prisoners was something of an accident – if there are accidents in these matters. We had, of course, helped to promote Amnesty International in Catholic circles for several years. When the Pope's message for the 1975 Jubilee Holy Year came out it had in it an appeal for amnesty for prisoners of all kinds. Maggie Beirne, an Amnesty worker, turned up one day, pointed this out and asked what we were going to do by way of a response. Thus was the Prisoners' Sunday Committee born, with representation from prison chaplains, from Amnesty and from political parties. Sir Hugh Rossi MP gave his time and moral support. Prisoners' Sunday became a regular feature of the Catholic annual calendar, though unhappily it has rather lost its original thrust and has tended to concentrate on remedial work rather than radical reform.

The Committee was the springboard which made me take a much more critical view of our domestic prison system. For instance, when we organized an exhibition, as part of the second Prisoners' Sunday programme, I saw a Home Office display indicating that something like 80% of current prisoners in Britain had never been guilty of violence against persons. Then, as now, I wondered why we went on pretending that locking people up, often in disgusting conditions, was the only effective punishment we could think of, especially for people not guilty of violence. The problem was that apart from of a few specialist groups, like the Howard League for Penal Reform, not many people were thinking of reform at all. When I sat on the unofficial inquiry under John Platts Mills QC investigating the Hull Prison Riots I got to know much more about our degrading system and to regret that so much official church concern centres around the prison chaplain, whose task was to make the system work as humanely as possible, not to challenge the system itself.

But there were lighter moments. In Westminster Cathedral one year we got permission to erect a cage. On it were the names of prisoners tortured in different parts of the world. In it we put a stool, a mattress, a thin blanket and a chamber-pot. The message was clear enough: get involved in Amnesty work. This display moved some people in ways we had not expected. When the time came to dismantle the cage we found that a substantial amount of cash had been thrown through the wire into the pot. When people with warm hearts don't know what else they can do to help, they often give money. Truly radical change will occur as they are helped to grow from immediate generosity and anxiety to relieve the symptoms of injustice towards rooting out its causes.

In these years Pax Christi was doing its best with teaching and preaching aids to promote the idea of an annual Peace Sunday in every parish, first called for by Pope Paul VI in 1968. Getting such a Sunday taken seriously to start with was uphill work, but it began to spread in some parishes and dioceses. Cardinal Heenan, initially not very interested, became finally so enthusiastic that just before his death he was calling for a peace week.

The subject of peace has its pitfalls. Preaching once on Hiroshima Day, I tried to make clear that though those involved in the atomic bombing were surely in good faith, nevertheless the Church did have some very specific things to say about direct assaults on civilians. So also did International Law. "How dare you?" said a recent communicant afterwards. "The Japanese deserved everything they got, and just think of all our boys who were saved!"

These years involved a great deal of international travel. I served at the time on the international executive of Pax Christi. This meant many visits to Utrecht for meetings under the kindly eye of the very lovable old Cardinal Alfrink, International President of Pax Christi, who was already between a stone and a hard place in the workings of the Vatican. He did not like rows and was tolerance itself, though in liturgical matters he personally was for Latin and proper rubrics. The only thing that ever got under his skin was the French Pax Christi lay representative, a M. Klein, who would have made any British Government official sound dangerously left-wing by comparison. No-one was going to touch the French Bomb while M. Klein was around, whatever else Pax Christi International got up to.

Such conservative reactions I had come across before on my one and only visit to the Pontifical Justice and Peace Commission in Rome, set up after the Second Vatican Council. This Commission had been neutered from the word go. The international guests who had been invited were told clearly that we were not members of anything permanent, just consultants for the occasion; we could not initiate business but must stick to the prepared agenda; above all we had no right whatever to issue statements to the public in our name or anyone else's. With these limitations we set to work for two days in 1970. There were great compensations. One was a free trip to Rome. Another was Séan MacBride, once an IRA Commander, then a lawyer and the Foreign Secretary of Ireland and co-founder of Amnesty International, and also the President of the International Peace Bureau. When I first saw him, I thought that a good gust of Rome wind would blow this frail figure into the Tiber. I soon learned that his frailty could be turned to advantage. When chairing a meeting, he knew very well how to move business forward – by turning down his hearing aid and sweeping through objections.

He taught me a great deal about the Vatican. In the course of our meeting, while the Bishop President was out of the room, he proposed that we should send a message to the Pope, all of 500 yards away, asking the Holy Father to intervene on behalf of some Dominicans who were being tortured in prison in Brazil. All agreed. A message was prepared and handed into the secretariat for typing before we left for lunch. When we returned it was to some confusion. The Bishop, on returning, had found the letter and had torn it up. Did we not know that we were not allowed to make statements? Who had authorized us to write to the Pope?

Séan took all this quietly and then passed around a note saying that if the message could not go from one Vatican Department to another he would pop down to the post office and send it himself to the Pope by telegram. About half of those who were attending put their names to this new improper message, and that was the last time most of us were invited to such Vatican consultations. The French priest who had to act as deputy administrator for the Vatican Commission clearly did not like this style of proceedings and stood out as a square peg in a Vatican round hole. He married not long afterwards and I wished him every happiness. With Séan I remained friends for many years. I succeeded him as President of the International Peace Bureau, shared the hospitality of Roebuck Castle, his Dublin home, as a fellow guest with Bishop Tutu, and stood in a wet Dublin cemetery at his funeral in 1988. The subsequent editorial in *The Times*, which was supposed to assess his life and work, was one of the most disgusting pieces of English establishment journalism I have ever read. It was entitled "His Infamous Career" and continued in the same spiteful vein. No wonder the Irish find us so self-righteous.

Pax Christi in those years also sent me on journeys which I would never have dreamed otherwise of taking. In 1973 a group of Catholics in Melbourne, Australia, wanted to gather from around the world Catholic voices which would not otherwise get a place on the programme of the 40th Eucharistic Congress. Melbourne was a conservative place with a very conservative Archbishop (later Cardinal) James Knox, and the Congress needed another dimension. So, along with others, including a black nun from the USA, I was invited. I prepared three speeches on militarism, underdevelopment and Church peace work, and set off.

Our arrival was a bit unfortunate. According to Australian custom, passengers leave the plane at Sydney while it is sprayed with some sort of bug killer. My white collar I left in the rack in front of my seat and found that it had not only presumably been sprayed but had been removed entirely. I could not, therefore, land at Melbourne even looking like a priest, and it was not my fault that the nun chose to give a Black Power salute to the cameras directly in front of me, so that I looked like one of her entourage.

It *was* my fault that after a series of questions about Ireland a journalist popped in a googly. What did I think of *Humanae Vitae*, the Encyclical on Birth Control, and its distinction between natural and unnatural methods of family planning? "I can't understand it" or something to that effect was my answer, and that, of course, was just what was splashed across the front page of the Melbourne *Age*. No matter. The meetings I went to were well attended and the trip was a great opportunity to meet like-minded people with another set of parallel problems. The main Congress activities went on alongside the smaller unofficial ones, and I marvelled at the grip that Catholicism had on Melbourne. Even the trams had Papal yellow and white colours flying on pennants at each side. The best part of the whole trip was the journey home. No-one with a spark of soul can fail to be moved by that long, long flight across the red Australian desert, with just occasionally a track or a water-course down below. My head was at the window, eyes glued, until we left Australia that night and headed up across Bali towards the airport luxury of Singapore.

In 1975 came one of the most moving trips of my life. I had always been fascinated by Professor Gordon Zahn's account of the life and death of Franz Jägerstätter, the Austrian farmer who had refused service in Hitler's army. The full account can be found in Zahn's *In Solitary Witness*. Jägerstätter lived in an Austrian village, divided only by a river from Germany. In 1938 he had been one of the few to oppose the annexation of Austria by Hitler. Married, with three little girls, he did undertake a first period of military training but was deferred because of the priority given to farm work. By the time his call to serve came again he, now a very convinced and devout Catholic, decided that he could not take the unconditional military oath which would commit him to total obedience to a regime which he thought unjust. Both his parish priest and his bishop tried to persuade him that such issues were too large for him and that his duty was to serve, like everyone else. He persisted in his refusal and was finally court-martialled in Berlin in July 1943 and sentenced to death. Unknown on the world stage, this very ordinary Christian was beheaded in Brandenburg on 9th August 1943. After the war his ashes were moved, by a priest who had also opposed the Nazi regime, to the little church in St Radegund where once Jägerstätter had served as sacristan. The account of this heroism was, by the 1970s, starting to go around the world. The Pax Christi Committee decided that something like a pilgrimage would be made to St Radegund with its tiny onion-topped church. We wrote to as many European peace organizations as we could think of, announcing that in Jägerstätter's village on 7th September 1975 there would be a Mass and a discussion about the significance of that lonely witness of thirty years before. Fr Reg Riley, one of the West London chaplains, along with other Pax Christi friends, joined me on this journey, and good value he was too with his non-stop range of songs and quite fluent German and French.

Our rendezvous turned out to be a memorable occasion. Individuals and couples came from Vienna, Warsaw and Paris, as well as smaller places in the locality. Perhaps twenty-five people came together, and we were joined by Jägerstätter's widow, later to be honoured by the Austrian State, and by two of his daughters. It is ironic that Jägerstätter, who said "No" at the greatest cost, is now a hero and may even be canonized, while Kurt Waldheim, who said "Yes" at just the same time, has ended his career as Austrian President but in international disgrace.

In 1977 a final long-distance trip took me to South Africa, sponsored by the Quaker-inspired Christian Fellowship Trust. This Trust was set up to help South Africans, of all races, to visit the United Kingdom and to enable British citizens to meet their counterparts in South Africa. It was not easy to make plans for this trip because the South African authorities kept suggesting that I needed a visa, which as a British subject I did not actually require. It was an effort to stop me from going, but finally I decided to go anyway and let them turn me back if they wanted to. After this a visa was in fact issued.

Until you see it for yourself, it is difficult to understand how divided a country can be. On my first morning in the seminary in Pretoria, I woke early and looked out of the window to see dozens of black figures walking up the street long before dawn. These, I learned, were workers coming in from the Townships miles away. During my six weeks in South Africa I got to know a great deal about Townships and Homelands. They were a different world from that of the white cities, with their wide streets, swimming pools and large houses. I started too to realize that in a few weeks I was seeing more of black South Africa than many white residents had ever seen, since to enter a Township meant applying for a pass. The illusions of some of the white parishes were extraordinary. In Port Elizabeth I was introduced to a sodality of white Catholic women. They told me how well they got on with their servants, how little apartheid actually meant and what a bond their religion was between them and black Catholics. The next day I was taken into the Township by some nuns to talk to a sodality of black women, most of whom were actually the servants of the type of ladies I had met the day before. Far from being united by religion or anything else, they were very angry when they talked about their conditions of work, the education of their children, and poor health care. Their white mistresses were under an entire misapprehension about the feelings of those with whom they were in contact every day.

What made my trip unlike many others to South Africa was the death of Steve Biko. I had never heard of him. In the black seminary at Hammanskraal, I was sitting in the chapel after Mass when a student dashed in and shouted "Biko is dead!" The place erupted and seethed. Biko had been a black activist: articulate, energetic, visionary. On him so many hopes had been pinned. Arrested, humiliated and brutally beaten, he had been taken half way across South Africa in the back of a van. His death was a direct result of the treatment he, not even charged or tried, had been given.

Twice I was involved in his funeral. From Johannesburg I was taken (again by the nuns) into Soweto for the service commemorating his life and death. The great barn-like church of Regina Mundi, an absolute contrast to the glittering Catholic cathedral in Johannesburg itself, was packed and African singing rolled in waves to and fro across the church. There were tears everywhere. The Master of Ceremonies interrupted to give out a warning. "There are people here," he said, "who have no right to be here. I give them three minutes to leave." For an awful moment I thought he was referring to me, another white priest and two white nuns. But he wasn't. He was talking about informers. For a few seconds there was silence as everyone looked around. Then three or four blacks from different places in the church dashed for the nearest door and vanished.

The day before I had met a white informer on a very personal basis. I had spent an evening with Beyers Naudé, the courageous Dutch Reformed Church minister who had had to give up his ministry because of his rejection of apartheid. Just before I spoke to a meeting he had organized through the Christian Institute he took me over and introduced me to a young white man. "This," said Beyers, "is our police informer. He comes to all our meetings." It all sounded much more amiable than it was. After I had left for home Beyers was placed under a banning order, a kind of internal exile.

But in September 1977 he was still free and he drove me down to King William's Town, a journey of hundreds of miles, to share in Biko's funeral. Cars carrying blacks were being turned back at road-blocks at every stage of the journey. Our white faces got us through. Thousands of Biko's people had come to an open-air stadium to pay their respects and to say farewell. The courage of those South Africans, denied all political rights and most social and economic rights, was astonishing. By comparison we in Western Europe, who thought we were challenging governments, were only playing games.

I returned to England in October 1977 with a headful of new ideas about leverage which we in England might bring to bear to help the victims of apartheid in South Africa. The demands of my new parish, however, meant that for the next three years my main interests were focused around one square mile of NW1 and WC1.

CHAPTER TEN

A People's Parish

Within three minutes' walk of Euston Station is one of the most attractive of the post-war London churches. Designed by an exceptionally modest modern architect, John Newton, who understands the nature of Christian community worship, it is a simple semicircular structure with a large porch, a ramp for wheelchairs and a hall below. The only design fault was that to get into the inner roof and to the gear which lowered the lighting in order to change bulbs, you were supposed to climb up a fifty-foot ladder, turn around on it and pop through a trap-door. At anything over ten feet I always feel sick, so it was with great relief that, when parish priest, I got the firemen of Euston Road to do the job for me. Thus I made contact with one of the best of the trade unions.

Unfortunately not many people wander up Eversholt Street from Euston, towards Mornington Crescent. If they did more would visit St Aloysius on the corner of Phoenix Road, the Catholic parish church for an area bounded on the north by Crowndale Road and on the south by Russell Square. The boundaries were not always very logical. The line on the south ran right through the Brunswick Centre and its many flats because, so tradition has it, the two parishes concerned could not agree which one was going to get the benefit of that new concentration of population.

St Aloysius himself, born in 1568, was a young nobleman from Mantua who, despite his father's opposition, joined the Jesuits and died at the age of twenty-three in Rome while nursing victims of the Plague. That story was good enough to provide the foundations for many a sermon, but even more interesting to me was that he was supposed to have refused to play with swords, guns and other war toys. A few more sermons were based on what I also hoped was accurate history. Today St Aloysius may be on his way to becoming the patron saint of AIDS sufferers.

It was to St Aloysius that I went early in 1977 as parish priest. Bishop Guazzelli, the courageous and independently-minded auxiliary bishop, had asked me to take this parish on. He saw no incompatibility between the kind of work I was doing for Pax Christi and the responsibilities of being a parish priest in a parish where there were several other priests to share the load. I could not have been more lucky in my fellow clergy. Michael Munnelly was not only incredibly funny but was also very pastoral, concerned about everyone and knowing almost the entire parish by name. Maurice Keane, who reached marriage more rapidly than I did, was a genius with the liturgy and a genuine radical, always asking "Why?" If not the idol of the traditionalists he certainly was of the younger people and the students who came in numbers to his very interesting Mass and discussion evenings. I can't remember a single row between our clergy team in three years, which is not bad going.

On my side, I was pining for a congregation and some sort of base. There are two sides to that coin. A priest needs a hospital or a prison or a parish and their down-to-earth human problems to keep his feet on the floor when he is dealing with large-scale issues. At the same time there is a certain seduction in being the kingpin in any world, however small. In a parish the priest is exactly that.

My hope was that St Aloysius would become a peace parish – a place where world-wide issues would be part of the accepted life of the community and where many justice, peace and human rights organizations would find a home. This ideal did not always work out perfectly in practice, but at times we had our successes. The "One World Shop" which we started in a spare room with access to Eversholt Street still exists at another location and is a good outlet for Third World gifts and literature. Peace and human rights groups began to make more and more use of the church. A group of Chilean exiles once asked me if they could use the church for a fast they wished to make in solidarity with fasting students, back in Chile, protesting at some awful Pinochet outrage. For the first few days some of the ordinary parishioners were quite upset. "Father, those Chileans, they aren't genuflecting in front of the Blessed

Sacrament." But as time went on, and things got more serious, everyone started to understand, especially when we reminded them of Terence MacSwiney. The Lord Mayor of Cork, he died in 1920 in Brixton prison while on hunger-strike for Irish freedom. The connections were made and much respect was then shown. By contrast, some members of the media would ring up to ask, "Do they look *really* hungry yet?" Only when they did, did the TV cameras turn up.

To St Aloysius hundreds came every Sunday – Maltese, Irish, Spanish, Filipinos, rich tourists from the Euston Road hotels and sometimes very poor single parents living in the great blocks of council flats. The area behind those major stations, Euston, King's Cross and St Pancras, is unknown to most people but there is more real drama and a greater sense of local community there than there ever is in *EastEnders*.

It was a parish with great traditions – the first church had been built by an active French emigré priest, the Abbé Carron, and it served the French community in exile during the days of the Revolution in an area which was then the outer fringe of metropolitan London, before the northern villages began. In 1830 came some nuns, the Faithful Companions of Jesus, who took responsibility for the schools which, in different forms, have lasted until today. I found this history fascinating and made sure that the old baptism and marriage registers were carefully rebound and repaired. They recorded the departure of the French and the arrival of the Irish and all the other nationalities who followed on. The History Corner which we created at the back of the church is still a mini-museum of Somers Town life.

Canon Welland, my predecessor, was himself part of that history, having served the parish with single-minded devotion and absolute authority from 1945 until I took over in 1977. He was, as a matter of fact, a slight surprise. Almost as an afterthought, the Vicar General said, when details of my appointment had been agreed, that the Canon would be staying on and living in the parish house. Queen Bees do not usually live in pairs. I had already heard of the Canon's reputation for gruff traditionalism and lack of interest in other churches and got quite worried. In fact it worked out well enough.

I promised not to interfere with the Saturday night Novena service, to which he was devoted, and made sure that he was warm, well fed and never short of a dose of brandy when he wanted one. On his part, he was willing enough to give way to new brooms who were reasonably polite, even though so many of his rules disappeared within days. Hence lay people were actually invited into the house, all kinds of parish parties went on in it and we had a Wednesday afternoon single parents' club which met sometimes in the priests' dining-room itself. Ours was an open-door policy.

One of the greatest of the revolutions was that I recruited teams of lay people to count the collection. This also had been a priestly preserve for many years, but I felt quite sure that plenty of lay people were capable of counting. They certainly were. The Canon had been a jam-jar accountant. All kinds of jars – labelled "candles", "missions", "schools" and the like – lined a shelf. But I think he had something there. Twenty years later, I am starting to return to jam jars for my domestic accounting. It seems to get the electricity bill paid, though I tend to end up with credit and debit reminders in the various jars. My Poll Tax jar usually owes something to all the others.

Life for our au pair girl was transformed. Instead of a live-in housekeeper, the Canon had cleaners and an au pair girl, usually a young Spanish or French student, whose task was to produce one meal a day. The tradition was that the au pair served the food through the hatch. The Canon would then fill her plate and pass it back. Thus we could see her eating in the kitchen, she could see us eating in the dining-room, and we pretended that we were eating separately. This did not, it seemed to me, fit too well with the idea that we were all supposed to be equal in the eyes of God, with no exceptions for au pair girls mentioned. So the au pair started to eat with us, and so did anyone else who happened to turn up. Full marks to the Canon for amazing adaptability. His tradition of thirty years crumbled within a couple of weeks, and he made no fuss when he could have been very difficult.

The main problem with the Canon was his dog. A previous curate had left behind as a gift an ageing white part-Labrador called Max. The Canon, with his limp and stick, was not one who could take

Max out for exercise. Indeed, that was a difficult thing to do since Max, once outside the house, had only one ambition and that, understandably, was to escape as fast as possible. This he did all too often, and I would get phone calls from police stations at all hours of day and night, as far apart as Harrow Road and Brixton, asking me to come and collect dear Max. I was tempted more than once to remove his collar and thus our phone number and address, and let him go, but the thought of his eventual fate in Battersea Dogs' Home put me off. No-one would ever have adopted poor old Max and he would have been in the front of the queue for the final needle. The further result of his confinement to the premises was that the underground car-park, which I saw as an immediate source of revenue, had been Max's private toilet for far too long and smelt like it. When finally Max, already in pain, had to go, the Canon looked at me reproachfully as if to say, "I know I'm next." He was far from next. Nearly two years later, after a good evening on the telly and a couple of generous brandies, off he went to bed. We found him the next morning lying over the bed, one sock on, one sock off, dead from what must have been an immediate heart attack. If there are happy deaths, I think he had one.

I missed the Canon when he was no longer there. He had mellowed a lot, enjoyed a joke and was the best Neighbourhood Watch there ever was. Forever popping into the church, he must have deterred plenty of those visitors whose aim was to open up the various wall-safes and make off with the proceeds given for candles, papers, flowers, the poor, missions and all the other good causes. Candles were, of course, a major industry and income. As soon as he got into the church in the morning the Canon would make sure that there were plenty of candles in their racks and that one candle was burning to encourage people to put others up as well. Mind you, I always thought it a slight cheat when he would blow them all out at night. If I light a candle I like to think that it's going to get a straight run and not be used again second-hand the next day.

Being close to Euston Station, we had a steady stream of beggars looking for handouts. I did not believe in giving out cash but I got quite expert in making cheese sandwiches. Large lumps of cheese and plenty of marge all pressed down firmly between two pieces of sliced bread. I could make them with one hand while answering the phone with the other. Some of my wodges were chucked into the basement area but most met a real need. It is not, however, easy to keep your temper while listening to long nonsense stories which will inevitably end up with a cheese sandwich. The most unlikely beggars all had grandmothers and mothers who had just died in Manchester, and therefore a British Rail fare was immediately needed to get her dear son or grandson to the funeral. There was a limit to my patience with grandmother stories. After I was very brisk with one boozed and offensive gentleman and shut the door on him, his bottle of much-strengthened Cyprus sherry smashed its way through our window. I saw his point.

But there were compensations. One of the regulars, a cheery little man with a red face, white hair and a beard, rang the bell one day looking very miserable. "Father," he said, "I've shit my trousers. Please help me." As a matter of fact I could. He stripped off in a basement bathroom and I popped him into the first hot bath he had had for a long time. With his brown-red face, white hair and pink body he looked like a small-sized Father Christmas. All the old clothes went into a black bag and he left in a set someone had just given us for the poor, very pleased with himself indeed, and clean for the first time in months. I have always believed that free, clean and numerous public toilets are as much a mark of civilization as cathedrals.

Somers Town was very much a community with its own network of pubs and clubs and families who had lived in the area for generations. To the Church of England, the Magdalen College Mission and in particular Father Basil Jellicoe, who died in 1935, goes the credit, in the years after the First World War, for improving conditions and building decent flats. The films and pictures of those days are hard to believe now. Bugs were a major problem and between the wars fumigation vans toured the streets, collecting and gassing all the furniture. In one film an old lady can be seen taking a picture off the wall. Behind it the surface was black with active cockroaches. Such were not, of course, the conditions of 1977, but they were conditions very well remembered by plenty of those who lived in the area. Even paid holidays, I discovered, were post-Second

World War developments for many of them, and the fear of getting ill was something they had not forgotten. Some had spent all their lives in that neighbourhood and indeed I once met an old lady who had never even seen St Paul's Cathedral, not more than two miles away.

Some of the flats housed Asian families, the latest generation of immigrants, and racialism was never far away. Pakistani waiters in West End restaurants had sometimes to take mini-cabs, at great expense for them, back to their homes late at night to be sure of getting there without being beaten up. One family was desperately persecuted and jeered at by young thugs after school. Abuse on their phone was normal. It was not unusual for excrement to be pushed through their letter-box. They, fearful, could not understand the hatred, and nor indeed could I.

Our parish did its best through influence at school, church functions and social life to provide a rather warmer welcome, but we were only a part of a wider community where racialism is rather more obvious than it is in the discreeter utterances of some politicians. Even in church circles it requires imagination to see how insular we can sometimes be. Before I went to St Aloysius Saturday evening socials would often conclude with the National Anthem – the Irish one. The Irish tradition was very strong and could be warm and welcoming. It could also operate as an invisible barrier facing anyone else. A black face would be so unusual in our social club as to cause heads to turn.

Ours was not just a social club – it was also a licensed one with club status. It was popular in the neighbourhood, not least because the drink was cheaper than in the local pubs. I have to say that it caused some headaches, since the parish and club worlds did not always mix easily. Some of the club members were active, enthusiastic parishioners, but others were not and looked on the parish hall as "their" hall, not to be interfered with by the parish priest for other purposes. At a Parish Council meeting a new timing was once suggested for the Maundy Thursday liturgy, but was strongly objected to by one of the club members on the grounds that this would interfere with the club activities – one of which being a devotion to music of a sort which boomed its way up into the church.

I thought enviously of the parish in West London where the priest got so fed up with club–parish conflict that he hired a bulldozer and levelled the club building early one morning. Not easy to do when the club is in a hall under the church. When I become Archbishop of Westminster I will propose that permanent licensed clubs on church premises come to an end and that when a dance or other social takes place the local pub be asked to get an "occasional" licence, as it used to be called, and provide the drink.

It was a small irony that the basement room in the priests' house also became home to a group of Alcoholics Anonymous. I never interfered with their affairs but marvelled at the devoted care that the members showed for one another.

St Aloysius was a very happy place in which to work, with plenty of interests, including a range of hospitals. My own special concerns were the Hospital for Tropical Diseases and St Pancras Hospital, once a workhouse and then a general hospital. Tropical diseases were just that, and people turned up with all sorts of bugs and infections very abnormal to London NW1. St Pancras was more down to earth, with several geriatric wards on the top floors. I could only admire the staff, but I hoped to God that I would never end up there. Many of the very elderly, some of them incontinent, would to all intents and purposes appear to be mentally disturbed. But not all. I remember one old lady, quite bed-bound, who was surrounded by others who clearly knew little about what was going on. But she herself was entirely lucid, an Egyptologist with her brain in 110% working order. I always stopped for a chat, and I know that the staff, run off their feet, did their best too. But what a fate! Once or twice a week a lovely girl would turn up with a guitar and tambourines, coax the old people into a circle and get them all to sing or at least to keep time to the music with the tambourines. They loved it.

It was, I think, in one of the geriatric wards that I got closest to a mini-exorcism or something like it. Very odd things were happening late at night. Towels landed on the floor. Beds rolled out into the corridors. Drinks were suddenly spilt. Entirely sensible nurses and sisters gave full details of all these odd activities and the word went round that the ward was haunted. The administrator sent for the C of E and RC chaplains. Why the nonconformists were excluded, I'm not sure. Perhaps they aren't so good at exorcisms. The two of us were asked to go up to the ward at about midnight, when most of these odd activities had taken place, and to set about praying. At last we had a role which everyone could understand. Leaking pipes – call the plumbers. Poltergeists – call the chaplains. We prayed away in turns for some time in the darkened ward, like two rival witch-doctors who had decided to collaborate for once. The administrator and nurses looked on with interest. Nothing moved, no beds rolled. In fact that was the end of all strange phenomena, and whatever cynics care to say, I would like at least to claim a share of the credit.

Paddy is my other lasting memory of that hospital. He was an alcoholic and had had both legs amputated and he was always good for a chat. He also demanded to go on my Holy Communion list and liked a blessing and a prayer. We remained friends after he was moved out into a nearby ground-floor council flat, which soon became the boozer for the wide range of Euston Station layabouts who made up Paddy's world. When I knocked on the door, I would already have been spotted from the window, and the kettle would have been put on. The place was always full of smoke from their awful tobacco and the beer tins were lined up all along the mantelpiece. I think Paddy drove his well-meaning social worker to desperation, but I gave up any attempt at reformation and we got on very well together.

Paddy was, till the day he died, also one of Sister Martina's flock. Sister Martina was officially the cook in the Phoenix Road convent, and a very good one she was too. But she also gathered under her wing a wide family of problem cases. There was no time, day or night, when it would be too difficult for Martina to take someone or something on. When I wanted to have a private lunch with Shirley Williams one day, she produced a magnificent meal and with the help of her community, turned the convent parlour into a first-class restaurant. But her strength was with the Paddys of this world, just as Sister Bernard's was with the elderly. Bernard must have been at least eighty, which did not stop her announcing regularly that she was just off to visit her "old people" – many of whom would be ten years younger than her. She took a great interest in the Friendship

Club, a regular Sunday afternoon social for pensioners. The participants were nearly all working-class widows who had a great time together – tea, a singsong, dancing, and the odd outing. From time to time a few men would turn up, but they were not essential. One old lady told me that yes, she had loved her George, but he had passed on a few years before. Now she had her pension and was having the best time of her life.

So was I, but I knew it could not last. I was getting too many calls on my time from out-of-parish concerns. I was, in fact, facing the same problem which had made me feel that I ought to leave the Chaplaincy six years before: my involvement in so many peace, human rights and international activities.

CHAPTER ELEVEN

Into the Deep End with CND

Much as I enjoyed the experience of being a parish priest and much as I tried to concentrate on parish affairs, by 1979 it was clear to me that I could not both do justice to St Aloysius and fulfil the many demands made on me, and willingly accepted, by Pax Christi, War on Want, CND, PROP (the National Prisoners' Movement) and the many other groups with which I was connected. In these pages I have several times mentioned Providence. Providence has been part of my life in so many strange ways. When I heard that Duncan Rees, the General Secretary of CND, intended to retire at the end of 1979 there came into my bones the conviction that he would not be easily replaced on the salary then offered and that CND was going to experience a rebirth and ought to be ready for it.

Duncan Rees, and Dan Smith before him, had had the unenviable task of keeping CND going through the very lean years of the 1970s. Membership had fallen steadily. Despite the constant escalation of the nuclear arms race, British Polaris submarines caused little public concern. There were no debates on nuclear policies in the House of Commons. Harold Wilson had brought the Labour Party well into the Atlanticist fold. CND activists had moved to other causes, in particular opposition to the Vietnam War. I kept up my CND membership out of moral conviction rather than with any hope of political change. In the late 1970s, when I had become CND Chairman, our Council meetings took place, thanks to the Sister Headmistress, in the staff-room of Maria Fidelis School on Phoenix Road. If twenty people came we were doing well. The Council was so small that we did not need an executive.

A few active groups in London, such as the one in Highgate, still existed, but there was no longer any real regional structure and our membership records, in a pre-computer age, were kept on postcards in a couple of shoe-boxes. If we then had as many as three thousand paid-up members, I would be surprised. Indeed, when in 1980 I began to go through our records I discovered that not a few "active" members were actually dead. The more praise, therefore, is due to those who slogged away for years without much political hope, keeping the moral issue alive. The 1978 neutron bomb campaign did give a shot of adrenaline to activists as they realized that this was an issue on which, together with other European groups, they could and did win.

This was the background, and yet I knew – I don't know why – that change was going to come and that when it did come I would do my best to make CND effective and to make more difficult the task of those who would want to marginalize it. Because of this conviction I went to see Cardinal Hume, who had not long before attended in our parish a showing of *The War Game*, Peter Watkins' epic film which had been jointly suppressed by the BBC and the Government in its day. It clearly moved him.

I told him that the position of Secretary of CND would shortly be vacant and that I was anxious to fill the post. I can't say that he thought this a wonderful idea, but in a tolerant way he said that if that was what I felt I ought to do then at least I ought to try it. I'm sure he hoped that this was an enthusiasm which I would get out of my system in a reasonably short time. It was a generous decision, but one which he clearly came to regret.

So it was that in January 1980 I started work in two tiny offices at the top of 29 Great James Street, the home of the National Peace Council. They were on the ground floor and a firm of solicitors occupied the floor between us. It was well within walking distance of the parish of St John's, Duncan Terrace, where Fr George Haines had offered me a room and much hospitality besides.

Each morning I would say the 7 a.m. Mass for the Marist brothers in their Duncan Terrace community house and on Sundays the 8 a.m. for the parish. To have found St John's was to have fallen right on my feet. I spent seven very happy years there, and it enabled me to keep in contact with ordinary parish and hospital life. It also meant that within twenty minutes I could get to the CND office. I shared this with two and a half other CND staff, none Christian, all of whom were half my age. They must have experienced a considerable culture-shock at the arrival on a daily basis of a middle-aged cleric. Apart from my bizarre interest in cleanliness (discovering cups of cold coffee with cigarette butts embedded in the surface crust was a regular horror), I think Sally, Caroline, Chris and I got on pretty well.

By February, I was well into begging. We needed to. We were working under awful conditions with clapped-out machinery. The photocopier was an ancient machine which required much coaxing and the infusion of a nasty yellow liquid into its plastic bag. If the mixture was properly prepared, it was true that copies could be made of a rather dim quality, visible in a strong light. A failure to prepare just the right mix meant that it would disgorge bits of almost blank paper which could have deceived even MI5. The total annual income of CND was under £30,000. £14,000 of that came from donations and most of those came from a loyal membership who were used to being bled dry twice a year with special appeals. As a major threat to the Western Way of Life we were non-starters. At that stage much of the work involved collecting our few copies of *The War Game* from various British Rail Red Star depots and sending them off again to other groups. They were very ancient copies, of course, and after every outing they got shorter and shorter as broken pieces of 16 mm film were sliced out.

By April 1980 I was complaining to the CND Council that too many people outside the Campaign thought it was dead and buried. Indeed, some of my predecessors did their best to promote that idea. I remember a John Collins broadcast in which he made it clear that in his judgement CND had died when he left it. I knew it had not, and I was looking forward to the 1982 United Nations Second Special Session on Disarmament and was urging CND Council to make this our opportunity. We had to make it clear that ours was, despite the name, not just an anti-nuclear movement but a pro-disarmament and peaceful solutions one as well.

Time for quiet forward planning was not ours to enjoy. Though we did not at once realize it, public opinion was massively on the move. I have always wondered why it was that the Government did not realize how much it was doing to boost CND's flagging fortunes. In December 1979 and January 1980 it announced that Britain would not only host American cruise missiles but, to replace Polaris, would also build Trident submarines with American missiles and British warheads. The cost was then put at £5 billion. The Government followed up this chilling news with an entirely ludicrous pamphlet called *Protect and Survive* which told the public what to do in case of nuclear war. Not only were the recommendations in themselves ridiculous (hide under the stairs for fourteen days, etc.) but the message was clear. The nuclear deterrence which we were told was foolproof was not so foolproof after all. If it was, then why all the concern for civil defence?

Their next mistake was to move the deterrence goal-posts themselves. Up to 1980 people were under the vague impression that nuclear weapons were dotted around Europe to deter anyone else from using nuclear weapons. It now began to dawn on a wider public that "our" nuclear weapons were there even to be used first in a conventional war. The glossy blue brochure produced by the MOD to sell cruise missiles to the public ("A vital part of the West's Life Insurance") made this "first use" function quite clear. The aim of using cruise missiles "would be to persuade the Russian leadership – even at the eleventh hour – to draw back". The idea that some rational purpose could be served by setting off a flight of cruise missiles, each carrying a warhead with about ten times the destructive power of the Hiroshima bomb, was not immediately convincing. The task was made worse for Government spokesmen and women by the public differences between General Haig and Caspar Weinberger as to the possible length of a future European nuclear war. Not a comforting discussion for Europeans.

This is not a history book and future historians will have to decide what were the principal factors in the revival of CND in 1980. We, at the receiving end of this new interest, were slow to grasp what was going on. Week by week arrived more letters, more membership applications, more callers, more journalists, more requests for speakers, more orders for badges and leaflets. One morning I popped out of our office to find half a dozen people queuing down to the level of the solicitor below us, to his displeasure, waiting to get in. Life was becoming impossible. Our two small office rooms, which can't have amounted to more than 300 square feet in total, were jammed with volunteers, Council members and existing staff. Early in 1980 CND had turned down the offer of a *Peace News*-owned office in Goodwin Street, Finsbury Park, on the grounds that it was too big. We had to go back to Harry Mister of *Peace News*, always a tower of strength, to tell him that we had changed our minds. By the end of 1980 we were in new offices, themselves soon becoming too small.

New memberships poured in by the hundreds every week. The graph which we had on the wall outgrew the wall and had to be taken across the ceiling. Many of those who had been activists in the 1960s returned to renew their subscriptions. Polly Toynbee wrote a rather touching piece in *The Guardian* about returning to the CND church of her youth, but unfortunately, under the influence of the SDP, she soon lapsed again. All over the country anti-cruise missile groups sprang up, most of which eventually turned themselves into CND groups. The old regional structures, many long deflated, began to swell once more. Because there was a constitution and a framework, the new growth at least fitted into a pattern, even if it was not exactly the one which I would have chosen. We were destined to lumber through the 1980s with a cumbrous decision-making structure and an annual resolution-orientated conference which must have sprung from the Labour Party roots of the 1960s. However, in the early 1980s there was no time to think of constitutional reform. It was enough that a constitution existed.

The real scale of the new growth was only obvious when the time came for our 1980 demonstration in support of the United Nations Disarmament Week, starting 24th October, which had been asked for by the 1978 General Assembly. So ignorant, incidentally, of anything that the UN might have said about disarmament were some of our right-wing critics that they assumed that if Eastern Europe was also having disarmament activity in October it could only be another proof of our manipulation by the Soviet Union.

In 1979, when I was still Chair, we had, with great caution, decided to hold this October event in the basement of Westminster Central Hall. With more caution still we decided that one of the two rooms, with about 600 seats, would be big enough. To be even more sure we organized not just on a CND but on a broad peace movement basis. To our great relief, when the night came the room was full. Amazing. Nearly 600 people. I also had a little foretaste of how respectable radicals actually felt about CND. Bishop Montefiore had been invited to speak but at the last moment, at the steps to the platform, he balked. This wasn't a CND event, was it? No, I explained, it was a broad-based peace movement event focused around the 1978 UN Report. So comforted, he was persuaded to climb up and speak. How many like him I have met since then, whose respectable radicalism could not quite embrace CND.

The decision to hold an outdoor rally in Trafalgar Square on Sunday 26th October 1980 was not easily made. It was taken at the April Council. I thought Trafalgar Square was over-ambitious. How stupid we would look if only a few hundred turned up. It is to the credit of Dr John Cox, a longstanding CND member who was later to have the honour of an acknowledged MI5 phone tap, that the Trafalgar Square decision was made. He said there would be a full square and convinced the doubters. We assembled in Hyde Park, as the Labour Party did in June of that year, for their disarmament rally. They got a downpour and a crowd of about twenty thousand. On our Sunday morning in October we already knew that we were on to a winner. Coaches were coming from all over the country, trains had been booked and there was an astonishing feeling of expectation. By the time we were on our way out of the park I was getting my first experience of politics. Labour MPs of all sorts were popping up, anxious to be photographed at the front of the march. Today, many of the same people would be hiding behind hedges till we were safely past.

It was an amazing, magical afternoon. The square was full and went on filling. As many as 80,000 people turned out on that day. Great banners kept on flowing down from Piccadilly like the sails of ships. By half past four it was already getting near dusk, and still they came. A number of invited guests and several uninvited ones made speeches. Philip Noel-Baker, Fenner Brockway (later to found the World Disarmament Campaign together) and the great Japanese monk Fujii Guruji, the inspiration behind the Milton Keynes and

Battersea Peace Pagodas, were lined up in their chairs. Edward Thompson thrilled the massed thousands with his great cry, "Feel your strength!"

Only slowly did people start to disperse towards Charing Cross, moving past the police horses barring Whitehall. The last hour, as the light faded, I spent with a few others putting rubbish into black bags and collecting broken banners. As reports began to come in of other European demonstrations I knew that something was on the move which was very positive indeed – people everywhere were starting to think again, and indeed to feel their strength.

No-one played a greater part in that process than Edward Thompson, the historian. It was his *Protest and Survive*, published in answer to the Government's civil defence absurdities, which put the match to a powder-barrel of alternative thinking. But we have also to thank Professor Michael Howard of Oxford University for putting the match to Edward Thompson. He wrote a letter to *The Times* on 30th January 1980 giving ringing support to the Government's civil defence programme. It was "an indispensable element of deterrence". People should be given "the greatest possible degree of protection in the worst eventuality". Our defence posture would be destroyed if we did not give evidence "of our capacity to endure the disagreeable consequences likely to flow from it". The phrase, "disagreeable consequences" was too much for our Edward. People who had seen *The War Game* and, better still, the appalling pictures of Hiroshima and Nagasaki, knew well what the proposed "disagreeable consequences" were likely to be and were deeply grateful for an Edward Thompson who could put their feelings into his burning words.

He gave us international vision as well as indignation. CND was still a very British-directed organization and, though there was in it a new interest in the work of the United Nations, it had a limited international perspective. The END Appeal, launched in 1980, gave us a new framework for a united, bloc-free Europe and a new idea of people's power. It also linked disarmament and human rights in a positive way which did at times have difficult side-effects for CND, by its constitution a single-issue disarmament campaign, not a general human rights movement. That Appeal clearly bore fruit in the next twelve months.

In 1981 the British UN Disarmament Week demonstration took place in Hyde Park on 24th October, and the park was full. It was, from the platform, an amazing spectacle, with moving crowds of people as far as the eye could see, right down to the edge of the Serpentine. We claimed 250,000 people, and that seemed a modest guess to me. In any event, we knew that whatever number we selected would at once be halved by the police, who only counted people on the march passing a particular point. People who came to the rally but did not go on the march or who joined the march at places other than the starting-point were not included in the totals.

Not that there was ever much trouble with the police, who in planning major public events invariably tried to be helpful. I was heartily glad to see the effective way in which they removed the more obnoxious and violent members of Class War from the 1981 demonstration. Individual policemen could, however, be amazingly silly. One Inspector had to be told loudly not to be so daft as he moved forward to arrest someone singing, on the grounds that he did not have a music licence from the Department of the Environment. No arrest was made.

The wonderful feature of 1981 was the news of other demonstrations in other European capitals. Always there was much less co-ordination than officialdom and the media actually imagined, and large numbers in Rome or Bonn or Paris were often as much of a surprise to us as they were to anyone else.

The biggest demonstration by far that I ever attended was in New York on 12th June 1982. It had been my dream to take a large group to New York for the UN Disarmament session – I even imagined chartering a Jumbo for the trip. Jumbo numbers we never managed, but the final party of sixty or so was impressive enough. Actually there was one more than we expected. A pregnant representative of Babies Against the Bomb (those were the days when there must have been everything from Undertakers to Dentists against the Bomb) actually produced a baby between booking her ticket and flying. This meant a long delay at John F. Kennedy Airport as the political affiliations of mother and child were assessed. This is not an entirely inane remark. Hundreds of people were refused entry to the United States who wanted to attend the UN Assembly, though such restrictions did not get much publicity.

Saturday 12th June was a clear, fine day and a marvellously encouraging one. People seemed to have come from all over the States. There were bands and trick cyclists and people walking on stilts. But there were thousands and thousands of ordinary people, carrying signs and posters saying "Bread not Bombs", "Stop the Arms Race", "No more Nukes" and the like. It was a joy to me to see the Catholic religious orders go past – Dominicans, Benedictines, Jesuits, Franciscan nuns and Sisters of St Joseph of Peace, too many to count. I could not fail to contrast what I was seeing in the States with the difficulties experienced in getting any official Church representation in England – unlike Scotland, I hasten to add, where a very different wind has always blown.

It was said that a million people came together in Central Park to listen to speeches and hear the bands. Who knows exactly? It was an enormous crowd and a most encouraging spectacle. It was also my second major activity in one week. On the Sunday before, 6th June, there had been a massive turn-out in London's Hyde Park to mark the Second Special Session of the UN General Assembly on disarmament, the arrival of President Reagan and opposition to the war, then coming to an end, in the Falklands. It was decided to connect me in New York by telephone to that London rally, and a very curious speech I had to make. I was put in a room with a phone by Cora Weiss and Bill Coffin, who between them seemed to manage the massive Riverside Church, right up on the side of the Hudson. The phone rang from London and a distant voice told me that I was now connected to a quarter of a million people in Hyde Park. So, alone in my small room, on a wet New York morning, I made my speech to the mantelpiece without a face to look at, without a cheer or a boo to break the proceedings. It all came out loud and clear at the London end, I am told, but it was quite the oddest speech I have ever delivered. Inspiring a mantelpiece standing in for a quarter of a million people six thousand miles away has its problems.

The danger of this sort of anecdotal history is that it may be thought that the only task of CND was to march large groups of people from A to B and then shout at them. This, of course, is exactly what critics want to believe about CND so that it can be dismissed as inconsequential. Of course marches are not discussion groups or seminars, but the wealth of informed CND expertise about arms control and disarmament is clear enough from the rows of books produced during the 1980s which still bend my shelves. Those who try to diminish the intellectual weight of CND diminish Dorothy Hodgkin, the distinguished physicist, Maurice Wilkins, a Nobel Prize winner, and the late Martin Ryle, Cambridge Astronomer Royal, to name but a few of our friends and supporters.

Most of my work was not at such an exalted academic level but consisted of articles, interviews, debates and an endless series of visits to local groups. The demand was unlimited. Sometimes I could spend six out of seven nights in various parts of the country. I have spoken to packed halls from the Channel Islands to the Shetlands. Usually I managed to get back to London on the same night so as to get to the office early the next day and flick my way through a pile of daily papers before starting work. Often enough this meant getting a sleeper, when such luxuries existed, from Manchester or Newcastle which would tip me out at 7 a.m. at Euston or King's Cross. Charlie, the little sleeping-car attendant on the Manchester run, became a good friend, always ready with a miniature Scotch before bed. One night as I walked up the platform I just about noticed a figure in naval uniform pacing up and down. When I had booked in Charlie wanted to know if, in my second-class berth, I was on my own. I was. "Then I can let the Admiral on board," he said. I'm not sure whether my companion was an Admiral or not but he had something to do with Faslane and submarines, did not go in for much chat when he realized who I was, and vanished quickly the next morning. One never knew who would be sleeping in the other bunk or who would try to get in. Geoffrey Howe once lost his trousers on a sleeper. I lost a lot of sleep one night on the train from Liverpool, trying to get a boozy fellow passenger to understand that I was not going to hear his confession.

One of the places I always greatly enjoyed visiting was the Army Staff College at Camberley, where courtesy to visitors and amazing efficiency are characteristic qualities. The dialogue that went on there was always entertaining. I don't suppose I ever convinced those future military high-flyers that we ought to dispose of British nuclear weapons, but some certainly shared with me the belief that wars could not be fought with them. It was at Camberley I first realized that Big Brother was watching over me. On the train down I started to talk to a friendly enough man in civilian clothes. He said he too was going to the Staff College. Awaiting me was a Major, a driver and a smart car. I suggested to the Major that we give our friend a lift and got in the car. Through the window I heard him decline a lift, saying quietly that he was from DS something or other at the MOD, down here to listen to me talk. Sure enough, in the auditorium there he was, at the very back.

All this welter of work, on which so many CND spokespeople (notably Joan Ruddock, who was elected Chair at CND's 1981 AGM) were engaged, was without doubt having its effect. Denis Healey, who had taken a rather snooty view of CND at its foundation in 1957, was generous enough in a December 1982 article to say that "CND has already achieved the most impressive victory for single issue politics in recorded history." Perhaps he was too generous, but clearly our numbers and success in debate, when one could find a serious Conservative with whom to debate, were looked at with interest by two groups of people. Trots, in the first place. When we first started to grow, Chris Horrie, editor of *Sanity*, the CND magazine, looked at the rising numbers on the membership lists and commented, "The Trots will soon come." I had no idea what he meant, but I soon found out how right he was. The Socialist Workers' Party, the International Marxist Group and probably many others whom I could not name began the infiltration process. They were, granted our numbers, more of a nuisance than a threat, but, being no St Francis of Assisi, I resented their take-over tactics and said so. At every demonstration a handful of them would turn up with thousands of posters marked with their name and message to be handed out to the innocent. Fortunately the innocent soon grasped what was going on and would use the posters, having torn off or folded over the Socialist Workers' Party name. The tendency to medieval incantation ("Maggie, Maggie, Maggie – Out, Out,

Out!" or in Scotland, "Maggie, Maggie, Maggie – Oot, Oot, Oot!")
also got up my nose. So also did the regular attempts by such
minority groups to swamp the front of any march, as if they had
organized it themselves.

I even took drastic action once when Youth CND was seriously
threatened. An astonishing number of new Youth members were
signed up in 1983 through the Oxford branch, just a few days before
the national youth's Annual General Meeting. The Trots, for so
they were, then took over the committee. I made it my business to
go to the first post-AGM meeting, discovered a row of irregularities
in the AGM process, declared the meeting null and void, and left.
Fortunately the CND executive meeting a few days later gave me
full support and a genuine AGM was convened a few weeks later.
Trot dangers were wildly exaggerated by some journalists. Thus
Peter Jenkins, then of *The Guardian* and the SDP, wrote a feature
article in December 1982 after our annual conference entitled
"How the Trots hijacked the CND". They had done nothing of
the sort, despite a certain amount of noise. The Trot conviction
that those "on the shop floor" were only too anxious to "get out
on the streets" seemed to me to fly in the face of the facts. Nor
did it seem to me that they ever understood the function of
single-issue campaigns. No-one, however, could fault them for
passion and persistence.

Our growing influence also brought us rapidly to the attention of
the British right wing – a far more sinister threat than the Trots –
who used every trick of misrepresentation and smear they could
devise. Lord Rawlinson, in a letter to the *Catholic Herald* in May
1983, said that the debate should be conducted "with charity and
personal respect". He went on to dismiss the idea that there were
smears about by quoting the legal saying, "If you have a bad case,
abuse the other's attorney." In other words, if you said that you
were being smeared that was yet more evidence of your own guilt.

I don't know where people like Lord Rawlinson were in the 1980s,
or what they thought their Conservative Party was doing. The sharp
end of Conservative attacks on CND came from a body called the
Coalition for Peace though Security. One of its founders is now a
Tory MP. Another, who did not manage to get elected, works for

Conservative Central Office. The Coalition, with its headquarters in Whitehall, would never reveal the sources of its own finance, but nevertheless made outrageous allegations about CND's funding. As defamers well know, it is very difficult to prove a negative. How could I possibly prove that some Mrs Smith who sent in £50 from Sidcup was not actually a Soviet agent? So early on in my career as CND General Secretary I decided that the best way to answer these accusations was to offer a prize, initially of £100, I think, to anyone who could produce evidence of Soviet funding of CND. The prize was never claimed, though that did not stop Sir Frederic Bennett MP claiming that he had the evidence but could not reveal it since to do so would put a Czech dissident in jeopardy. A safe smear.

However, lack of hard evidence did not bother those who wanted to throw mud. Lord Chalfont, much more establishment than the members of the Coalition, used the House of Lords in 1981 to say that "It would be strange indeed if the CND were not substantially assisted from Communist sources . . ." He also claimed that the Soviets spent £100 million a year "financing peace movements in Western Europe". If they were, it was certainly not getting to our grotty little office in Finsbury Park. This, by the way, was the same Lord Chalfont who in better days had said in *The Times* that British nuclear policy had "No military significance . . . is based on a false sense of national pride, and . . . puts existing and future arms control agreements at risk."

The Coalition left no stone, large or small, unthrown. One of their most tasteless activities was to turn up at Burghfield, the nuclear bomb factory in Berkshire, on Hiroshima Day, 6th August, at the end of my 1986 Long Walk from the nuclear submarine base at Faslane, and play loud music during the minute's silence for the dead of Hiroshima and all wars. Had it not been for some very nonviolent women, the kind of brawl which the Coalition was hoping for might well have taken place. Its activities were well known to officials of the Conservative Party. Mr Harvey Thomas, an evangelical Christian working for Conservative Central Office, said in 1983, "We keep in touch with the Coalition. There is a friendly relationship between us." Did he really not know what was going on? Apart from trying to link me with the IRA in one of its first leaflets, the

Coalition then sent a spy, Francis Holihan, to our office. He was rapidly exposed. "We regret that," Julian Lewis of the Coalition was reported to have said. "If you're going to spy on somebody you've got to do it efficiently." MI5 did actually do it efficiently and, but for brave Cathy Massiter, who left the Service and blew the whistle, we might never have known that nice old Harry Newton, who stuffed envelopes as a volunteer, was actually a Government informer. Not that there were many secrets to reveal. I used to chat with him over the sink at 11 Goodwin Street, and for my pains he reported me to his superiors as a pseudo-Marxist, which sounds even worse than being a real one.

The Coalition were more obvious. In 1982, on a spring speaking tour in the United States, I discovered that a team of men, apparently young Republicans, headed by Edward Leigh, now a British MP, were shadowing my progress. On several nights I had to tell local journalists, who had clearly been primed, that I was not a Communist, did not come from a Communist peace movement, and did not call for the unilateral disarmament of the West. Hunting down Communists and ex-Communists in CND was a major task for those who wished to denigrate us. We refused to take part in these witch-hunts, which Mr Heseltine, misusing the Security Services, brought to a fine art before the 1983 election. Cathy Massiter, MI5 agent, was so disgusted by the way that security information was being used for party purposes that she left the Service. Heseltine would have been more impressive if he had understood that our CND Council consisted of over a hundred representatives and not the twenty or so on whom he based his sample. What CND had actually said and done, with the support of its Communist members, in relation to the Soviet Union, he did not want to know about. Listening to him, no one would realize that we had condemned the invasion of Afghanistan and the deployment of SS20s, and both as an organization and through END, spoken up for the victimized independent peace groups of Eastern Europe. Our representatives to the Prague peace conference of June 1983 were actually assaulted by secret police when they tried to make contact with members of Charter 77.

Much more entertaining than the Coalition was Lady Olga

Maitland. I really liked dear Olga. She knew very little about the complexities of the disarmament process, the technology of the arms race, or the work of the United Nations. Hers was a clear world of us against the Reds. She never tried to be personal; she was just astonishing. I think she saw herself as Mrs Thatcher's Light Cavalry, well ahead of the rest of the troops, hacking away at the Forces of Darkness, and if possible doing it in front of TV cameras. I had to frustrate her wiles once during a very cold snow-bound vigil at Molesworth. As I trudged round in my wellies, trying to keep warm and chatting with some of our frozen thousands, Olga hove in sight, with a camera crew lugging their equipment behind her. I turned tail. "Bruce, Bruce!" she cried. "I want to talk to you!" "But I don't!" said I, and increased my pace. She could probably have outrun me, but her TV crew had not signed up for a hundred yards sprint through the snow and gave up the chase.

Despite the abusive letters, nearly all anonymous, which I received in those ten years, I was very rarely in physical danger. Once a very large sailor recognized me at Chatham Station, said I was an effing Commie and told the rest of the carriage that he was going to knock my block off. Fortunately, before he could get on with this work, the effing train began to move and he had to get off in a hurry. The greatest moment of danger came with a rather curious parcel which, when half opened, aroused my suspicions. The bomb squad were sent for and identified it as an incendiary, which happily my letter opener had not set off. They gave me a severe ticking off for not taking it to the yard at the back of the office and out of the way of the rest of the staff. I thought the ticking off was a bit unfair. Parcels don't arrive marked "Bomb".

More damaging than any direct assaults was the steady drip of the main-line media. It did not seem to matter what was said at meetings or demonstrations. What mattered was how many were arrested, what went wrong, how few came, and what the negative police comments were. Long before I arrived on the CND scene, the media had divided the world into two camps – the multilateralists against the unilateralists. The former were good; the latter were bad. It did not matter much what the proposal was or who had made it. If the Government was against it, it must be unilateralist. If the

Government was for it, it must be multilateralist. The United Nations had said in 1983, "There is no either/or choice between unilateral and negotiated measures of disarmament. Both are needed in view of their complementary nature." But this made not the slightest difference. No one had read this UN report. To be against cruise missiles was to be a unilateralist. To be for Star Wars was to be a multilateralist.

This bogus opposition between two parts of one process was carefully fostered by the propagandists of the right, and it did them much good until both Mr Gorbachev and Mr Bush in due course began to make their own unilateral steps. Then it became more difficult for the media to use "unilateral" as a term of denigration. But not impossible. The resolution which I moved at the 1989 Labour Conference, and which was overwhelmingly passed, calling for a reduction in military expenditure, was marginalized by some as a "unilateralist" resolution.

To be honest, some of our CND fundamentalists had also turned the word "unilateral" into a touchstone of orthodoxy. Purists were always wanting to know if someone was or was not "selling out" on unilateralism, as if it were an end, not a means. I sometimes wondered, so strong was the insistence on the word, if they would really approve of disarmament if it came about in any other way. The whole uni/multi ding-dong was clearly a complete waste of effort. The great majority in CND knew perfectly well that some steps on the road to a less militarist world could and should be taken independently, some bilaterally, some regionally, and some multilaterally. The real discussion, rarely allowed to surface in the media, ought to have been about which steps belonged where.

When the media were not dividing the uni's from the multi's they were concentrating on "balance". Theirs was a bean-counting world, and of course the answers they came to about balance depended on the military beans they chose to count. That both East and West were already admirably equipped to blow up the world did not seem to matter. What mattered was how many of *this* they had compared to how many of *that* we had. The implication was that the arms race proceeded in a planned way, with one deployment matching or balancing another. No wonder the media swallowed and passed on to a believing public the idea that cruise missiles somehow "answered" SS20s. Rarely does anything answer anything else. When about to deploy a new technology, which had probably taken about ten years to develop from drawing-board to production, each side regularly justified it on the grounds that it was a response to something else. All this is ancient history now, but, for the benefit of those who accepted Whitehall propaganda at the time, General Bernard Rogers' evidence to the US Senate Committee on Armed Services may be of interest. Said Rogers: "Most people believe it was because of the SS20 we modernized. We would have modernized irrespective of the SS20 because we had this gap in our spectrum of defence developing and we needed to close that gap." "Closing the gap" meant that there was thought to be a rung missing on the ladder of nuclear escalation.

Few people, however, now believe that flexible response policies make any sense. From Denis Healey to Robert McNamara, those who supported such strategies now repudiate them. In his magnificent but barely reported Strasbourg speech of 1979, Lord Mountbatten commented on the idea that nuclear weapons could be used without triggering an all-out nuclear exchange: "I have never found it credible." He went on to say of nuclear weapons: "Their existence only adds to our perils because of the illusions they have generated."

Nevertheless, cruise, the great bone of contention of the early 1980s, was part of the ladder of escalation demanded by those who believed that nuclear war could be made a rational option. The United States "must possess the ability to wage war rationally" said Colin Gray of the US National Security Council in 1980. His words were echoed by Field Marshal Sir Nigel Bagnall in front of an Edinburgh audience in 1990: "The idea of flexible response is, you don't actually blow the world up. You may blow it up, and that's what you rather hope the opposition thinks you will do, but you do it in a graduated, controlled way." No wonder the Edinburgh students fell about laughing at what should never have been a laughing matter: the irrationality of nuclear policy.

Field Marshal Bagnall did not stand alone in having to defend nuclear nonsense. General Sir John Hackett wrote a best-selling book about a NATO/Warsaw Pact military conflict. His scenario involved the use of a British Polaris missile to destroy Minsk, which was itself rather odd, since the official line was always that if Polaris were ever used it would have failed in its purpose. The blame for this fictional use was placed by General Hackett in a TV debate in 1983 squarely on the Soviets: "If they'd done their sums correctly they wouldn't have made their fatal mistake." Our deterrent was evidently only as effective as the Soviets' ability to do their sums correctly.

These were the issues which should have been publicly aired. Granted the nature of our media and the use to which they were put by the Government of the day, I do not think that there was a genuine debate about nuclear policy in the 1980s. To criticize NATO or British assumptions and policies was simply to be soft on the Soviets. Full stop.

One of my most lively media experiences happened when I was returning from a meeting in Brussels of other European peace groups. That day there had been a terrorist bomb at Harrods planted by the IRA, and it had claimed its victims. On the same day over in the East End of London a CND group had obstructed traffic, or marched, or done something to protest at the arrival of cruise missiles. The *Evening Standard* had the bold banner headline, "CND holds hands with the IRA". The theme of the story was the allegation that we had helped the IRA by diverting police to the East End. I knew nothing about all this until I got on the late plane at Brussels. Every passenger had been given a free copy of the *Evening Standard*. As I walked down the aisle people looked up from their papers with their banner headlines, recognized me and glared. It was an uncomfortable flight. Eventually the *Evening Standard* had to apologize, but apologies do almost nothing to right damage done.

Years later the same paper published an article by Professor Minogue of the London School of Economics, in which he claimed that Tony Benn, Vanessa Redgrave and I had only one paradise left in Eastern Europe – Albania. Having never maintained that there were any paradises in Eastern Europe, let alone Albania, I felt somewhat miffed. But the Press Council said there was nothing to be done. The law of libel is apparently, like the Savoy, open to everyone.

CND did back one successful action for defamation, but had it not been for our cool solicitor, Geoffrey Bindman, we would have chickened out even of that action. The Federation of Conservative Students in some leaflet had claimed that one of our elected officers, Dan Smith, was a Communist. Since he was a Labour Party member and a defence expert whose professional knowledge was being sought by the Labour Party, he had in this instance been defamed. But he had to wait for nearly two years before the action came to court, by which time the costs were in the region of £50,000. Panicking, I thought we ought to pull out and cut our losses, but braver judgements prevailed. On the second day of the hearing, Counsel for the Conservative students involved said his clients wanted to settle, apologized and paid the costs and some small amount in damages. With wealthy backers one can take chances. Without them it is better not to risk the courts.

Looking back over those ten years, I sometimes wonder what the paranoia was really all about. Paranoia there certainly was. I do not forget Sir Frank Cooper's sudden outburst. Invited to chair a meeting of the establishment Council for Arms Control at which Sir Francis Pym was to speak, he spotted me, an invited guest, near the front row. Frank Cooper's face began to flush and he gave up official Ministry of Defence urbanity. That is Bruce Kent, he told the audience, and no one has done more to delay the disarmament process. It was an astonishing piece of personal rudeness. The dignitaries on the platform looked at their shoes and said nothing. The next day, to be fair, the Secretary of the Council rang up to apologize. The problem, I am sure, for the Coopers of this world was that CND was challenging some of the assumptions on which they had built their lives, and was doing so in a way which took the discussion out into the market-place and made it possible for ordinary people to join in. Not surprisingly, ordinary people felt quite passionately both about the risk of nuclear annihilation and about the incredible costs of the East–West arms race, nuclear and conventional.

Today, so much that was official gospel in the 1980s now looks slightly incredible. Who really believed then that the Warsaw Pact – a disparate collection of assorted tyrannies and opposing national-isms all of which were being bankrupted by the arms race – actually intended to overrun Western Europe, and that having done so, it would be able to run what was left of the show to its own advantage? Yet, that the Soviet Union was poised for a massive westward strike was the endless assumption of journalists and politicians. "Their" malign intentions had, it seemed, always to be determined by their massive capabilities. Our benign intentions, on the other hand, were to be accepted by the Soviets without question, despite our equally fearsome capabilities.

Such double standards were rarely challenged. Media conformity was the order of the day. Graham Greene in 1969 said, "If only writers could maintain that one virtue of disloyalty, so much more important than chastity, unspotted from the world."

Disloyalty would have told the public about the other war which was going on in the 1980s and for decades before – the economic war. It was Sir Francis Pym who once said in the Ministry of Defence to Lord Hugh Jenkins, active Chair and Vice-President of CND, and I that the West would eventually destroy the Soviet economy. He was quite right. That is exactly what has happened. At the same time, the public had to be persuaded that what was going on made some military sense. The US 1984–1988 Fiscal Report even urged "preparations for winning an extended nuclear war against the Soviet Union and for waging war effectively from Outer Space". But that is yesterday's history and many of the dogmas of those days are now widely doubted. Some of the credit for those doubts is due to CND and similar movements in other parts of the world. There is a "one world" perspective in the intellectual and ethical air today and, despite any mistakes which may have been made, the peace movement has played its part in creating it.

Lord Kennet, then Wayland Young, was once a CND enthusiast – so much so that he was, according to A. J. P. Taylor, even bitten by a police dog on his way to Downing Street after the first great CND meeting in Westminster Central Hall. In 1961 he wanted CND to change its direction and said, "There is a tremendous fund of energy, right feeling, good thought and organising ability in CND. If ever it seemed that this fund were being wasted on an irrelevant or minor battle that would be tragic." I do not think it was wasted.

My ten years gave me a unique overview of groups and individuals of vision, humour, knowledge and commitment. I am proud to have met so many wonderful people, unambitious for themselves, and for the most part unknown to the rest of the world. A bishop once visited the Pax Christi office, long before I became deeply involved with CND, and said that one of the troubles with Pax Christi was that it did not have any important people in it. If that was a weakness, CND had a similar one. Important people tend to be respectable people, and respectable people like to be respected, especially by those with power. Theirs was not the world of Pax Christi or of CND, to which I became something like an unofficial parish priest.

In those ten years I met determined campaigners, old and young, who refused to give up. I have grieved with parents whose campaigning children have died in tragic accidents. I have visited prisons where those with more courage than I will ever have were sent. I even found myself one Christmas in a home-made nativity scene. I was visiting a caravan just up the hill from the vast American base of Lakenheath and found two young parents at a peace camp watching over their new baby by candle-light.

One of my great privileges was to work with James Cameron, that principled, modest journalist who never compromised. James would have enjoyed his own funeral. CND ordered a wreath to be delivered to Golders Green in the shape of a large floral CND symbol. The wreath arrived all right, but it was not the CND but the Mercedes Benz symbol which had been prepared. James would certainly have known the difference. His coffin moved off with a major symbol of modern capitalism on top. One afternoon, calling at his Swiss Cottage home, I met him with the Australian journalist Wilfrid Burchett, the first to smash the propaganda wall which had been erected around Hiroshima. It was he who, for the first time, thanks to the Beaverbrook Press, was able to reveal some of the details of radiation deaths.

There were so many other, less well-known names. Lucy Behenna of Crawley, for instance, a retired teacher and a Quaker. By dint of endless persistence she founded, with her friend Marion Mansergh, Mothers for Peace and began East–West exchanges on a very human level. Cuthbert Leigh of High Wycombe collected signatures on petition forms in shopping centres from his wheelchair, which eventually we pushed to the door of number 10 Downing Street. Jack Sheppard of Ledbury drove us all mad with his enthusiasm as he set about building his world-wide pensioners' network. Harold Bearston from North London made his money out of kitchen knives and gave it away, just as easily as he made it, to peace and justice organizations. An early visitor in 1980 to our Great James Street office was Edwin Haig from Berkshire. An upright, proper, very British and very meticulous man, he persisted in writing and talking about the relevance of international law to illegal modern weaponry when few were interested. Only recently Sybil Cookson of Worthing died in her eighties. It was she who persisted in promoting the work and charter of the United Nations when most of the peace world was ignoring the UN as an expensive irrelevance. The list is a long one indeed, but let me just add the name of Robin Tanner. Educationalist, etcher and deep lover of England's countryside and traditions, he knew how to call barbarism by its proper name. These people, and so many others, were the backbone of CND, even though the media always wanted to focus on spokespeople and leaders.

I remember the day in 1986 when an almost spontaneous demonstration was called in London to protest against the raid on Libya and the use of British bases by the American Air Force for that illegal operation. We first of all went to Grosvenor Square, but then a substantial part of the large crowd moved to Oxford Street and sat down there for an hour of silent indignation. The senior policeman came up to me and asked me if I would please move my people on. I could not get him to understand that they were not "my" people who would move at my orders. They would do what they thought right to mark the murders of a few days before. If they were my people it was only in the sense that they gave me and others, put into leadership positions, such wonderful support.

I remember travelling to London on an Intercity train one evening and munching through the sandwich I had just bought from the train's buffet. Looking up, I saw the chef, a large man in his white apron, looking a bit grim and walking rapidly down the aisle towards me. When he got alongside he suddenly stopped, leaned down, grabbed my right hand and shook it firmly, saying "God bless you."

He turned in a flash and was gone, leaving in my hand a curled-up piece of paper – a £10 note.

In its second phase CND managed to avoid the splits over "direct action" which had damaged the campaign of the 1960s. A conference resolution was passed supporting "considered" nonviolent direct action, and thus we avoided the trap which had so divided Collins and his followers from Russell and his. Nearly everyone in CND phase two knew well that there were circumstances in which national law ought to be broken. Luther King broke the law and became an international hero. So did the conscientious objectors of the First World War, who suffered dreadfully for their principles. So did the Pankhursts and their companions in the early days of this century.

The issue as I saw it was what laws, in which circumstances, and with what effect? There were those in CND, overestimating, I thought, our numbers and national support, who gave to direct or illegal nonviolent action too high a priority. I never did. It was winning the battle of ideas, not the number of arrests, which mattered. Indeed I was convinced that direct action could sometimes have a negative effect unless its purpose was very clear. It was, of course, very difficult to get a hearing in court for our key conviction that nuclear weapon policies are themselves illegal. Very rarely were courts willing to listen to arguments from international law. In May 1985 some of us undertook an action which we thought might have forced the courts to have considered such matters. Twenty-two assorted inciters to disaffection, including our witty ex-military secret weapon, Air Commodore Alastair Mackie, read out a statement to the few servicemen in sight and some rather chilly MOD policemen on the other side of the Molesworth wire. Our message urged them "to refuse to obey illegal orders such as those requiring you to guard, maintain or transport any nuclear weapons of first use such as cruise missiles". Though we were clearly inciting disaffection in a way which would normally have earned us a generous prison sentence, the Director of Public Prosecutions took no action and the Government ignored us.

I tried once again to get international law raised as a defence in a British court after I took part in a Snowball action at a United

States standby base in Sculthorpe, Norfolk, in January 1988. "Snowball" was the name given to a series of symbolic actions designed to expose the criminality of national nuclear policies. It was hoped that thousands would eventually join in, and that thus such issues would be raised in courts around the country. The hope was a vain one, however interesting the idea. The kindly judge whom I faced in Norwich Crown Court later that year, asked the jury to leave the court during my international law defence and when they returned he put two questions to them only. Did I have a hacksaw blade? Was I going to use it? One juror, a CND member, was in tears as she agreed to a guilty verdict. She had been given no choice. But issues of international law will not go away and steps are now afoot to take these questions to the World Court.

Perhaps it was the Greenham women who most imaginatively broke the law in defence of the law with their various escapades inside and outside the base. Theirs is, of course, a tale to be told in full by someone else. It is my own conviction that one day the courage, humour and determination of those women will be recognized and honoured in our national history. The effect they had on women around the world was incalculable. In remote towns in Australia, through translators in Japan, at private meetings in the GDR, I would often be asked before any other question was put, "How are the women of Greenham?" That incredible day in December 1982, when the entire nine-mile perimeter fence was ringed by women, was one of the most remarkable of those ten years. They left that Greenham wire covered with pictures, poems, photographs of children and grandchildren, and thousands of touching reminders of our common humanity.

My own contribution was minimal. When the walkers from Wales first arrived at Greenham (and for the record at that stage the group was mixed) in the autumn of 1981, they said they were going to stay until they had met the Minister of Defence or someone of that ilk. I remember urging them to lower their sights and settle for the Mayor of Newbury. They wouldn't be able to stay for more than a couple of weeks, said I, so they ought to choose a more achievable target. Two weeks turned into more than ten years. It was ten years of abuse, harassment, physical cruelty and defamation. At one stage, thanks to someone called Yossef Bodansky, who wrote a piece for *Jane's Defence Weekly* in January 1986, all the main-line media sprouted with ludicrous stories about the Soviet Spesnatz, who were supposedly managing to pass themselves off as Greenham women. The story lasted for forty-eight hours and vanished along with Mr Bodansky.

It would be dishonest to suggest that feminist exclusiveness at Greenham did not cause problems for some CND supporters, or that later divisions amongst the women themselves were not inexplicable to outsiders. So what? Those ten years of courageous witness have empowered women everywhere. To Greenham women critics I commend this little ditty which is said to date from the time of the enclosures in English history:

> *The law condemns the man or woman*
> *who steals the goose from off the common;*
> *But lets the greater felon loose*
> *Who steals the common from the goose.*

My own education in feminist thinking started in a small way many years before when I was a university chaplain. Two students went to work for the holidays on a temporary basis in Harrods. The boy was paid £18 and the girl £12 a week for the same hours and the same work. Rather odd, I began to think. Then one day, when I was in the Pax Christi office, a priest with a reputation as a liberal rang up and was answered by the General Secretary, Valerie Flessati. Hearing a female voice, he asked if there was someone of "some calibre" to whom he could speak! Rather rude, I thought. CND meetings increased my awareness as I began to notice that, unless checked by Joan Ruddock with her own special blend of gentle strength, male CND Council members would regularly talk over female ones without even noticing. My lessons from Greenham have been all part of a process. Now, when I see male domination so obvious in the law, in the Church, in the military and in political and commercial life, I begin to understand some of the indignation.

The two great disappointments of the 1980s were the general

elections of 1983 and 1987. Though CND policy was to urge people to vote for the candidate who, in the voter's opinion, would do most for disarmament, outside Wales and Scotland that in effect meant a Labour vote. In 1983 the media had so effectively carved up the Labour Party and ridiculed its leader that the mess the Party made of the defence issue hardly mattered. Opportunities were thrown away by the barrelful. I remember ringing the Labour HQ at Walworth Road in the middle of the campaign to ask when they were going to start to expose the Tory record on arms sales, on the Non-Proliferation Treaty, on a nuclear test ban, on the Trident escalation and on the recommendations of the 1978 UN General Assembly Special Session. Soon, I was promised, but soon never came. James Callaghan, as disloyal as any Militant and just as dangerous, finally torpedoed Michael Foot's attempts to defend a non-nuclear policy by making it clear in the middle of the election that he did not agree with what was then Labour policy. No Walworth Road Star Chamber has ever called for his head.

In 1987 Labour produced a defence and nuclear policy which was doomed from the start. It challenged none of the assumptions of the Cold War, or the presumption that nuclear weapons enhanced security. All it did was to promise that Britain would get rid of hers while compensating with more conventional weapons and sheltering under what was claimed to be an American nuclear umbrella. The umbrella theory itself was an odd one. It assumed what was highly unlikely – that an American president would risk Washington or New York for London or Rome. It was a dog's dinner of a policy and it got the fate that unconvincing stitch-ups deserve. The sad fact is that the Labour Party and many, but not all, of its supporting unions have never set about the process of internal education about international relations and disarmament which must precede a policy change. Something very different happened in Sweden, which could also easily have become a nuclear weapon power. In 1957, 40% of the Swedish public wanted a Swedish bomb, 36% did not, and 24% were uncertain. Twelve years later in 1969 only 17% were still in favour, 69% were against, and 14% were still uncertain. The shift in opinion was no accident. It was the result of pressure group and political campaigning and education. Even now in Britain the nationalism which led Ernest Bevin to say, "We've got to have this thing over here, whatever it costs. We've got to have a bloody Union Jack on top of it," is still our dominant political fixation.

CND cannot escape its own share of responsibility for failing to move public opinion further, as it might have been moved, despite the media odds against us. It was too easy to assume that popular opposition to cruise missiles, civil defence and Trident submarines meant that people had come to realize that British nuclear threats were both immoral and pointless, decreasing rather than increasing our security. This was always the key issue. Nuclear weapons were still discussed as if they were weapons. We did not get over to enough men and women on the Clapham omnibus that promising to blow up your own house is not a very intelligent way of dealing with burglars; or that threatening to fire Chernobyls at one another does nothing to enhance real security. Had we, however, had the help of those thousands of respectable radicals – environmentalists, academics, aid workers, church leaders – who never hesitated to sign up for more generalized disarmament good causes but avoided the one which would directly confront British nuclear weapon policies, things might have been very different. It may well be that rust and the state of the economy are now as likely to take Britain out of the nuclear club as anything else. Trident is a rather expensive bit of pretension for a middle-range European country with a very unhealthy economy.

"Sunset for CND" said a Sunday paper headline after the 1983 election. Some sunsets take a long time to come. Far from having nothing to do, CND has as much to do as ever in a very different world situation. The Non-Proliferation Treaty is under grave threat. The break-up of the Soviet Union has resulted in the appearance of yet more independent nuclear weapon states. And new claims are being made for nuclear weapons themselves. It is now suggested that getting rid of them altogether is a utopian dream, not part of the world of real politics. Thus Sir Michael Quinlan, one of the principal architects of deterrence theory in the Ministry of Defence (and also a Christian), speaking to Soviet military leaders in 1990 about nuclear weapons, referred to "their unique value in war prevention". That is not what the Non-Proliferation Treaty had to say about them. That treaty commits us "to pursue negotiations in good faith on effective measures relating to the cessation of the nuclear arms race at an early date and to nuclear disarmament . . ."

Despite the long list of post-1945 wars, the defeat of nuclear America by non-nuclear North Vietnam, the attack on the Falklands and thus on nuclear Britain by non-nuclear Argentina, the Soviet humiliation in Afghanistan, the indifference shown by Saddam Hussein to the nuclear might of America and Israel, Michael Quinlan's conviction is the one still shared by very many powerful figures in the world today. Nuclear weapons, they are convinced, have a "unique value in war prevention". Why then, CND has to ask, are they not made freely available to everyone?

Clearly, the gap is widening between those who think of security as a national problem, primarily military, and those who like CND think of it as a global one of threats we all face. For the latter, nuclear weapons are part of the problem, not the solution. Already the human race is trying to face environmental and development issues on a global basis. There is no other way of facing issues of military insecurity.

CHAPTER TWELVE

Changing Vocations

When I started work as the full-time General Secretary of CND in 1980, not for one minute did I think that seven years later I would, as a result, be going through the trauma of resigning from the priesthood. At the end of those seven years I did not think I had any choice. At the beginning it did not even occur to me that there might have to be one. To resign was no easy matter. When, on that morning in February 1987 I wanted to tell George Haines, the immensely kind parish priest of St John's, Islington (where I had been living), that I was resigning and why, I could not speak to him for tears. It was an appalling day. I knew that one part of my life was over and that I no longer fitted into the priesthood as others saw it. Thirty years of a life is a long chapter and that chapter had ended.

It was an unreal morning as I walked with a suitcase in one hand along the Islington canal to the CND office near Old Street. The canal was as dirty as ever and the ducks looked much the same, but everything else was upside down. I was outside the official framework of the Church, on my own, not knowing how others would react, without any kind of security or pension. The Mennonites of Highgate, a small but active peace church, had offered me a room until I sorted myself out and Meg Beresford, our CND secretary, went back to St John's to pack up my books and clothes. The Cardinal issued a statement which simply said that I was right. A choice had to be made, though he much regretted that, in his judgement, I had made the wrong one.

The whole thing was less than a seven days' wonder in the press. There are always bigger fish with larger problems in the world and the media soon moved on. Plenty of letters started to come in and most of them were very encouraging. Some were hostile, a few downright cruel. One longtime Catholic family friend wrote to say how glad he was that my mother was dead and thus would not have to experience this disgrace. An odd idea of heaven, I thought to myself, or does he think that news is censored there as well? Many priest friends were sympathetic and even sent personal cheques. Others whom I had known well said nothing and broke all contact. They could have handled things more easily had I robbed a bank or been charged with indecent exposure. Many lay people could not have been kinder but some whom I had known since school days simply cut all links. Such breaks were very painful.

Though I had used the word "retire" in my resignation letter, I knew perfectly well that I was not going back. It seemed to me that while I was still sound in wind and limb, with my marbles more or less in place, I had a job to do for which I was well equipped. Happily it was not of the slightest interest to most people in CND what my ecclesiastical status was as long as I stood with them in the Campaign. Many Catholics had similar views. I still get letters addressed to Fr Kent, and Monsignor Kent, and occasionally to Monsignor and Mrs Kent, now that I am married. In fact, when I did marry a year later and was getting another dose of press hassle a nice old Irishman dashed around the corner one day to warn me about a photographer: "Monsignor," he said, "watch out! They're trying to get a picture of your wife!"

How did 1980 turn into 1987? Progressively I felt more and more isolated and alienated from the official Church in which I had once been so much at home. The process started with the 1980 National Pastoral Congress in Liverpool, which gave such high hopes to all of us who had survived the 1970s and still believed in the community Church which we had seen outlined in the conclusions of the Second Vatican Council. The Congress ought to have been the jewel in Archbishop Worlock's crown. It was held in Liverpool in May of 1980 and I was proud to have been asked by Cardinal Hume to represent my diocese in the Peace, Defence and Disarmament sector. It was a good meeting; many different points of view were represented and respected. Some of our recommendations were platitudinous and others perhaps too radical for many in the Church.

But plenty were reasonable and possible. A national collection on Peace Sunday for peace organizations approved by the Hierarchy was not an extraordinary suggestion. To ask the Catholic Fund for Overseas Development (CAFOD) to include "substantial information" about the arms race in its development education programme was not too revolutionary. To propose a Congress peace scholarship, perhaps at Bradford University's School of Peace Studies, would not have broken the bank.

In the end it mattered not the slightest what the Liverpool Congress proposed. It was immediately made clear by the bishops that the recommendations of the Congress were no more than that. An event which had taken two years of preparation in the parishes at the request of the bishops was now over. Too many of my friends from then on said "Why bother?" and took their energies elsewhere. As a Christian, a priest and a CND worker, I felt an enormous sense of lost opportunity. My endless round of public meetings and contact with local groups had made me realize how active, committed and self-sacrificing people of all ages could be when they believed in a cause. Christianity for me was such a cause, but by contrast too often Church life was conservative, top-down and middle-aged. It was a great sadness that the churches in general, and not just the Catholic Church, were unable to enter into generous dialogue with the growing peace movement, which included in its ranks large numbers of active Christians. We in CND knew from a professional survey that 25% of our members were also Christians active in their churches. I felt that they were kept at arm's length by the Church leadership when they should have been warmly welcomed. There should have been a sharing of ideas instead of polite silence. The episode at Cheltenham is symbolic to me of the mood of the early 1980s. The local CND group wanted to hire a church hall for a showing of *The War Game*. Not one church could or would make its hall available and the showing eventually had to take place in something like a cricket pavilion. The only serious lengthy discussion I had with a religious leader critical of CND on ethical and strategic matters in all those years was with the Chief Rabbi.

I felt this isolation acutely. Only one Catholic bishop made an official visit to CND's office to see what was going on, and I had to take the initiative to make that visit happen. Statements were made by bishops about peace and nuclear matters without any hint that our views might even have been relevant. Yet I knew the professionalism and first-class quality of CND's and Christian CND's research on these issues.

Worse, the statements that did come out always had an escape clause somewhere inserted. The 1983 statement by the Bishops of England and Wales marking the arrival of cruise missiles said that their deployment "would appear to make it more difficult for HM Government to demonstrate its commitment to a policy of progressive and mutual disarmament". What on earth did that mean? Clearly nothing that worried HM Government. The 1982 statement on Trident said that it was "another grave warning of the trend towards escalation". So what, I wanted to know? The first 1980 statement on Trident said that it was "a frightening reminder of present international tensions. We would ask our government and the governments of other nations to use every means at their disposal to check this terrible escalation of nuclear capacity before it is too late." Whatever the significance of that, it was not a clear demand that the Government should change its mind about Trident.

And so it went on over the years. When people wrote to Archbishop's House asking for a Church call for an end to nuclear testing, or for the abandonment of nuclear first-use policies, they got answers which might well have been drafted in the Ministry of Defence. Many of these letters were signed on behalf of the Diocese of Westminster by a spokesman who was in fact a retired army officer. The contrast between these statements and the specific comments made by the bishops on a complex subject like embryo research could not have been more striking.

The reality was that the bishops were doing their best to square official Church teaching with what our Government was actually doing. The official Church line was that nuclear deterrence could not be morally acceptable as a permanent policy but only as "a stage towards progressive disarmament". Those are fine words. But in England they did nothing to stop Cruise or Trident. At the Vatican level no specific Western nuclear escalation was ever criticized. The 1985 Pontifical Academy of Sciences report prepared by twenty-seven international scientists which was critical of Star Wars was suppressed. There was no Vatican call for reciprocal action when Mikhail Gorbachev started his unilateral eighteen-month nuclear test moratorium in 1985. By instinct the friends and advisers of bishops were in the British Foreign Office and Ministry of Defence rather than at peace camps or in grubby peacenik offices. Despite all the language about the temporary nature of deterrence it became clearer and clearer to me that this temporary state of affairs had an eternal quality about it. Nuclear threats were, as Archbishop Silvestrini, the Vatican representative, had said at a Stockholm conference in 1984, in the real world a "necessity".

There were, of course, splendid individual exceptions like Bishop Guazzelli, President of Pax Christi, who did nothing for his own career when he challenged the Apostolic Delegate on my behalf in 1983. Bishop McMahon of Brentwood broke ranks in 1984 with a courageous individual pastoral letter which urged "a first step by Britain in a scaling down, a de-escalation, a reduction in tension, leading to multi-lateral disarmament". A first step was exactly what we were asking for and constantly failing to get. The steps Britain was actually taking were moving us in the opposite direction. Even when the UN asked for an International Year of Peace in 1986, with educational and other programmes to be promoted by governments, the British Government made not a penny available. I doubt if many at the top end of the Church even realized that such a year might have been on the agenda. Though Pax Christi proposed a parallel "Pastoral Year of Peace" this was never taken up.

The problems of the Catholic Church were not unique. The Church of England was only different in that it had in its ranks Archbishop Habgood, with a scientific training no Roman Catholic bishop could match. He wanted no serious dialogue with the kind of peace movement which CND represented. Once I got him to give us an hour of his time, but he brought with him another Anglican bishop whose presence made serious dialogue with Habgood impossible. On defence matters Habgood was an Establishment man through and through, who believed in what he called "the present robust nuclear deterrent umbrella". I never had the opportunity to ask him why in 1978 the United Nations had said "enduring international peace and security cannot be sustained by a precarious balance of deterrence . . ." Was it precarious or was it robust? That might have been an interesting discussion but it never took place.

We now know that Harold Macmillan in 1958 asked Dr Charles Hill, later of the BBC, to mobilize support for Government nuclear policies against the first wave of CND. Hill reported thus to Macmillan: "Steps have been taken to gather together a group of distinguished churchmen and Conservative backbenchers to organise the public expression of support for the Government's attitude." It has taken thirty years for us to find out a little about the use made by the Government of the Church in the late 1950s and early 1960s. It will be another twenty years before we learn something about the process which operated in the 1980s.

In 1983 the Church of England Synod refused to accept the unilateralist recommendations of the committee, headed by the Bishop of Salisbury, which had produced *The Church and the Bomb* report. A substitute resolution was passed which said "that even a small scale first use of nuclear weapons could never be morally justified . . ." That resolution might have meant something if it had ever been applied to actual operational policies, in particular by military chaplains. NATO, after all, openly reserved the right to nuclear first use. The Synod resolution had not the slightest discernible effect on NATO policy. Indeed, the Diocese of Peterborough, shortly after the Synod, was discovered to be trying to sell land to the Ministry of Defence to enable the Molesworth cruise missile base to be enlarged.

To go through all this now may sound vindictive or petulant, but it is not meant to be. Unless the background is known some of my reactions may seem to have been rather curious. Just to show how nice I can be I won't even name the Nonconformist church leader who actually refused to meet a CND delegation at any time during his entire period of office. Those who read this account, perhaps critically, have got to realize how it felt to be marginalized as we were marginalized by just those people whom we thought would be sympathetic friends, whether they agreed with every proposal we made or not.

The crisis for me began to come to a head in April 1983 when Cardinal Hume issued a press release in the run-up to the election. Clearly he was under pressure from a number of right-wing Catholics. Lord Rawlinson had said that my position in CND was "a grave scandal". Michael Brotherton MP announced that I was "doing the work of the Kremlin". John Biggs-Davison said I should resign "in loyalty to the Pope". The Cardinal's press release did no more than buy time both for him and for me. In it he said, "Should the political aspects of CND develop further and become predominant in its work it would be difficult for a priest to hold responsible office in the direction of the movement . . . Although recent developments have caused me serious misgivings, I do not feel that at the present time the grounds for my decision [to allow me to work as CND Secretary] have been invalidated."

The pot, however, really began to boil when the Apostolic Delegate weighed in with a circular letter which effectively ranked me with the "useful idiots" who serve the interests of the Soviet Union. I need hardly say that he had never at any time discussed with me CND or its work. Cardinal Hume gave me generous support, making it quite clear that he entirely disagreed with the Apostolic Delegate's personal criticism. He even went out of his way to arrange a meeting at Archbishop's House on the occasion of a visit by the American Pax Christi President, Bishop Thomas Gumbleton, at which we showed a united and friendly front. But media speculation did not end.

I started to feel like someone stuck in a shell-hole between two front lines. Heavy artillery shot over my head in all directions. I was dissected, analysed, assessed and sometimes rubbished. Everyone had an opinion. I received plenty of kind letters but not a few stinkers as well. "What a self-righteous prig you are, full of your own importance, you over-blown pansy, the Pope would always find you a rat-hole in the Vatican . . ." (sic). I was not at all sure that the Pope would have done anything of the sort. Had I needed a hide-out it would probably have been in Scotland, where church people with a tradition of independence from Westminster know how to express themselves. In 1986 a delegation from the Scottish churches delivered a lovely letter to the Queen which started: "Madam, your

Government's aid programme is a disgusting charade, an insult to the poor; its reliance on Trident is totally unchristian . . ."

The 1983 election came and went and the storm blew over. CND was meant to have been annihilated. Paul Johns, a Methodist management consultant, succeeded Joan Ruddock as Chair. I gave way as Secretary because I knew that CND needed good internal management and it was not getting it from me. Three quarters of my time was being spent outside the London office and I was rarely even able to pay a visit to CND regional offices elsewhere. We had and have a devoted team of paid staff and volunteers who have always had to put up with cramped conditions and highly unreasonable hours. We also had a network of committees, sub-committees and working groups, all of which were meant to keep the wheels of democracy turning and sometimes managed to do so, while consuming quantities of paper. All of this needed management – an unfashionable term in radical circles, since it is thought to carry with it overtones of the whip. An oil can would be a better image of the kind of management I had in mind. I well knew, in an organization which had grown from three to over thirty staff in five years, whose membership had got somewhere near the 100,000 mark in the same period, which had a trading company and a monthly magazine, that a General Secretary was needed who would not have to be sought out either in BBC or ITN studios or visiting groups in different parts of the country. It was with pleasure and relief, therefore, that I handed on the post to Meg Beresford, whom I had first met in 1980 in Oxford when Campaign Atom was getting off the ground there and the wave of protest was mounting.

But I was not giving up in the way that Cardinal Hume clearly hoped that I would. Had there been any indication that my Church was, as a community, making peace and disarmament a priority, perhaps I might have thought of doing so. But I saw no such signs. On the contrary, I was getting more and more disenchanted with a Church with its own clear political focus of which nationalism, especially Polish, and anti-Communism were central features. It seemed to me that to be against Communism and to be for persecuted Christians was not enough. For Christians to have a positive vision of what society might be was equally important, and there seemed to be little thinking along those lines. "The Market" of current Capitalism was not an alternative to which I felt I could subscribe.

The hullabaloo of 1983 only postponed conflict by a few years. In fact until the October of 1986. Then, with another election on the horizon, Julian Lewis of the Coalition, about which I have already said too much, opened a new campaign in the form of "An Open Letter to Cardinal Hume" in the conservative *Salisbury Review*. It was a direct challenge to the Cardinal to make up his mind about me. To let me go on as CND Chair (which I had become), could, according to Lewis, "only be construed as the exercise of bias in favour of the CND position". I knew that the Lewis piece was only round one in another anti-Kent campaign which would rumble on during the pre-election months. I also knew that I could not cope with it. I had had enough of being prodded and dissected by every journalist and politician with half an hour to spare. If there was a problem for the Church it lay in the contrast between the official idea of what a priest ought to be and what a priest actually was in many parts of the world. Support for Solidarnosc in Poland was priestly. Support for the Sandinistas in Nicaragua was not. To be Bishop of HM Forces was not political. To be CND Chairman was. My position was an impossible one. Many of my fellow Catholics, and other Christians, told me that what I was doing as a priest gave them hope, though I knew that most of my bishops did not think my work *was* priestly.

By December 1986 I had made up my mind to resign. One winter's night I went to see our Vicar General and almost had the feeling that I was expected. He was extremely kind, and so was the Cardinal when a brief final interview took place. Compromises were not suggested, I suppose on the good grounds that everyone knew that there were none to be made.

The fiction, however, continued that everybody wanted to get rid of nuclear weapons but that the CND way was the wrong way. The reality was, as I knew, quite different. Mrs Thatcher had already said that she would "not stand for the denuclearisation of Europe". It was not a conflict between uni's and multi's which put me on the front steps of Archbishop's House, Westminster, on my way out for good on 11th February 1987. It was a conflict between those who believed in the Bomb and those who did not, with the official Church uncomfortably in the middle. In my public retirement statement I said:

I no longer find it possible to cope with the strain resulting from the tensions between my pastoral role which means so much to me and what is thought to be an unacceptable political role. That strain can only increase as a General Election approaches ... I simply cannot continue in my present dual role. To do so is to force my superiors into an impossible situation since I cannot offer them the obedience expected.

That was the crux of the matter. I knew that if I had been ordered to leave CND I would have resigned rather than obey. It did not seem to be very fair to force people to give orders which in conscience I knew in advance I could not accept.

Rumour being what it is, events had to move fast. The news leaked a day earlier than I had planned, and I fled for Paddington and friends in Oxford. The noon edition of the *Evening Standard* already had my face plastered on the front page, but happily no one in my carriage seemed to have bought one. I told myself that I had not committed murder or done nasty things to widows or orphans. Nevertheless a chapter had closed in my life and a great door banged shut in my head. "My refuge, my stronghold, the God in whom I trust" would look after me, and so he has.

My Mennonite friends in Highgate gave me their spare room for a month and could not have been kinder. Then CND friends in Cricklewood lent me their house for a couple of months while they were on holiday. Going to Mass in a declericalized state was an experience, but not the ordeal expected. There was a certain amount of head-turning and often some nice hand-shaking afterwards. After nearly thirty years of delivering, I was now on the receiving end of sermons. Now I was the one to whom collection plates would be passed rather than the one to whom, when full, they would be returned. Not knowing what my canonical status might be, I did not go to Communion, and I have not done so since, though I try to be a co-operative parishioner in our north London parish, with its marvellous mix of Irish, African, Asians and even English. Whatever my canonical status was then, it has clearly got much worse since I married a year later, in April of 1988. In the Cardinal Heenan tradition there is supposed to be a woman behind most clerical problems. But had it been a simple case of leaving to get married I would probably have left a long time before. In fact my wife Valerie Flessati, whose name already appears in these pages, did not even know about the choice I had made when I went to speak to the Vicar General in 1986. Having left, I could have lived out my life as a rather odd bachelor or have found the love and companionship of marriage. Thank God I was lucky enough to find the partner I have.

CHAPTER THIRTEEN

Visions and Dreams

It is now five years since I stood on the steps of Archbishop's House, Westminster, on my way out. I have since adapted to a new life. Thanks to generous friends, my family and my own savings I was able to find myself, in the summer of 1987, a north London, ground-floor, one-bedroom flat. Never had I had a garden of my own before. Now I can sit outside in the summer, smelling jasmine, and checking up on each new weed and flower is an unsuspected joy. No vines and no fig-trees, but the calming effect is much the same. The garden, however small, has also meant an ongoing guerrilla war with the cats of the neighbourhood, who are unwilling to give up ancient privileges.

It has been a five years during which I have learnt much more about money, or the lack of it, than I had learnt at any time in the past. As a priest, there were few problems about paying bills. Each week generous collections meant that there was plenty in the kitty, and there were few others to check up on how it was spent. That parish cheque-book was a great source of power. Deciding now what subscriptions can no longer be afforded, if the gas should be paid before the electricity, and whether a holiday abroad is on the cards are new experiences. By the standards of many I will never be poor, but to have to worry about personal money at all has been part of a new world. An old one, for most people.

It has even made me rather more cautious about church collections. For instance, my Labour Party subscription costs £15, as does my membership of Amnesty and CND. But in all three organizations, as a result of that membership, I have some kind of democratic access, however minimal, to the formation of policy. In the Church, I realized soon enough that if I was putting £1 a week into the offertory plate I was making an annual contribution of over £50 to an organization over which, except at the level of the basic needs of my new parish, I had no democratic control whatsoever. My lay friends tell me that I should have thought of this before.

My change of status did not bring the world to a halt in 1987, nor did an election which I watched as a new Labour Party member, with my head in my hands. There are some issues, like nuclear disarmament, on which a principled position has to be taken and argued for. It did not take the journalists long to notice that there was something odd about a Labour policy which suggested that Britain did need nuclear protection but would prefer to get it from the Americans. I was glad, after that election, to fill the rest of the year with a great deal of travel, to Ireland, to the Highlands, to France, and finally to make long journeys first to New Zealand and then to Australia.

New Zealand was a real shot in the arm. That small country, where some of the smaller towns look like slices of a 1930s England recreated near the South Pole, had defied American pressure, refused to accept nuclear warships, and had done so on a popular vote. The treaty which was supposedly insuring its security against hypothetical Soviet assault was, as a consequence, in the process of collapsing, and yet the sky had not fallen in. I wished that the entire opposition Front Bench could have made the journey with me to see for themselves what was possible with a little determination.

It was already clear that the Labour Party was gearing up to drop the defence policy which everyone was telling them had cost them the election. It certainly had not cost them the election in Scotland, but the Scots, and the Welsh, were assumed somehow to be different. Throughout 1988 there were hints and nudges that CND was no longer the flavour of the month. If the British people wanted nuclear weapons, then the new Labour Party would find a way of providing them. James Lamond MP had at one time been a supporter. He was also a Vice President of the pro-Soviet World Peace Council. I met him one night at a reception in the Embassy of the German Democratic Republic and he told me, almost in an aside, that he no longer went in for that unilateralist business. The writing was on the wall and we wondered when it would appear in print.

It did so when the Labour document, *Meet the Challenge, Make the Change* appeared before Labour's 1989 conference. The section on defence had been carefully drafted by Gerald Kaufman and the result was presented as if it was a response to the new Gorbachev climate of detente. If so, it was an odd response, since on the key issue – Trident – it said that though Trident was not a deterrent, Britain would now keep three Trident submarines in order to assist in the process of disarmament negotiations. Two years later Kaufman added, in a *Guardian* article of July 1991, a new gloss to what had been agreed by the 1989 Labour Party Conference. Britain, he said, in order to be able to stay in the negotiation club, would retain nuclear weapons until negotiations were "finally concluded with an agreement by all thermo-nuclear powers completely to eliminate these weapons". In short, we would have them as long as anybody else did. This was a full, 180-degree about turn, but few outside CND were really interested in that or in Paddy Ashdown's just as thorough but less noticed reversal of policy. Leader of the Liberal Party's opposition to cruise missiles, he still maintained, as late as September 1986, that an independent British nuclear deterrent makes "neither political nor military sense".

Getting into Government was the overriding Labour ambition, and anything thought to stand in the way was going overboard. My dismay at such an unprincipled performance was made worse by the politically foolish reaction of the Labour leadership to the 1989 conference resolution calling for cuts in defence expenditure down to the European level, with the savings spent on real social needs. The very idea was received by the Front Bench like an indecent suggestion made to a collection of maiden aunts, yet it ought to have been warmly embraced, at least in principle. Fields of votes are out there waiting to be harvested by anyone with the courage to say that Trident is to be scrapped and the resultant savings spent on the NHS, pensions or housing. It was a mild pleasure to me, after the warm reception given to the speech I made at the 1989 conference, to find myself next to a pale, silent, unsmiling Peter Mandelson, whose manoeuvrings had for once come unstuck. It must have dawned on him that we might be photographed together and he vanished like the White Rabbit.

It may sound perverse, but it was my Labour experiences in 1989 which made me listen to a suggestion that I ought to stand as a Labour candidate and which in May 1990 led to my selection for Oxford West and Abingdon. I had met many decent, conscientious Labour supporters and so I knew that the Front Bench did not represent the Party on every issue. If they did I would never have been selected as a candidate. Whatever the electoral compromises at the top, I knew that there was a yearning for peace, disarmament and social justice in the Labour rank and file which outstripped anything that the modern Conservative Party had on offer. I also wanted to be able to show that, as a minimum, arguing from conviction does not lose votes. At least the new-look Labour Party does hold out the hope of a nuclear weapon-free world. The Conservatives have never put that on their agenda.

British politics were not my only preoccupation. By the end of 1987, Valerie and I had agreed that we ought to get married and I had been given to understand that no dispensation would be issued by the Vatican in a case like mine. I was no longer sufficiently interested to want to argue the legalities, though it did seem to me that the Vatican wanted to have its cake and eat it. I was not prepared to finish out my days as a kind of half cleric. But how to get married without once more bringing an army of reporters down on our heads? Since a Church wedding was not an option, we soon discovered the advantages of the £52 special licence. A helpful registrar at Camden Town Hall explained that if our notice was recorded as late as possible on a Tuesday evening, the wedding could take place as soon as the doors opened on a Thursday morning. Providentially, no one from the press read our entry in the notice-book on Wednesday 6 April, which warned anyone interested about what was going to happen on the next day. At 9.55 precisely I popped through the front doors of the Town Hall and at 10.00 on the dot on Thursday 7th April we stood in front of the registrar and made our promises, as binding and as sincere as if they had been made in any cathedral. It was all quite quick, with only a few good friends present as witnesses. I remember a bunch of tulips and a picture of Venice on the wall, but not much else. A three-day honeymoon on the French coast meant that by the Monday I was back at my CND desk and

Valerie was in Italy with relations, waiting to ride out the inevitable media storm.

On the Monday morning a reporter from Cambridge rang to say that he had heard a silly story about me getting married. Would I mind denying it? I would. Within an hour the phones were hopping and I was getting juicy and lucrative invitations to tell my story. A young man from the *Daily Mail* kept up a hopeless vigil in the front garden for nearly a week and the *News of the World* ran a colourful and imaginative account of an interview with an in-law which had never taken place. Eventually the dust settled, the dogs stopped barking and the caravan moved on.

There was a lot of planning to be done. In 1986 I had started a pattern of Long Walks, the first from Faslane, the nuclear submarine base in Scotland to Burghfield, the nuclear bomb factory in Berkshire. It took about five weeks. On the day I started I really wondered if I was going to make Dumbarton, let alone Glasgow. Soon I discovered that I could manage a brisk twenty miles a day, broken into four slices of five. Better still, I found out that if I washed and powdered my feet every day and wore thick woollen socks, I could avoid even the suspicion of a blister. Nevertheless, I received all kinds of alternative helpful advice. Some thought I should dip my feet in hot paraffin. Others wanted them rubbed with cold soap. Yet more wanted them smeared with Vaseline. I couldn't oblige everyone. Before I started I suggested, during a radio interview, that I would get all the energy I needed by eating a Mars Bar a day. The next day a large box of Mars Bars arrived from the makers. Now that I have mentioned them here in print, a much more permanent medium, I shall expect at least a crate.

That walk raised over £100,000 in sponsorship money and a lot of interest, since we had public meetings every night. I slept in many a strange bed – one of which was in a room looking out over the shop where Mrs Thatcher grew up in Grantham. Towards the end of that Walk, I was joined for a day by one of the straightest men in British public life – Ron Todd of the Transport and General Workers' Union. Despite his National Service in the Marines, his feet had grown a little soft, but blisters or not, Ron bashed on bravely through Newbury towards Burghfield. I treasure the photograph of the pair of us standing with mugs of coffee in the significantly named village of World's End.

It sounded like one of their jokes when a year later Meg Beresford and other members of the CND staff suggested that a walk across Europe in 1988 might not be a bad idea. From Warsaw (of the Pact) to Brussels (of NATO), for instance, calling for a united bloc-free Europe, while fund-raising for UN projects for child victims of war.

It soon ceased to be a joke. The two CND members who had so carefully planned the 1986 Walk, David Rumsey and Wendy Pullum, took on the enormous task of planning this trans-European expedition. The political problems were immense. There were many in Poland for whom disarmament and peace meant first and foremost getting the Soviet Union out of their country. I am not sure if she still is, but at that stage Mrs Thatcher was thought by many Poles to have saint-like qualities. If we opposed Mrs Thatcher we must clearly be pro-Soviet. That took a lot of explanation and negotiating. Some in the West would have been only too delighted if our walk had been denounced at the start by opposition groups in Poland. A difficult discussion took place in a church hall in the Warsaw suburbs, but when it was finally agreed by everyone that on our first day some young Poles would come with us with placards carrying the names of conscientious objectors serving prison sentences, an understanding was reached. The day we started, 11 July 1988, the Polish police behaved with some sense. A red car with plain-clothes police in it kept turning up in side streets as we made our way out of Warsaw, but no one bothered us or the courageous young Poles. Malcolm Harper of the British United Nations Association and Francis Khoo, then General Secretary of War on Want, walked with us for the first day, and very encouraging their support and the significance of their presence was too.

But the officials of the GDR had also to be squared. We can't have Bruce Kent passing through our country "like the Pied Piper", said one. Eventually they said yes, but on their own terms. After walking for two and a half weeks, twenty miles a day, we reached the GDR border at Gorlitz, where we were welcomed by the official GDR peace council and given a route which made quite sure that we passed no centres of population. In no position to argue, we spent a few days in the GDR walking through unpopulated country-side and meeting surprised farmers before heading south over the mountains into Czechoslovakia and thence into West Germany. As we walked through the mile of corn-fields which represented the no man's land between East and West, a party of Hungarian tourists in a large car was travelling in the same direction. The driver wanted to know what traffic conditions would be likely to be in Scotland. Someone, I thought, was not taking the Cold War seriously enough.

Altogether it took nearly eight weeks before we reached Brussels on 31st August and delivered at NATO Headquarters a copy of the letter which we had left in Warsaw for the Warsaw Treaty Organization. It called for an end to confrontation and proposed nuclear disarmament, the dissolution of the two military blocs and the dismantling of divisions like the Berlin Wall. A great deal of this started to happen in 1989, but adequate credit does not yet appear to have been given to me, Dave or Wendy. Perhaps the Nobel Prize committee was on holiday at the time.

The most moving moment of that entire walk was to stand on Nagasaki Day, 9th August, in the box at the Nuremberg stadium where Hitler had harangued his rallies in a frenzy of mad nationalism. The railings were rusting, weeds were pushing up through concrete slabs, and there was a sports pitch at the far end. All I could hear were awful ghosts. In thirteen years one man had ruined the lives of millions. He could not have done it had he not had a culture of nationalism, militarism and anti-Communism on which to build. "What's new?" I thought to myself. The same culture is not far below the surface today, and not only in Germany. History soon gets forgotten. I have now to remind people even in Oxford that it was in that city that an appeasement election was fought in 1938, and it was the appeasers of the Conservative party, unwilling to confront Hitler with military force, who won. Not many now remember that the *Daily Mail* was, in those days, a pro-Hitler newspaper.

That thousand-mile expedition was not the end of my walking. In 1989 I spent two happy weeks circling London from Aldermaston to Burghfield, with a ferry across the Thames at Tilbury. Every night we again had well-attended public meetings, but I also saw a

lot of unexpected nature. Within an hour of leaving Aldermaston
we saw deer grazing in Berkshire fields. Rarely did we walk on
roads, though we were never more than thirty miles from Piccadilly
Circus, in wonderful country with magnificent views. Perhaps I
should get a job with the Ramblers' Association.

A final expedition took place in 1990 when an international group
of about twenty-five set out from the ancient pilgrimage centre of
Vézelay in France and headed down through Burgundy and over
the Jura to Geneva. This was not just a jolly camping holiday, though
it was that as well. It was an attempt to raise interest internationally
in the Review Conference of the Nuclear Non-Proliferation Treaty
due to open in Geneva on Monday 20th August. We left Vézelay
on Hiroshima Day, 6th August, in a temperature of forty degrees
centigrade, and arrived, much thinner in most cases, in Geneva on
Sunday 19th. Outside the Palais des Nations hundreds of Swiss and
other assorted nationalities were there to give us a warm welcome.
The reaction of the diplomats the next day was rather mixed when
they saw this strange crowd of visitors in disarmament tee-shirts in
the public gallery. The Irish officials made a great fuss of the Irish
members of our expedition. The British Foreign Office representatives took a slightly more guarded view of me and their other com-
patriots with the large CND symbols, who had suddenly appeared
in the conference chamber.

It was not a successful conference. The Mexicans insisted on
reality, and made a bland final statement impossible. They, and
other non-nuclear powers, were not going to let the United States
and Britain, both anxious to continue nuclear weapon testing,
off the hook. Today the treaty has only three years to run to
1995, and even its renewal is in doubt. The Cold War may be
over, but the dangers of nuclear proliferation must be obvious
to all.

These were issues I had often heard discussed in Geneva at
meetings of the International Peace Bureau of which I had succeeded Séan MacBride as President. There is a certain sense of
trusteeship in heading an international peace network which now
has well over a hundred membership organizations from all over
the world, which had its first committee meeting in Berne on 1st

December 1891, twenty-three years before the outbreak of the First World War.

I doubt if any of us, during that 1990 walk, had the slightest idea of the dreadful consequences which would follow from the invasion of Kuwait by Iraq on 2nd August. It then looked like a very small cloud on the horizon. This surely was an issue which could be settled by negotiation and with economic pressure. In fact no negotiations were ever allowed and, despite the clear provisions of Article 42 of the UN Charter, economic pressure was never given a chance. Once more the futility of war as a means of solving problems has been made shockingly obvious. Despite billions of dollars, and hundreds of thousands of dead, with many more innocent post-war victims yet to die, Saddam Hussein remains in power and the UN is seen by many as no more than the political instrument of its largest paymaster. The Pope will once more have realized how inconsequential his appeals for peace are if they do not fit in with the politics of the day. Around the world there were many calls by Church bodies for a negotiated settlement. Unhappily, in England mainline Church leadership fell in once more behind Government policy. There comes a time when "ifs" and "buts" and "on the other hands" simply will not do. It is too late afterwards for bishops and moral theologians to discover that the accurate bombing which television showed us was not nearly as accurate as a docile media made out. Too late afterwards to learn from Pérez de Cuellar himself that "this was not a UN war".

In media terms I had something of an Indian summer, being hauled off to TV studios time and again to "balance" General X or weapons expert Y. Since the Gulf war was a non-stop twenty-four-hour media spectacular, it was assumed that a genial chatty commentary could be provided at any hour of day or night. During those weeks Marjorie Thompson, our new active CND Chair, Alastair Mackie, myself and other peace movement representatives did not get much sleep. Just as in the Falklands crisis of nearly ten years before, independent Labour Party and Trade Union voices of opposition were few on the ground. Just as it happened during the Falklands war, I got my invitation to appear on "Question Time" and was able to wave my copy of the UN Charter in front of millions.

But if it takes yet another war to get me on to "Question Time" again, then that is a privilege I can do without.

In one lifetime I have already had more than my share of privileges. Above all I have been blessed with a sense of purpose which still hasn't faded. In the field I know best there is still much to do in a world which can spend even now nearly a trillion dollars a year on war and the preparations for it. One day it is going to dawn on the human race that war is as barbaric a means of resolving conflict as cannibalism is a means of coping with diet deficiency. If we had only read the right parts of the right books we might have learned that long ago:

> A King is not saved by his great army,
> A warrior is not delivered by his great strength.
> The war horse is a vain hope for victory
> and by its great strength it cannot save.
>
> *Psalm 33*

"One day" can be a long way off. However, it seems to me that we are now in the middle of a Copernican revolution in understanding, which some have not yet begun to notice. Too many political leaders have not given any more than lip service to this new perspective. Indeed, during the 1992 general election – a disaster for Labour and a disappointment for me personally – one would have thought that Britain was the world and that beyond our shores lay only outer darkness.

Today, world interdependence becomes more and more obvious. The debt crisis which highlights the injustice between poor and rich countries, the spiralling of population, the pollution of our oceans, reckless chemical emissions and consequent damage to the ozone layer, the danger of nuclear weapon proliferation: all these are threats to everyone. The nation state has become too small in a world where we have not yet built the structures of law and democratic decision-making which we so desperately need. Barbara Ward, the great economist, twenty years ago ridiculed those who could not see that nonviolent solutions to problems are both necessary and possible. "All the procedures proposed for disarmament – elimination

216

of private control of arms, the subsidization of police forces, courts of law, mediation, arbitration ... are in fact practised every day inside domestic society. To say that mankind is not capable of this is simply nonsense. Most of the time this is actually what it does."

The enthusiasts of today – those protecting rain forests, guarding whales, working for economic justice, fighting racism, striving to remove weapons of mass destruction, trying to reform the United Nations – are all globalists. There is no other way. Chernobyl was the most dramatic lesson of our mutual interdependence that we have had so far. It was something we should have learned when we first saw the picture of our small blue-green globe floating in the darkness of space. There was a time when all respectable, sensible people knew perfectly well that the sun went round the earth. Not so long afterwards all respectable, sensible people knew perfectly well that the earth went round the sun. An equivalent shift in our understanding of our citizenship, from local to global, is going on right now. In some small way I hope I have played a part in changing perspectives. This, however, is an autobiography not an obituary, and I hope to help the process along for some time to come. It gives me a great sense of vocation and that is just as vital as laughter and the love of friends. Mind you, friends have been important. My father used to tell us to make friends on the way up since we would meet them all again on the way down. I've been lucky in both directions.

Bibliography

Clement Attlee, *As It Happened*, William Heinemann 1954.

Hugh Dalton, *High Tide and After: A Book of Memoirs 1945–1960*, Muller 1962.

J. E. D. Hall, *Labour's First Year*, Penguin 1947.

Kenneth Harris, *Attlee*, Weidenfeld and Nicholson 1982.

Adrian Hastings, *A History of English Christianity 1920–1985*, Collins 1986.

Dennis Healey, *The Time of My Life*, Michael Joseph 1989.

Philip Laundy, *The Office of Speaker*, Cassells 1964.

Charles Preece, *Woman of the Valleys: The Story of Mother Shepherd*, Mother Shepherd Project 1988.

Viscount Tonypandy, *George Thomas, Mr Speaker*, Century Publishing Co. Ltd 1985.

Parliamentary Reports, Hansard, House of Commons

Index